MRS ROBINSON'S DISGRACE
The Private Diary of a Victorian Lady

In France in the late 1850s, Gustave Flaubert was prosecuted for corrupting public morals with *Madame Bovary* – a novel considered 'too repulsive' for publication in Britain. In England, the 1857 Matrimonial Causes Act made divorce for the first time a civil matter, affordable to the middle classes. And the godless ideas Charles Darwin was formulating about natural selection, published to accusations of heresy in 1859, would further undermine the religious and moral tenets of Victorian England.

The story of Isabella Robinson's fall from grace unfolds against this backdrop of dangerously shifting social mores, in which cherished ideas about marriage and female sexuality were coming increasingly under threat. For a society dealing with such radical notions by clinging ever more tightly to its traditional values, Mrs Robinson's diary and the lawless ideas about love expressed in it were nothing short of scandal.

A compelling story of romance and fidelity, insanity, fantasy and the boundaries of privacy, *Mrs Robinson's Disgrace* brings brilliantly to life a complex, frustrated Victorian wife, longing for passion and learning, companionship and love in an unsettled world which – as yet – made no allowance for her.

BY THE SAME AUTHOR

The Queen of Whale Cay

The Suspicions of Mr Whicher

MRS ROBINSON'S DISGRACE

THE PRIVATE DIARY OF A VICTORIAN LADY

KATE SUMMERSCALE

BLOOMSBURY

LONDON • BERLIN • NEW YORK • SYDNEY

First published in Great Britain 2012

Title page illustration, *A Wife* by Sir John Everett Millais,
Private Collection/The Bridgeman Art Library

Family trees by Phillip Beresford

Bloomsbury Publishing Plc
50 Bedford Square
London
WC1B 3DP

www.bloomsbury.com

Bloomsbury Publishing, London, Berlin, New York and Sydney

A CIP catalogue record for this book is available from the British Library

ISBN 978 1 4088 1241 9 (hardback edition)
ISBN 978 1 4088 1563 2 (trade paperback edition)

10 9 8 7 6 5 4 3 2 1

Typeset by Hewer Text UK Ltd, Edinburgh
Printed in Great Britain by Clays Ltd, St Ives plc

In memory of my grandmothers, Nelle and Doris,
and my great-aunt Phyllis

The wife sat thoughtfully turning over
A book inscribed with the school-girl's name;
A tear – one tear – fell hot on the cover
She quickly closed when her husband came.

He came, and he went away – it was nothing –
With cold calm words on either side;
But, just at the sound of the room-door shutting,
A dreadful door in her soul stood wide.

Love, she had read of in sweet romances, –
Love that could sorrow, but never fail,
Built her own palace of noble fancies,
All the wide world a fairy tale.

Bleak and bitter, utterly doleful,
Spreads to this woman her map of life;
Hour after hour she looks in her soul, full
Of deep dismay and turbulent strife.

Face in both hands, she knelt on the carpet;
The black cloud loosen'd, the storm-rain fell:
Oh! Life has so much to wilder and warp it, –
One poor heart's day what poet could tell?

'A Wife' by 'A' [William Allingham],
in *Once a Week*, 7 January 1860

CONTENTS

THE ROBINSONS

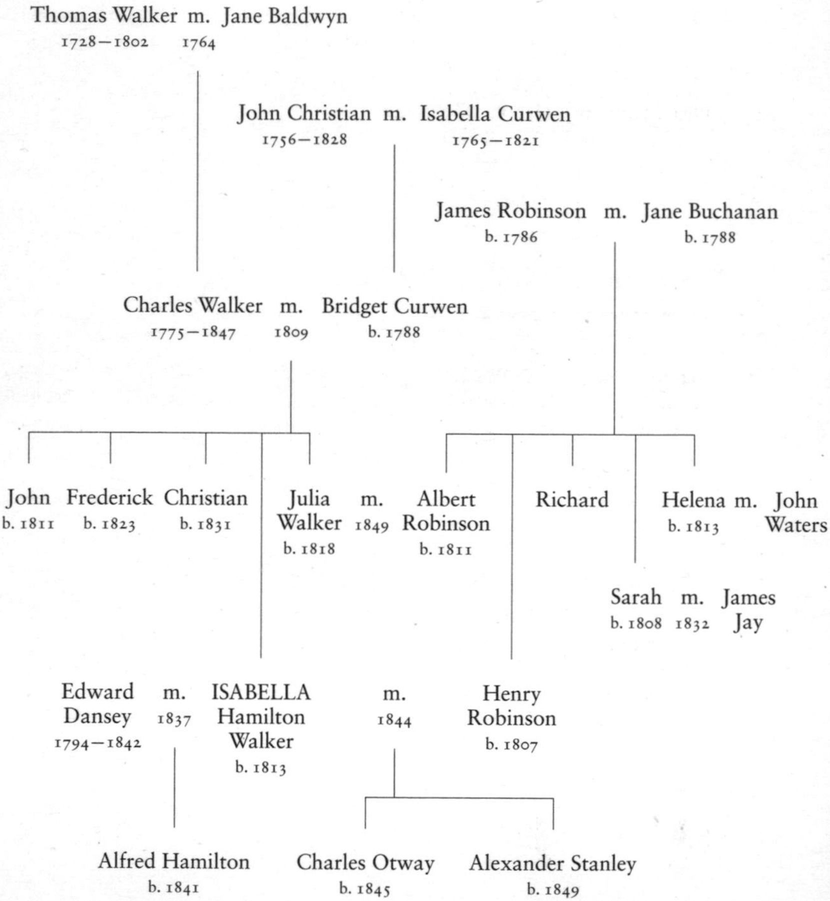

Thomas Walker m. Jane Baldwyn
1728–1802 1764

John Christian m. Isabella Curwen
1756–1828 1765–1821

James Robinson m. Jane Buchanan
b. 1786 b. 1788

Charles Walker m. Bridget Curwen
1775–1847 1809 b. 1788

John
b. 1811

Frederick
b. 1823

Christian
b. 1831

Julia Walker
b. 1818
m. 1849
Albert Robinson
b. 1811

Richard

Helena m. John Waters
b. 1813

Sarah m. James Jay
b. 1808 1832

Edward Dansey
1794–1842
m. 1837
ISABELLA Hamilton Walker
b. 1813
m. 1844
Henry Robinson
b. 1807

Alfred Hamilton
b. 1841

Charles Otway
b. 1845

Alexander Stanley
b. 1849

THE LANES

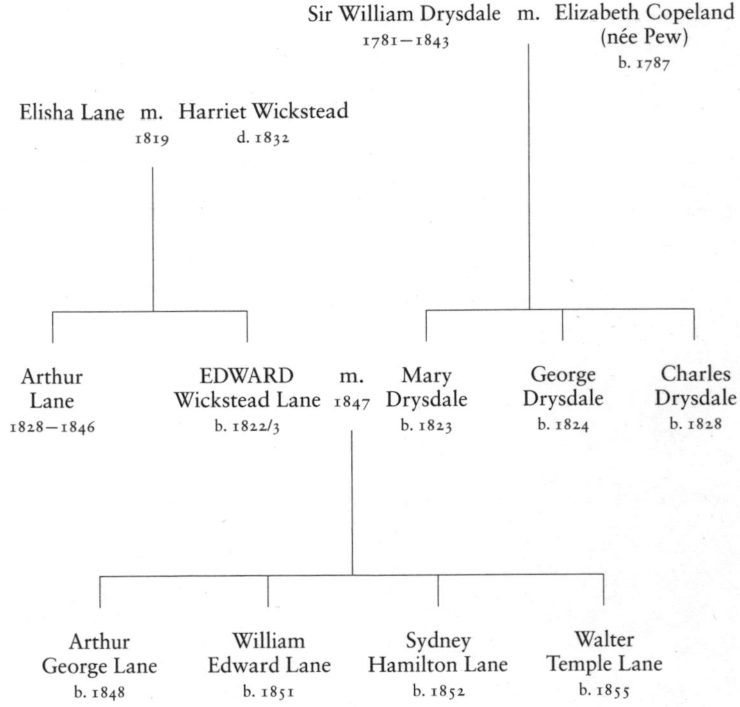

Sir William Drysdale m. Elizabeth Copeland
1781–1843
(née Pew)
b. 1787
Elisha Lane m. Harriet Wickstead
1819
d. 1832
Arthur
Lane
1828–1846
EDWARD
Wickstead Lane
b. 1822/3
m.
1847
Mary
Drysdale
b. 1823
George
Drysdale
b. 1824
Charles
Drysdale
b. 1828
Arthur
George Lane
b. 1848
William
Edward Lane
b. 1851
Sydney
Hamilton Lane
b. 1852
Walter
Temple Lane
b. 1855

LIST OF LAWYERS IN THE ROBINSON DIVORCE TRIAL

THE JUDGES

Sir Alexander Cockburn, Bt, Chief Justice of the Court of Common Pleas

Sir Cresswell Cresswell, Judge Ordinary of the Court of Divorce and Matrimonial Causes

Sir William Wightman

THE BARRISTERS

For Henry Robinson

Montagu Chambers QC

Jesse Addams QC, DCL

John Karslake

For Isabella Robinson

Robert Phillimore QC, DCL

John Duke Coleridge

For Edward Lane

William Forsyth QC

William Bovill QC

James Deane QC, DCL

PROLOGUE

In London in the summer of 1858, a court of law began to grant divorces to the English middle classes. Until then, a marriage could be dissolved only by an individual Act of Parliament, at a cost prohibitive to almost all of the population. The new Court of Divorce and Matrimonial Causes was able to sever the marital bond far more cheaply and quickly. To win a divorce was still difficult – a man had to prove that his wife had committed adultery, a woman that her husband was guilty of two matrimonial offences – but the petitioners came in their hundreds, bringing their stories of betrayal and strife, of brutish men and, especially, of wanton women.

The judges were presented with a singular case on Monday 14 June, a month after they had heard their first divorce suit. Henry Oliver Robinson, a civil engineer, was petitioning for the dissolution of his marriage on the grounds that his wife, Isabella, had committed adultery, and he submitted as evidence a diary in her hand. Over the five days of the trial, thousands of Isabella Robinson's secret words were read out to the court, and the newspapers printed almost every one. Her journal was detailed, sensual, alternately anguished and euphoric, more godless and abandoned than anything in contemporary English fiction. In spirit, it resembled Gustave Flaubert's *Madame Bovary*, which had been published in France in 1857 after a notorious obscenity trial, but was considered too scandalous to be translated into English until the 1880s. The diary, like Flaubert's novel, portrayed a new and disturbing figure: a middle-class wife who was restless, unhappy, avid for arousal. To the astonishment of those who read the extracts in the press, Mrs Robinson seemed to have invited, and lovingly documented, her own disgrace.

BOOK I

THIS SECRET FRIEND

'Why have I gone back to this secret friend of my wretchedest and wickedest hours? Because I am more friendless than ever; because I am more lonely than ever, though my husband is sitting writing in the next room to me. My misery is a woman's misery, and it will speak – here, rather than nowhere; to my second self, in this book, if I have no one else to hear me'

From Wilkie Collins's *Armadale* (1866)

CHAPTER ONE

HERE I MAY GAZE AND DREAM

Edinburgh, 1850–52

In the evening of 15 November 1850, a mild Friday night, Isabella Robinson set out for a party near her house in Edinburgh. Her carriage bumped across the wide cobbled avenues of the Georgian New Town and drew up in a circle of grand sandstone houses lit by street lamps. She descended from the cab and mounted the steps to 8 Royal Circus, its huge door glowing with brass and topped with a bright rectangle of glass. This was the residence of Lady Drysdale, a rich and well-connected widow to whom Isabella and her husband had been commended when they moved to Edinburgh that autumn.

Elizabeth Drysdale was a renowned hostess, vivacious, generous and strong-willed, and her soirées attracted inventive, progressive types: novelists such as Charles Dickens, who had attended one of the Drysdales' parties in 1841; physicians such as the obstetrician and pioneer anaesthetist James Young Simpson; publishers such as Robert Chambers, the founder of *Chambers's Edinburgh Journal*; and a crowd of artists, essayists, naturalists, antiquaries and actresses. Though Edinburgh was past its glory days as the hub of the Scottish Enlightenment, it still boasted an energetic intellectual and social scene.

A servant let Isabella in to the building. Within the hallway, gas flamed in a chandelier, throwing its light on to the stone floor and the polished iron and wood of the banister bending up the staircase. The guests took off their outdoor clothes – bonnets, muffs and mantles, top hats and coats – and proceeded up the stairs. The ladies wore low-cut dresses of glinting silk and satin, with smooth bodices pulled tight over lined, boned corsets. Their skirts were lifted on petticoats, layered with flounces, trimmed with ribbons and ruffles and braid. Their hair was parted in the centre and drawn back over the ears into coiled buns sprigged with feathers or lace. They wore jewels at their throats and wrists, silk boots or satin slippers on their feet. The gentlemen followed them in tailcoats, waistcoats, neckties and pleated shirt fronts, narrow trousers and shining shoes.

Isabella came to the party eager for company. Her husband, Henry, was often away on business, and even when he was home she felt lonely. He was an 'uncongenial partner', she wrote in her diary: 'uneducated, narrow-minded, harsh-tempered, selfish, proud'. While she yearned to talk about literature and politics, to write poetry, learn languages and read the latest essays on science and philosophy, he was 'a man who had only a commercial life'.

In the high, airy reception rooms on the first floor, Isabella was introduced to Lady Drysdale and to the young couple who shared her house: her daughter Mary and her son-in-law Edward Lane. The twenty-seven-year-old Mr Lane was a lawyer, born in Canada and educated in Edinburgh, who was now training for a new career in medicine. Isabella was enchanted by him. He was 'handsome, lively and good-humoured', she told her diary; he was 'fascinating'. She chastised herself later, as she had done many times before, for being so susceptible to a man's charms. But a wish had taken hold of her, and she was to find it hard to shake.

In the same month that she met Edward Lane, Isabella took a trip to the North Sea coast and sat on the beach meditating on her many flaws. A well-born Englishwoman of thirty-seven, she had, by her own account, already failed in every role that a Victorian lady was expected to fulfil. She listed her deficiencies in her diary: 'my errors of youth, my provocations to my brothers and my sisters, my headstrong conduct to my governess, my disobedience and want of duty to my parents, my want of steady principle in life, the mode of my marriage and my conduct during that marriage, my partial and often violent conduct to my children, my giddy behaviour as a widow, my second marriage and all that had followed it'. She had been guilty, she said, of 'impatience under trials, wandering affections, want of self-denial and resolute persistence in well-doing; as a parent, as a daughter, as a sister, as a wife, as a pupil, as a friend, as a mistress'.

She then quoted a verse by Robert Burns:

Thou know'st that thou has made me
With passions wild and strong;
And listening to their witching voice
Has often led me wrong.

Some of Isabella's ruthless catalogue of her faults can be mapped on to the recorded facts of her life. She was born in Bloomsbury, London, on 27 February 1813, and christened Isabella Hamilton Walker at St Pancras Church that May. Her father, Charles, was the second son of a former Accountant General to George III; her mother, Bridget, was the eldest daughter of a Cumbrian coal-mining heiress and a Whig MP. When Isabella was a baby her father bought an estate in the Shropshire village of Ashford Carbonel, near the English border with Wales. It was there, in a red-brick manor house by the River Teme, that she grew up, defying her elders and annoying her siblings.

Isabella's mother later portrayed their home, Ashford Court, as an idyll for children: there was 'a large pretty Garden', she told a grandchild, 'plenty of green Fields & pleasant walks & a long River, & a Boat upon it', as well as 'young Lambs & Cows & Sheep & big Horses, & little Horses; & Dogs & Cats & Kittens'. The house was set in 230 acres of meadows, pastures, paddocks, hop fields and orchards. A lawn sloped down to the banks of the river, with a view of hills crested with trees. Isabella's father, the local squire and a Justice of the Peace, owned all of the land in the village, and he gradually bought and leased further acres, of which he farmed a hundred and rented out the rest.

Isabella and her seven siblings were looked after by a nurse and then by a governess, in whose care the four sisters remained while the four brothers were sent away to boarding school. A governess typically taught modern languages, arithmetic and literature to her charges, but her main task was to turn out accomplished young ladies, proficient in dancing, piano-playing, singing and drawing. Isabella, the eldest of the girls, felt limited by this training. From her earliest years, she later recalled, she was 'an independent & constant thinker'.

In August 1837, a few weeks after Queen Victoria's accession to the British throne, Isabella became the first of the Walker girls to marry. The ceremony took place in St Mary's Church, half a mile up the hill from her house. Isabella was twenty-four and her bridegroom, Edward Collins Dansey, was a widowed Royal Navy lieutenant of forty-three. Her disparaging reference to the 'mode' of her marriage suggested that it was not a love match; she later said that she had married on impulse, propelled by 'headstrong passion'. It was none the less a mutually advantageous union. Edward Dansey was from an ancient local family, the former lords of the manor in which Isabella's father had purchased his estate. He brought £6,000 to the marriage, which Isabella almost matched with

£5,000 settled upon her by her father. This capital would have yielded a comfortable income of about £900 a year.

After their wedding the couple moved to the nearby market town of Ludlow, where Isabella gave birth to a son, Alfred Hamilton Dansey, in February 1841. Early in the nineteenth century, Ludlow 'had balls in the assembly rooms', Henry James reported. 'It had Mrs Siddons to plays; it had Catalini to sing. Miss Burney's and Miss Austen's heroines might easily have had their first love affairs there.' The Danseys' house – built in 1625 and re-fronted with eight Venetian windows in the mid-eighteenth century – was next to a ballroom in Broad Street, a picturesque road that careered down to the River Teme. Isabella and her new family were installed at the heart of Shropshire society.

In December 1841, though, Edward Dansey suddenly went mad. Isabella's mother told a relative that 'Poor Mr Dansey' had become 'perfectly deranged' and 'required constant restraint & incessant vigilance'. She reported that Isabella's eighteen-year-old brother Frederick had gone to stay in the Danseys' house in Ludlow 'in order to attend to the poor sufferer & to console his sister under this most painful of all trials'. Five months later Dansey died of 'a diseased brain', aged forty-seven.

Edward Dansey had already settled money on Alfred, but everything he owned upon his death passed to his son by his first marriage, Celestin, a young lieutenant with the Royal Bombay Fusiliers. Isabella inherited nothing. She probably returned with her baby to Ashford Court.

Isabella lived as a widow for two years before she was introduced to Henry Oliver Robinson, an Irish Protestant six years her senior. The couple may have met through Henry's sister Sarah, whose husband was a solicitor and alderman in Hereford, twenty miles south of Ludlow. Henry came from a family of itinerant and entrepreneurial manufacturers. As a young man in Londonderry, the city of his birth, he had run a brewery and distillery that produced 8,000 gallons of spirits a year, and he was now in business building boats and sugar mills with a brother in London. Henry had since 1841 been an associate of the Institute of Civil Engineers, a body that regulated a relatively new, fast-growing profession; by 1850, there were about 900 engineers in Britain.

Isabella twice refused Henry's proposals of marriage, but when he asked for a third time she accepted: 'I suffered my scruples & dislike to be talked away by others,' she later explained in a letter, '& with my eyes almost open I walked into the bonds of a dreaded wedlock like one fated.' As a thirty-one-year-old widow with a child, she was not in a position to be picky. This marriage would at least offer her the chance to travel beyond the bounds of her corner of the country, to see new places and meet new people.

After a wedding in Hereford on 29 February 1844, Henry and Isabella moved to London, where their first child, Charles Otway, was born in a house in Camden Town just under a year later. He was christened Charles after Isabella's father, but there seems to have been no precedent for the name Otway in either of his parents' families. Isabella may have chosen it in tribute to the popular Restoration dramatist Thomas Otway, who wrote plays – dubbed 'she-tragedies' – about virtuous and afflicted ladies. Her pet name for this second and favourite son was Doatie, and she doted upon him.

Soon after Otway's birth the family moved to Blackheath Park, an expensive new estate just outside London. Their house was two miles south of Greenwich, from which a ferry regularly made the crossing to the Robinson iron works on the north bank of the Thames. Henry and his brother Albert designed and built steam-powered ships and sugar-cane mills at Millwall, amid the scrub and marsh lining the river east of the city. They turned out sheet metal, engines and parts in their manufactory, and employed several hundred men to construct boats and mills on site. In one project, which brought in £100,000, Albert designed five craft for the River Ganges, which were built and dismantled at Millwall, shipped to Calcutta (a four-month journey), and reassembled there under his supervision. In 1848 the Robinson brothers bought the iron yard for just £12,000 (it had been purchased for £50,000 more than a decade earlier). Their younger brother Richard joined the business, as did the pioneering naval architect and engineer John Scott Russell. The company, now known as Robinson & Russell, launched a dozen sea-going ships over the next three years, the first of them the *Taman*, an iron packet commissioned by the Russian government to ply the Black Sea from Odessa to Circassia. On the day of the *Taman*'s launch in November 1848, a large crowd gathered, many in steamboats and rowing boats, to watch the ship edge down the ramp, slowly at first, and then with a final, fast swoop into the river.

Henry's marriage to Isabella had secured him money as well as status. Just before their wedding, Isabella's father had settled £5,000 upon her 'for her sole and separate use', as he had done on her first marriage; this was a common means of circumventing the law that gave a man rights over all his wife's property. The interest from this fund – about £430 a year – was paid by the trustees (her father and her brother Frederick) into an account in her name at the banking house of Gosling & Co. in Fleet Street, London. Almost immediately after the marriage, though, Henry suggested that Isabella sign all her cheques and hand them over to him; he would then cash them as he saw fit, to pay for their domestic and personal expenses. Isabella assented. Henry was 'a person of very imperious temper', she explained later, and 'to prevent as far as possible any difference from arising' between them, she was willing to let him have his way. Henry gave Isabella cash to pay the tradesmen's bills and the wages of their female servants, as well as to buy household goods and clothes for herself and the children. He supplied her with some pocket money, and instructed her on how to keep accounts. The Robinson family's expenditure was about £1,000 a year, which placed it in the richest one per cent of the population and in the higher echelons of the upper middle classes.

Henry's appropriations of Isabella's money did not stop there, she said. When her father died at the end of 1847, leaving her an additional £1,000, Henry immediately withdrew the whole amount with one of the blank cheques that Isabella had signed, and invested it in his own name in London & North Western Railway stock. Though he arranged for the interest to be paid into Isabella's account – to which he in any case had sole access – he kept the capital. Isabella claimed that Henry also tried to suppress the surname of his stepson, Alfred Dansey, in order to make himself the heir to his legacy, and annexed £2,000 of the boy's settled property. In the face of Henry's greed, Isabella said, she was 'irresolute': 'chafing; yet still passive'. 'With every knowledge that my partner was mean & grasping,' she wrote, 'I made no stand against his encroachments, but suffered him to take from me one thing after another.'

In February 1849, Isabella gave birth to her third and last child, Alexander Stanley. At the time of his birth she was staying in a terrace in the seaside resort of Brighton, Sussex, two hours from London by the fastest train. She had probably taken lodgings there for the sake of her health. That year she tipped into a deep depression of spirits, accompanied by severe headaches and menstrual problems, and Dr Joseph Kidd in Blackheath identified her ailments as signs of 'uterine disease'. Henry was away on business in North America for six months in 1849. Isabella began to keep a diary: a friend in loneliness and in sickness, a companion and confidant.

'I know not where to turn for help,' she told her diary, 'and a dull load of dejection and nameless oppression weighs down my very soul. I have no sympathy, no love, for I do not deserve it. My darling boys are the only ray of comfort I possess.'

Though she sometimes behaved badly towards her sons – striking them in anger, favouring Doatie over the others – her love for them rescued her from the darkest moods. She said that she shared with them a bond 'of *no common* strength'.

Isabella, like many nineteenth-century women, used her journal as a place in which to confess her weakness, her sadness and her sins. In its pages she audited her behaviour and her thoughts; she grappled with her errors and tried to plot out a path to virtue. Yet by channelling her strong and unruly feelings into this book, Isabella also created a record and a memory of those feelings. She found herself telling a story, a serial in daily parts, in which she was the wronged and desperate heroine.

The Robinsons chose to move to Edinburgh after Henry's return from America because the city was renowned for its liberal and moderately priced schools. Here, their boys could be well educated without having to board away from home. Henry rented a six-storey granite house for his family at 11 Moray Place, at a cost of about £150 a year. Moray Place was the most lavish development in the New Town, a twelve-sided circus of houses built on tilting ground; just to the north, the land sheered down to the Water of Leith, through pleasure gardens planted with rhododendrons and hazel. The heavy grandeur of Moray Place was not to all tastes. 'It has been objected,' noted *Black's Guide Through Edinburgh* in 1851, 'that the simplicity of style and massiveness of structure which particularly distinguish these buildings, impart an aspect of solemnity and gloom repugnant to the character of domestic architecture.' The Robinsons kept four servants: a manservant, a cook, a maid and a nurse.

Inside 11 Moray Place, a broad staircase led to the reception rooms on the first floor and to the bedrooms above. The living rooms were wide, deep and panelled, with large windows that afforded views of a round, green park to the front of the house and a triangular garden to the back. At the top of the stairwell, a stucco frieze adorned a domed skylight: some of the cherubs in the frieze cavorted among the stylised foliage; others perched primly on the leaves, reading books.

A narrower staircase continued up to the children's rooms on the top floor. From the back windows of her sons' bedrooms, Isabella could see the roof of 8 Royal Circus, and past it the tower of St Stephen's, the church in which three years earlier Edward Lane had married Lady Drysdale's daughter Mary.

Isabella became a frequent visitor to the Lanes and Drysdales' home. Their house lay a quarter of a mile north-east of her own, a journey of a few minutes on foot or by carriage. She was invited to the family's parties – on one evening in Isabella's first year in the city Lady Drysdale held a huge children's party, on another a 'strawberry feast' – and she became acquainted with others in their circle: successful lady novelists such as Susan Stirling and influential thinkers such as the phrenologist George Combe. Lady Drysdale was 'a great patroness of everything scientific and literary', according to Charles Piazzi Smyth, the Astronomer Royal for Scotland. Another friend, the art critic Elizabeth Rigby, described her as '*unique* in my estimation in the act of diffusing happiness . . . I never met with so warm-hearted and unselfish a woman.' Lady Drysdale was a keen philanthropist who loved to take the dispossessed into her fold – Italian revolutionaries, Polish refugees, and now Isabella, an exile from her own marriage.

Isabella had never loved her husband; by the time they moved to Edinburgh, she despised him. A photograph of Henry in this period conforms to her description of him as narrow and haughty; he sits stiff and upright in a jacket, waistcoat, shirt and cravat, clutching a silver-topped cane in his right hand; he is skinny-chested, tight-waisted, a sure-looking man with a long nose in a long face. Isabella said that she tried not to pry into Henry's private life, but by now she had discovered that he had a mistress and two illegitimate daughters. She had come to believe that he had married her only for her money.

Within months, Isabella was visiting the Lanes and the Drysdales almost every day. She talked to Edward Lane about poetry and philosophy, debating new ideas and encouraging him to write essays for publication. Henry, by contrast, had no interest in literature, Isabella complained in a letter to a friend; he was quite unable 'to parse & interpret any line of poetry I might have quoted – either of my own or other people's!'. She used to invite the Lanes' eldest boy, Arthur, to play with her sons, especially after Mary Lane gave birth to a second child, William, early in 1851. Edward, in turn, often invited Isabella and her sons to accompany him and Arthur on drives to the coast – 'Atty' was a delicate boy, and Edward tried to strengthen him with regular rides to the sea in a phaeton, a fast, open carriage with a springy body and four high wheels. By the beach at Granton, a few miles north-west of the city, Isabella and Edward sat discussing poetry while they watched the children play on the rocks and sand.

In the grey afternoon of Sunday 14 March 1852, Isabella took a turn through the New Town on foot. The three-year-old Stanley probably stayed home with the nursemaid, an Irishwoman called Eliza Power, but Otway and Alfred, aged seven and eleven, accompanied their mother. The group climbed the hill from Moray Place and carried on over the summit and down to Princes Street, a wide avenue on the southern edge of the New Town. A terrace of houses ran along one side of the street. The facing pavement was reined in only by an iron railing, beyond which lay a steep drop and a far view over the dip of the ravine to the blackened tenements of the Old Town on the hill beyond: 'the city, dimly visible, lay before us', wrote Isabella in her diary, 'spires, monuments, streets, the port of Leith, the Frith, and in the front ground small unventilated dwellings, and houses of ten-storeys high'.

Isabella was gazing across a gulf from rich to poor, from the sparse, clear streets of modern Edinburgh to the busy, vertical slums of the old. The area between the New and Old towns had been drained and levelled at the beginning of the century, and in 1842 a railway line had been laid into the gorge. Though a few shops had set up along Princes Street, there was a lonely luxury to the thoroughfares along which Isabella walked with her sons. On a Sunday, the area was desolate. The shops were shut up and the blinds of the houses drawn. Isabella wished that she could enter the secret warren across the tracks. 'Oh, thought I, each of these roofs conceals human life with all its mysterious joys and sorrows. Doubtless, many a sojourner in these dwellings has a private history, thrilling, exciting, strange. If I knew them, some of them might make me feel less sad, less lonely. There might be hearts as much discontented with their lots as mine; few, I think, more weary of life.

'I walked home with my boys,' she continued. 'At heart I love and value them, and were it not that my darling Otway would be taken from me I would leave my husband for ever.' If she and Henry were to part, she would retain custody of Alfred, the child of her first husband, and perhaps of Stanley – the Custody of Infants Act of 1839 for the first time allowed a separated woman to petition for custody of any of her children who were under seven, as long as she was of good character. Doatie, though, would be certain to remain with his father.

Isabella reached her house at half past five, and tried to calm her troubled spirits: 'played psalms, wrote Journal, read, smoked cigar; boys with me till nine. Felt rather less sad'. To read, to play the piano and to spend time with children were conventional pastimes for a middle-class Victorian woman; to smoke a cigar, though, was a distinctly rebellious, unfeminine act.

On Saturday 27 March 1852, Isabella organised an outing for herself and her children. She invited Edward to accompany them, and hired a carriage and driver to pick up both families after lunch. Henry was away.

The morning was cold and bright. 'Resolved to get ready early for the drive,' Isabella wrote, 'to which I could not help looking forward with pleasure, not unmixed with a *dread* that something seemed to mar the pleasure I had promised myself, as it nearly always does with me.' The day started badly: she got up late, which meant that she missed an appointment, and a glass of sherry before lunch gave her 'a confused headache'. She became annoyed by her sons' rude behaviour in the garden. 'I dined in haste,' she told her diary, 'and left home immediately, not to lose the fairness of the day.'

On reaching 8 Royal Circus, Isabella discovered that her dread had been justified: 'after some delay and confusion, I found Mrs L— was to go too, and I knew well that all hope of a pleasant *tête-à-tête* was over for that day. I could hardly bid her and Atty welcome, or affect good humour, much less gaiety.' Isabella had become used to having Edward to herself.

The two families set out by carriage, with the three boys outside on the box and the three adults inside. They headed north towards the sea and then west along the coast, passing the new harbour at Granton. Inside the carriage, 'the talk was formal and confused. Mr L— read scraps from Coleridge and Tennyson.' They discussed an essay by Edward 'on the error of sudden judgments unfounded on knowledge', written at Isabella's suggestion, which had appeared in that morning's number of *Chambers's Edinburgh Journal*. Five miles on, the carriage drew up near a line of whitewashed cottages in the seaside village of Cramond, at the mouth of the River Almond, where the party scaled a steep path to a sheltered sunny corner on the bank. There they laid out their books and their plaids. To the north lay the rocky grassland of Cramond Island, to which day-trippers could walk at low tide across the sandy flats.

Mary Lane took the boys off to gather gorse, leaving Isabella and Edward alone, but 'no real cheerfulness came to my heart', said Isabella. She and Edward talked – 'of life, of Cana, of property, of riches, and of birth . . . of dejection, education, poverty, etc.' – and read out 'a few disjointed passages from our poets', including, Isabella remembered, Samuel Taylor Coleridge's 'Dejection: An Ode'. The poem described a mood that resembled her own: a 'smothering weight', 'A grief without a pang, void, dark, and drear,/ A stifled, drowsy, unimpassioned grief'.

'We rose to go when the sun got low,' wrote Isabella. 'Got into the carriage and kept up a conversation . . . wholly without interest on my part; duly admiring the views which were fine.'

Back in the city, the carriage dropped the Lanes at Royal Circus, where Isabella's 'starved boys' climbed off the box and got inside. They arrived back at Moray Place at half past six, with Isabella feeling 'as much vexed, dispirited, chagrined, and cast down as I ever remember to have been'.

Isabella remonstrated with herself for leaving a bad impression on the Lanes. 'Mrs Lane looked several times cold and puzzled,' she wrote; 'he was constrained; the child was tired; no one was obliged or pleased.' She usually presented a composed front to her friends, and unburdened herself to her diary, but on this day her dissatisfaction had been all too visible. 'I had spent 8 shillings for worse than nothing,' she wrote, caught between self-pity and self-disgust. 'Good God! Why is it everything I plan or wish for is turned to such bitterness? Surely it must be my own fault. I long for things I ought not to prize. I find it impossible to love where I ought, or to keep from loving where I ought not.

'My mind is a chaos,' she confessed, 'a confused mingling of good and evil. I weary of my very self, yet cannot die.'

Isabella then received a note – a 'cold line' – from Edward. She had intended to accompany his family the next morning to hear a sermon by the Rev. Dr Thomas Guthrie, one of the leaders of the Free Church of Scotland; but Edward told her that the service had been cancelled. Isabella retired at midnight 'to a sad and lonely couch, sick and low at heart'. The diary, at least, offered her solace, salvaging something from the ruins of her expedition: 'Felt a sad relief in thus writing the history of a lost day.' By putting words to her discontent, she felt it lifted from her. The diarist heroine of Anne Brontë's *The Tenant of Wildfell Hall*, a novel of 1848, notices the same phenomenon: 'I have found relief describing the very circumstances that have destroyed my peace.'

A fortnight after the outing to Cramond, Isabella was again tormented by her feelings for Edward Lane. 'Very fine, clear, agreeable day,' she recorded on Wednesday 7 April. 'Miserably and unusually depressed.'

Isabella got up late. Henry was bad-tempered and rude, and she wrote a letter to her mother complaining about him. She then called on Mary Lane at Royal Circus. 'Mrs L— very kind; she is a sweet, amiable temper, and shines when there is any sorrow to be soothed.' Upon joining the rest of the family, though, Isabella was wounded by Edward's seeming indifference. He 'chatted with every one in the room, and was more gay and talking than usual' but 'careless in manner, and hardly looked at me'. The Lanes saw her home in a fly. 'I was wretched; and as I got out of the fly at my house and shook hands with them with a hand cold as marble, I felt that I was not fit for their society.' She stole in to the house and up to her room, avoiding Henry. Like many upper-middle-class couples of the time, she and he had separate bedrooms. Isabella heard from the nursemaid, Eliza, that the boys were all well, and then 'retired to rest thoroughly mortified'.

After such disappointment, the renewal of Edward Lane's attentions only thrilled Isabella the more. She rose at eleven on 13 April, a fine, warm Tuesday morning, and sat in the garden reading a book by one of the Schlegel brothers, the founders of German Romanticism and advocates of love and freedom. Alfred was at school, but Otway was unwell and had been kept at home with Stanley. At four o'clock, Isabella went shopping and at five she picked up Atty Lane from Royal Circus and took him to her house. 'Children played in garden,' she wrote. 'St— very quarrelsome; his temper is excitable and passionate.' She returned Atty to Lady Drysdale at eight in the evening, and then went with Edward, Mary and 'Miss R', another friend, to a lecture on Homer. This was one of a series of talks given that April at the Philosophical Institution in Queen Street by John Stuart Blackie, Edinburgh University's new Professor of Greek. Professor Blackie, by his own account, could be an 'elastic and buoyant' public speaker, inducing in his audience 'a state not merely of delighted attention but of manifest exhilaration and glee'. In the lecture hall, Isabella sat on one side of Edward and Mary on the other. The professor's talk was 'amusing and original', wrote Isabella. She and Edward chatted before and after the lecture. 'We talked of nicknames and of grave characters, and I was merry, much excited by his presence. We laughed much.'

They continued to talk on the ten-minute walk back to their houses. 'Mrs L— and Miss R— walked on in front out of hearing. We spoke of weather, quoted poetry on the subject, discussed Homer, Shakespeare, talent, etc.' Isabella reached home in a state of high and agitated pleasure. 'These dark walks are very exciting,' she wrote, 'and on retiring to my lonely bed, I was too much roused to sleep, and tossed about for hours.'

At the party at Royal Circus on 15 November 1850 Isabella had also met the publisher and writer Robert Chambers, a bear-like man with swathes of wavy hair. They were neighbours: the back windows of the Robinsons' house overlooked the back windows of Robert and Anne Chambers's house in Doune Terrace. Robert was one of the city's leading literary men; he and his brother William ran the popular progressive magazine *Chambers's Edinburgh Journal*, which sold more than 80,000 copies a week. Within two months of meeting the Robinsons, Chambers had twice dined with them at Moray Place, and the Robinsons had twice attended parties at Doune Terrace. The next May, while Henry was away, Isabella went to a dinner party at the Chambers' house at which the other guests included the bestselling author Catherine Crowe, another near neighbour, and the young actress Isabella Glyn. At about this time Isabella Robinson began to submit poems to *Chambers's Edinburgh Journal*.

The only published verse that can be identified as hers, 'Lines Addressed to a Miniature, By a Lady', appeared under the initials 'IHR' in the number of 2 August 1851. The poem describes a woman's secret longing for a man who belongs to another. Unable to gaze openly upon the man himself, she dwells instead on a miniature portrait of him. Unable to disclose her feelings to him, she confesses herself to his image. She tells the picture: 'In vain I met, I knew, approved, and loved/ Him whose most truthful likeness thou dost bear.' For all the poem's high romance, there is no mistaking the narrator's physical yearning for this man: 'How sweetly on those closed and manly lips/Firmness and love together hold their sway!/ Thy form I see, with strength and courage braced./ Thy glance with all its native energy!' Her beloved, like the miniature painting, is innocent of her desire for him – 'calm and unmoved, unconscious of my eye' – and she burns with jealousy of the woman he has chosen over her. 'My heart is rent,' writes the love-struck lady, 'my inmost spirit seared.'

Isabella's journal was the equivalent of this miniature, a memento of the man she loved, a place where she spoke privately in order to keep her public silence. The lady in the poem vows to conceal her feelings – 'prayer and silence shall alone be mine' – though by putting words to her thoughts she has already half-broken her pledge. The diary, like the poem, exposed as well as buried Isabella's secrets. But she insisted on her privacy: '*Here* I may gaze and dream, and fear no blame,' her poem says. '*This* I may love and prize unseen – alone.'

CHAPTER TWO

POOR DEAR DODDY

Edinburgh, 1840–52

Edward Wickstead Lane, the object of Isabella's love, was born in 1823 into a Presbyterian family on the French-speaking island of Terrebonne, Quebec. Soon after his birth the family moved to the neighbouring city of Montreal, where his father, Elisha, found work as a clerk to a Scottish-born wholesaler. When Edward was nine, his mother died, leaving him and his four-year-old brother Arthur in their father's care. Elisha Lane and his boss built up a business importing liquor, meat and grain to Montreal and by the late 1830s Elisha was rich enough to send his sons to Edinburgh to be educated. Within a decade his company had assets valued at £70,000.

The Lane boys lodged with a family in the New Town and attended the renowned Edinburgh Academy, where Edward became a close friend of Elizabeth Drysdale's son George. While Edward was a sociable boy, George Drysdale was intense and self-conscious. Both were outstanding pupils. In 1840 Edward was named 'Dux of the Academy' – the highest honour in the school – and the title passed the next year to George. Edward won prizes for his achievements in French and English, both as a writer and as a speaker, George for

Latin, English, French, mathematics and arithmetic. Afterwards George read Classics at Glasgow, where he won six prizes in his first year. Edward read Law at Edinburgh University, where he continued to be praised for his eloquence and was elected in 1842 to the celebrated Speculative Society debating club. As a student, Edward took rooms at 30 Royal Circus, a few doors along from the house that the Drysdales had occupied since it was built in the early 1820s. He became intimate with several members of the family: George's parents, Sir William and Lady Drysdale, his younger brother, Charles, and – especially – his elder sister, Mary.

Mary was a small, sensitive young woman, clever, affectionate and trusting. She appears frequently in Isabella Robinson's diary as an innocent figure, seemingly oblivious to her friend's passionate interest in her husband. But Mary and Edward were bound together by shared sufferings that Isabella, in her anxious self-attention, may have failed to catch. These concerned George, Mary's beloved brother and Edward's best friend, and they began in 1843, when he was nineteen.

George was at university in Glasgow when his father, Sir William, died of cholera in June 1843; two weeks later, George's older half-brother William Drysdale died of the same disease in India. George suffered a breakdown, abandoned his studies and returned to his mother's house in Royal Circus.

The family and their friends rallied round. To help George recover his strength and spirits, his brother Charles and his friend Edward, who had just taken his law degree, accompanied him in 1844 on a walking tour of Europe. But while they were staying in Vienna, George disappeared. Charles and Edward's desperate search for him ended only with the discovery of George's clothes lying on the banks of the River Danube. His body was not recovered and his companions returned to Scotland with the news of his death. 'The deceased's mother and friends were in the deepest distress,' reported Lord Cockburn, an eminent Edinburgh judge who lived in Royal

Circus; George, he said, was 'the ablest and the most amiable boy I almost ever knew.' The newspapers announced that George had died while bathing in the Danube, and his tragic end became the subject of prize poems that year by students at the Edinburgh Academy.

Just under two years later, in March 1846, George reappeared. He begged his family's forgiveness. He had faked his death, he confessed, in lieu of taking his life. Lord Cockburn, in a letter to a friend, reported that George had been 'in a state of grievous despair of fulfilling the kindly expectations he had excited, and thought it would be less grievous to his friends to lament his death than his failure; and that therefore he had combined this with avoiding suicide, by *pretending* to be drowned'. Wolfgang von Goethe's late-eighteenth-century novel *The Sorrows of Young Werther* had supposedly inspired a spate of suicides by young men anxious to emulate its hero, and Cockburn speculated that George had been afflicted by 'a sudden Germanising of the noddle'. But he was baffled that such a beloved boy could have behaved so irrationally, and cruelly: 'the heartlessness of his conduct is the incomprehensible part of it'. The Drysdales' 'horror of his resurrection', claimed Cockburn, was 'perhaps greater than their grief for his death'.

George had tried to achieve a strange kind of annihilation in which, instead of ending his life, he shed his identity and his past. Amid their joy at his return, his mother and his siblings must have experienced some of the confusion and hurt that Cockburn attributed to them. But Mary, in a letter to a friend in Tasmania, expressed only compassion for her lost little brother: 'our dearest, our idolised boy did not perish in the Danube, but is *alive* and *well* & at present with us, having reached us only last Thursday . . . Poor poor fellow, dear Doddy, he has suffered much since we parted both in *mind* and *body*, but now through the mercy of the Almighty Father he has been conducted safe back to his happy family.'

Although not yet quite well, she said, he was getting much better, and his mind was 'purified, humbled, yet strengthened by the trials he has undergone'.

John James Drysdale, Sir William's son by a previous marriage, came from Liverpool to see George. John, at forty, was one of the leading homeopaths in Britain, the editor of both the homeopathic manual *Materia Medica* and the *British Journal of Homeopathy*. The theory of his chosen branch of medicine – which was contentious even among the liberal medics of Edinburgh – was that solutions of medicinal substances, diluted so as to be almost undetectable, would effect cures. After examining his half-brother, John Drysdale diagnosed a nervous collapse brought on by overwork and instructed the family to keep George clear of books.

Mary reported to her friend that over the previous two years, George had 'suffered under a temporary pressure on the brain, occasioned by overstudy, which rendered *impossible* to him any reflection on the step he was taking, & impelled alone by a feeling of suffering, he travelled to Hungary, where he has ever since been living, acting as teacher of English to the only son of a nobleman there, & treated by the family with the greatest kindness, nay even affection and confidence'. Eventually, the pressure on George's brain subsided '& then he could not rest till he shd see us all once more'.

The family was dazed with delight at seeing George again. 'We cannot gaze at him nor listen to him sufficiently, poor fellow,' wrote Mary; 'the past seems to him & to us like a fearful dream, from wh. we have just awakened to know what happiness & thankfulness are.' She found him gentler, kinder, more warm-hearted than ever. 'Our dear Mama looks with happiness many years younger since our darling one has returned, & dear Charlie's sad face has cleared up, & we all feel so very happy that we would not exchange places with any human being.' Their homeopath brother John reassured them that George's health would improve and that one day he might even be able to take up a profession. In the meantime, they were to 'guard him well from any temptation to study'.

The Drysdale family and Edward Lane must have known something of the truth. George's condition stemmed not so much from intellectual stress as from what he called his 'secret shame': a sexual neurosis. In an anonymous work he later published, he described himself as having been a young man 'of active, studious, and erotic disposition, but of almost feminine bashfulness'. 'In Scotland,' he explained, 'where there is a stricter sexual code than in perhaps any other country, and where the lusts of the flesh, as they are called, are stigmatised and controlled as much as possible, sexual shyness and timidity constitute a great *national* disease, and cause more unhappiness among young people, than can well be conceived.' At fifteen he accidentally discovered masturbation, and found that the practice offered an 'easy mode of satisfying his passions, which had long been the source of unrest and torment to his vivid imagination'. For about a year, George masturbated two or three times a day. As he moved on to university in Glasgow, at the age of seventeen, he began to discharge semen involuntarily at night: he became terrified that his compulsion had started to control him, to sap his strength and to push him towards madness. It was at this point that his father and his half-brother died and he returned home in distress.

On his trip to Europe with Edward and Charles in 1844, George found that he was still a slave to his vice. This so disturbed him that he decided to stage his own death. Afterwards, while living secretly in Hungary, he underwent a series of operations to cauterise his penis – that is, to deaden or destroy its nerve endings by inserting into the urethra a thin metal rod coated in a caustic substance. He submitted himself to this procedure seven or eight times.

Even in 1846, having returned to his family in Scotland, George continued to seek a cure. In May, he travelled to the

Continent for treatment. That summer Mary wrote a letter to the publisher John Murray, who knew the family, entreating him to help George; her brother was alone in Paris, she explained, waiting to consult the French doctor Claude François Lallemand. She did not mention that Lallemand had recently published a work that identified compulsive masturbatory urges as marks of a dangerous illness. In his study of involuntary ejaculation, printed in French in 1842 and in English in 1847, the doctor argued that both body and mind were corrupted by the excessive discharge of semen. The work of Lallemand and other French researchers set off a moral and medical panic about onanism that was to continue throughout the century. Masturbation was the dark corollary of the individualism so prized by Victorian society, an embodiment of the dangers of privacy and self-reliance: a man like George Drysdale might lose himself in books and dreams, folding inwards into a dissolute imaginary realm.

Mary explained to Murray that Edward Lane had travelled to France with George but had 'been obliged to hurry home'. She asked that Murray encourage a friend in Paris to call on George at his hotel, and so 'prevent him from feeling so lonely as he does at present poor fellow'. She and her family dreaded 'the evil effects so much solitude may produce on dear George's spirits and health'. Her reference to the 'evil effects' of solitude may have been an allusion to the suicidal impulses to which George was prey; or perhaps Murray was aware of George's sexual compulsions. Mary added a postscript in which she appealed to the publisher to be discreet: 'pray do not mention to your friend any circumstances connected with his past history as we are anxious he should himself forget it poor fellow'.

Edward Lane's sudden flight from Paris that summer was probably occasioned by a tragedy in his own family. His younger brother Arthur had graduated from the Edinburgh Academy in 1845, and returned to their father's home in

Canada. On 26 June 1846 he went to Quebec's Theatre Royal to watch a chemical diorama – a show in which scenes painted on huge sheets of linen were lit and layered in ways that made them seem magically to alter and dissolve. As the curtain fell at the end of the evening, it brushed against the flame of an overturned camphene lamp and almost instantly the stage and then the auditorium were alight. The audience rushed to the exit but the passage was narrow and the fire too fast: within minutes, forty-six men, women and children were dead. A bystander saw the eighteen-year-old Arthur in his final moments, 'overturned, in a half-recumbent position, with both feet firmly wedged in the mass of writhing humanity under it'. He 'appeared to struggle hard; soon the surrounding flames hid him from sight'.

A year after Arthur Lane's death and George Drysdale's resurrection, Edward Lane and Mary Drysdale were married. The ceremony took place in June 1847, when both bride and groom were twenty-four. George came to the wedding in Edinburgh, but then made for Europe again, and Edward and Mary met up with him while they were on honeymoon in Strasbourg. Mary said that she had never seen her brother look better: 'he was in high spirits', 'quite overjoyed' at seeing her, 'for by that time he had become quite tired of solitude'. In the book that he later published, George explained that he had taken Lallemand's advice to try coition, with astonishing success. Intercourse with prostitutes, he discovered, quite cured his urge to masturbate.

Outwardly, George remained awkward and reserved. He was later remembered by a young woman of his acquaintance as 'kind but shy, gentle but oppressive; he had a hard, Scottish face, and was silent, grave, serious, learned, a moral and mental impregnability like a vast mountain or a granite wall'. After the crisis his family kept close by him. Though Edward completed his legal training and was admitted to the prestigious Faculty of Advocates in 1847, he and the Drysdale family moved that year to Dublin, where George had decided to study medicine. Charles Drysdale, having spent one year studying mathematics in Edinburgh (where he came top of his class) and another in Cambridge, enrolled at Trinity College Dublin to train as an engineer. It was a strange time to move to the city: Ireland was in the throes of a great famine, triggered by a potato blight, and hundreds of thousands of Irish were dying of hunger and disease or fleeing the country.

Mary became pregnant in Dublin, and Lady Drysdale asked her Edinburgh friend James Young Simpson to recommend a local doctor who could administer chloroform during her daughter's labour; Simpson had discovered the anaesthetic properties of the gas that year in an experiment conducted in his house in the New Town. In Dublin in 1848, Mary Lane gave birth to a boy. She and Edward named him Arthur George, in tribute to their two brothers.

The family moved back to Edinburgh in 1849. Edward, having lost his own mother when he was nine, submitted gladly to Lady Drysdale's benign dominion at 8 Royal Circus. He decided to abandon the profession for which he had spent the previous seven years preparing, and instead to follow George into medicine. Perhaps the sufferings of his brother-in-law inspired him to take up doctoring, as well as his interest in the new sciences. A medical degree was then the only scientific education available in Britain, and the Edinburgh course was known to provide a practical as well as an intellectually rigorous training. Both young men enrolled at the university in the autumn of 1849.

As a medical student, Edward worked at the Edinburgh Royal Infirmary, which drew most of its patients from the working classes. He was dismayed by what he saw on the wards and became convinced that conventional medical interventions – with leeches and enemas, laxatives and mercury – were usually useless and sometimes actively damaging to health. The Royal Infirmary, as he pointed out in his final thesis, even exposed the sick to infection by putting contagious patients in general wards; he said that he knew of two people who had died as a result of this practice. Though he did not detail the ineffective and painful treatments administered by the infirmary's physicians, he witnessed plenty. One patient – a seaman in his thirties – was admitted with an abdominal aneurism in 1849, and for the next four years was bled, cupped and stuck with leeches (up to fourteen at a time) until eventually he put himself out of his misery with an overdose of aconite.

Edward noticed 'the total dearth of *books* of every description' on the wards of the Royal Infirmary and deplored 'the perfect mental blank' this inflicted on the patients: 'The effect on the spirits, it is clear, is as bad as possible . . . and the depression of spirits does its work on the health.' To combat this evil, he asked Charles Dickens to supply the hospital with free copies of his weekly magazine *Household Words* and Robert Chambers to provide *Chambers's Edinburgh Journal*. Both agreed. The new bestseller *Uncle Tom's Cabin*, by Harriet Beecher Stowe, was also popular with the patients.

During his time on the wards, Edward began to conceive of more humane and natural ways of treating illness, methods of healing the mind and the body in unison. He became convinced that environment could transform a patient's prospects of recovery. The sick were much more likely to get better, he argued in his thesis, if housed in hospitals in the suburbs or the countryside, where they could exercise gently in daylight and pure air, surrounded by the sights and sounds and smells of nature. The inmates of the Royal Infirmary had access only to 'the prison-gloom of a damp back-green, overgrown on every side with rank grass, and shut out from the rattle of a busy thoroughfare by a dingy wall'. He asked his fellow doctors to recognise 'the immense resources possessed and wielded by nature towards her self-cure, as compared with the pigmy, tentative, and too often only hap-hazard means, which the very best human skill can furnish'.

Edward's brothers-in-law were similarly sceptical about traditional medicine. John, the homeopath, was expelled from the Liverpool Medical Institute in 1849 because of his insistence on administering homeopathic remedies to cholera victims – with, he claimed, great success. George had discovered for himself that medical interventions failed to cure onanism; only the natural cure of sexual intercourse had saved him. He abandoned university again in 1851, this time to start work on a clandestine project, his book about sex.

Like George Drysdale, Isabella Robinson was excitable and depressive, ambitious and anxious. Like him, she was disturbed by her sexual appetites. Her lust, she believed, had hastened her into two bad marriages and was now snaring her in longing for Edward Lane. He was not the only object of her affections: another – unidentified – married gentleman in their circle claimed that Isabella besieged him with letters in an attempt to seduce him, and that he eventually disentangled himself by begging his wife never to let her in their house again. In Edinburgh, Isabella at least found a new way of thinking about her erotic urges. Her teacher was George Combe, a luminary of the Drysdales' circle and the pioneer of phrenology in Britain. The sixty-two-year-old Mr Combe was a thin, tall man, with a wide mouth, strong cheekbones and a huge, high forehead. He lived in the New Town with his wife, Cecilia, a daughter of the actress Sarah Siddons.

When Isabella met Combe in 1850 she adopted him as a surrogate father – her regard for him, she said, was 'quite filial in its character'. She believed him to be 'the exponent of a clearer, & more spiritual creed, than any yet preached to man'. Mrs Combe's cousin Fanny Kemble agreed that he was 'a man of singular integrity, uprightness, and purity of mind and character, and of great justice and impartiality of judgment; he was extremely benevolent and humane, and one of the most reasonable human beings I have ever known'. Marian Evans, later to become famous as a novelist under the pseudonym George Eliot, was also a friend and an admirer: 'I often think of you,' she wrote to him, 'when I want some one to whom I could confess all my difficulties and struggles with my own nature'.

Combe's book *The Constitution of Man in Relation to External Objects* (1828) had sold 90,000 copies by 1851, most of them in an edition published by Robert Chambers. An enormously controversial work, it proposed that man should accept his subjection to the laws of nature; the secrets of health and happiness, it implied, lay in science rather than religion. In *A System of Phrenology* (1843), Combe argued specifically that people's feelings were located in their heads, that their characters could be deduced from the contours of their skulls. The bump-reading aspect of phrenology was often ridiculed, but the principles of the new science were radical and influential: Combe insisted that the mind was located in the brain, that the mind and body were indivisible, that different parts of the brain had different functions and that human nature was based in matter rather than spirit. The defining image of the theory – a brain split into numbered segments – was a model for a new science of the mind.

Soon after they met in Edinburgh, Combe examined Isabella's skull. He informed her that she had an unusually large cerebellum, an organ found just above the hollow at the nape of the neck. The cerebellum, he explained, was the seat of Amativeness, or sexual love – men typically had larger cerebella than women, discernible in their thicker necks, just as highly sexed animals such as rams, bulls and pigeons had fatter necks than other creatures. Another of Combe's subjects, the nine-year-old Prince of Wales, had a similarly shaped skull: when Queen Victoria and Prince Albert consulted the phrenologist about the upbringing of their children, he observed that the young prince's 'Amativeness is large and I suspect will soon give trouble'. Combe's own amative region, he said, was small – he had not known the 'wild freshness of morning', even in his youth.

Josef Franz Gall, the Viennese physician who invented phrenology in about 1800, claimed to have identified the amative region while attending a nymphomaniac widow. 'In the violence of a paroxysm,' explained George Combe in *A System of Phrenology*, 'he supported her head, and was struck with the great heat and size of the neck.' Combe declined to go into further detail on the subject in his book for the general reader, but he pointed 'medical students' to his translation of Gall's *On the Functions of the Cerebellum* (1838), in which he elaborated on the story of the quivering widow: 'she fell to the ground in a state of rigidity to such an extent that the nape of her neck and vertebral column were strongly drawn backwards. The crisis inevitably ended with an evacuation [an orgasmic emission], accompanied by a convulsive voluptuousness and a veritable ecstasy.' The cerebellum had since become the most established of the phrenological faculties. In *On the Management and Disorders of Infancy and Childhood* (1853), a mainstream medical manual, Thomas John Graham asserted: 'The appetite of love is seated in the cerebellum, at the base of the brain; and when excited by any cause, it does, under certain circumstances, if not indulged, become greater and greater, until it induces derangement of various functions, and hence hypochondriasis, convulsions, hysteria, and even insanity may be the result.'

Combe pointed out that Isabella's large Amativeness was made the more dangerous by her small faculties of Cautiousness and Secretiveness, positioned just above the ears on the sides of the skull; these suggested that she was liable to be impulsive and indiscreet. Perhaps most worryingly of all, she had a small organ of Veneration: the crown of her head was depressed, which suggested that she lacked reverence for earthly and heavenly authority. Isabella was not only sexually enthusiastic, then, but she was also indifferent to law, religion and morality.

Yet Combe identified two areas of Isabella's head that indicated a craving for the good opinion of others: her Love of Approbation and her Adhesiveness were both over-sized. The Love of Approbation was visible in the full, broad undulations of the back of her upper skull. Combe claimed that this faculty was often large in women and in French people, as well as in dogs, mules and monkeys. It suggested that Isabella was eager to please, and needed to guard against vanity, ambition, a hunger for praise. Her well-developed Adhesiveness – just below her Love of Approbation, and also typically larger in women than men – indicated her inclination to form strong attachments, sometimes to unsuitable objects or people. To illuminate the qualities of this part of the brain, Combe cited a piece of verse by Thomas Moore:

The heart, like a tendril accustomed to cling,
Let it grow where it will, cannot flourish alone;
But will lean to the nearest and loveliest thing
It can twine with itself, and make closely its own

Phrenology taught Isabella that the conflicting chambers of her brain accounted for the turbulence of her nature – her surges of desire and collapses into despair. It offered her a scientific explanation for her emotional difficulties, and a project for her own reform. Josef Gall had promised that his new science would 'explain the double man within you, and the reason why your propensities and your intellect . . . are so often opposed to each other'. By decoding her constitution, Isabella hoped to adjust it, enlisting the higher faculties – the intellectual and moral sentiments – to contain and control the unruly parts of her brain. She resolved to free herself from the 'self-love' instilled in her in youth and to become 'reasonable, moderate, self-possessed'.

'I could only wish and strive to amend,' Isabella wrote in her diary in February 1852, although she admitted that 'with ardent feelings, with love of approbation beyond the common, with an ill-balanced mind, and the early misfortune of a bad education' she found this 'unusually difficult'. On the one hand, phrenology suggested that people had the capacity to manage their wayward selves; and on the other that they were powerless animal organisms, at the mercy of their physiology. Isabella often felt in thrall to her misshapen brain. 'I know not how I can make myself anywise different,' she wrote. 'My heart clings to those that cannot help me, and rejects those whom I ought to love. God help me! How useless and hapless is my life; how much am I discontented with myself, and yet I persist in evil.'

The novelists Anne and Charlotte Brontë shared Isabella's belief in phrenology. The heroine of Anne's *The Tenant of Wildfell Hall* notices that her promiscuous, dipsomaniac husband has a dip at the crown of his skull, where the organ of Veneration should lie: 'The head looked right enough, but when he placed my hand on the top of it, it sunk in a bed of curls, rather alarmingly low, especially in the middle.' The heroine of Charlotte's *Jane Eyre: an Autobiography* (1848) argues that all human beings 'need exercise for their faculties'. Like Isabella, Jane is driven by passion. 'Who blames me?' she asks. 'Many no doubt; and I shall be called discontented. I could not help it. The restlessness was in my nature; and it agitated me to pain sometimes.'

Phrenologists, unlike most scientific thinkers, believed that men and women's emotions and compulsions were essentially similar. 'Women are supposed to be very calm generally,' says Jane Eyre; 'but women feel just as men feel.'

George Drysdale and Edward Lane remained intimate while Isabella was living in Edinburgh. They took walks in the city or to the sea, by themselves or in the company of their friend Robert Chambers. All three sailed from Hull to Sweden in the summer of 1851, during a violent storm, in order to witness a total eclipse of the sun. 'It was a ghastly spectacle to behold,' reported one of their party, 'a black sun surrounded by a pallid halo of light, and suspended in a sky of sombre leaden hue.' Edward Lane measured the exact duration of the eclipse with a box chronometer; the darkness was so complete that he had to light a candle to read the time.

The friends shared a keen interest in scientific phenomena. Robert Chambers, as well as being a successful publisher and journalist, was the anonymous author of the bestselling *Vestiges of the Natural History of Creation*, a proto-evolutionary, daringly materialist account of the Earth's formation. *Vestiges* was condemned by many: its author, raged the *Edinburgh Review*, 'believes . . . that mind and soul . . . are all a dream – that material organs are all in all – that he can weigh the mind as a butcher does a joint . . . He believes that the human family may be . . . of many species, and all sprung from apes.'

The authorship of *Vestiges* had been the subject of speculation ever since it was published in 1844. George Combe, as the most famous of their group, came under suspicion of having written the book, as did Catherine Crowe, whose *The Night Side of Nature* (1848) attempted to find physical explanations for apparently supernatural phenomena. Mrs Crowe was known to participate in outré scientific experiments, exploring the links between the mind and the body, visible and invisible forces. Hans Christian Andersen saw her inhaling ether at the house of Dr Simpson in 1847. 'Miss [sic] Crowe and one other poetess drank ether; I had the feeling of being with two mad creatures – they smiled with open dead eyes.'

George Combe's phrenology, Edward Lane's theory of medicine, Robert Chambers's geology, Catherine Crowe's psychical research and George Drysdale's sexual philosophy all came from the same basket. They dealt in the idea that the world and its inhabitants were not fixed but dynamic, that they were ruled by natural rather than supernatural laws and that they changed over time.

In his journal of 1839, Combe described how he put his hand to the pulsing brain of an eight-year-old girl in New York, the victim of an accident that four years earlier had cracked open her skull and exposed its contents to the air. When he provoked various emotions in the child – bashfulness, pride, pleasure – Combe felt the different faculties swell beneath his palm, giving him 'a sensation in the hand when placed on the integuments, as if one were feeling, through a silk handkerchief, the motions of a confined leech'. It was as if he were touching the child's thoughts, feeling her feeling, as if her emotional world had been made flesh.

Combe's attempts to probe the skull for clues to the life it enclosed were akin to Isabella's attempts to decipher her life by recording her experiences in a diary. Like the economist and philosopher Herbert Spencer, who described his memoirs as 'a natural history of myself', she was charting her personal evolution. By writing and reading her journal, Isabella hoped to understand her alienated, conflicting self from the outside in, to get inside her own head and under her own skin.

CHAPTER THREE

THE SILENT SPIDER

Berkshire, 1852–54

A crisis in Henry Robinson's business affairs compelled the family to leave Edinburgh in the spring of 1852, taking Isabella far from the friends who had sustained her. Albert and Richard Robinson were pulling out of the London iron yard, and Henry was forced to accept part of his share of the company in machinery and to surrender the rest. On top of this, it fell to him to pay their father the £3,000 that he had put in to the business. To recoup his losses, Henry set up in an office in Moorgate Street, in the City of London, negotiating the sale of sugar mills to colonial plantations.

Henry's father, James, had patented his first mill in 1840. His advertising material promised plantation owners that the mills would crush and boil sugarcane more efficiently than the 'careless' 'attendant blacks', who pushed in the stalks 'intermittingly and in unstratified bunches, now too little and then too much'. Since the abolition of slavery in the British Empire in the 1830s, planters had become keen to find alternatives to paid labour. The Robinson mills were exported to Java, Cuba, Mauritius, Bourbon, Barbados, Bermuda and Natal; in Tirhoot, India, the workers nicknamed their three massive machines Rattletrap, Blowhard and Goliath of Gath.

Henry refined his father's device. In 1844, the year that he married Isabella, he was granted a patent on a design to fix the parts of a mill on to an iron base plate, increase the number of rollers that squeezed the juice out of shredded cane, and tighten the seal on the vacuum pan that converted the juice to syrup.

For three months in 1852, while Henry worked to establish an independent business in London, Isabella and her sons moved from place to place. They toured the Scottish Highlands and stayed for a while in a hotel in Scarborough, a fashionable resort on the Yorkshire coast. Isabella liked to be near seas and rivers. She preferred the Highlands to the 'bold and beautiful' valleys of South Wales, she told Combe in a letter, because of 'the general absence of water in the Welsh landscapes'.

Isabella and the boys visited her family home in Shropshire, which she gave out to her Scottish friends as her address for correspondence. A railway station had opened in April at Ashford Bowdler, less than a mile from Ashford Carbonel, making it easy for the family and their visitors to come and go. The household at Ashford Court was much depleted. Two of Isabella's younger siblings – Caroline and Henry – had died in the 1830s; her older brother, John, had emigrated to Tasmania in the early 1840s; and her sister Julia had moved to London upon her marriage to Henry Robinson's younger brother Albert in 1849. The widowed Bridget, at sixty-three, now shared her home in Shropshire with her sons Christian and Frederick, aged twenty and twenty-nine. Frederick had qualified as a barrister in November 1847, but when his father died a month later he had been obliged – as the eldest son still in England – to take over the management of the estate.

Early in the summer, Isabella recorded in her diary a day on which the Lanes were staying as her guests at a house in the country. The house may have been Ashford Court, since

Isabella seemed to take a proprietorial pride in showing her visitors the grounds and surrounding country. But she made no mention in the diary entry of her mother or brothers, so it is possible that the Lanes were visiting her in a rented property elsewhere. Henry, as usual, was absent.

At eleven in the morning of 30 May – Whit Sunday – Mary and her children came into Isabella's bedroom. Mrs Lane was 'very kind', wrote Isabella, 'and as the little group (joined by her pet spaniel) visited my bed, I felt how charming was their happy, affectionate spirit, and longed to love and enjoy life as they did'. The Lanes had decided to skip church that day. Edward was in his room, writing, but later in the morning he and his family headed out of doors. Isabella rose at noon and joined them in the garden, where she 'answered their humorous condolences on my not being well'. She seemed to have been suffering from a hangover, given her friends' teasing sympathies and the conversation that ensued: 'chatted on selfishness, indulgences, and habits'.

While the boys played, Isabella took Edward and Mary to see a 'flowery mound' in the garden, which they admired. Then they sat and talked about 'great men' such as Samuel Taylor Coleridge and George Combe. They discussed the issues that Edward had addressed in his article in *Chambers's Edinburgh Journal* the previous March: 'pliancy of character, decided opinions, legal caution, mental reservation, and both sides of any question'. In his essay he had urged his readers to listen carefully to all versions of a story. 'There is so much bias from self-love,' he wrote, 'so much recklessness about truth in general, and so much of even a sincere faithlessness of narration, that no partial account of anything is to be trusted.' People could fool even themselves, he pointed out; they could be sincere in their misapprehensions.

'Mr L was not in the buoyant spirits of the day before,' observed Isabella, 'but he was very gentle and charming. We went round by road after a little scramble, and round into steep meadow above. Here we paused to admire the lovely view.'

They soon went back to the house, where Edward read Isabella a passage from an essay on the imagination by Percy Bysshe Shelley – a new edition of the poet's prose had been published that year. Isabella was not convinced by the essay's argument; 'as a phrenologist', she told her diary, she had a different account of human psychology. When Mary came in with the boys, they convened for dinner. Many upper-middle-class families by now had luncheon at midday, tea in the afternoon and dinner in the evening, but the Robinsons adhered to the older convention of having a large meal in the afternoon and tea at night. Sunday dinner was a particularly lavish affair, and Isabella was pleased with the food prepared by her servants – beef, pigeon-pie (plucked pigeons laid on a bed of beef steak and baked in puff pastry), dumplings (boiled balls of suet and flour) and vegetables. They finished with coffee and eau-de-vie, a clear fruit brandy. 'The only drawback,' Isabella said, 'was Atty's bad conduct, and he annoyed us all day. At last we all went out.'

In the meadows and lawns around the house, in 'fine, cool, shadowy weather', Isabella and Edward walked together. Implicitly, hopefully, she ascribed to him the unspoken desire that she felt. They stopped 'a good while' at a swing in the grounds: 'I had a long turn, and Mr L sent me very high; Mrs L looking on.' One of the Lane boys was brought over by his nursemaid and his 'papa' gave him a ride on the swing.

Edward and Isabella continued alone. They stopped to sit silently side by side in the shelter of a steep bank: 'F, the spaniel, was on my lap, and Mr L next me. It was the very scene I had often longed for and pictured to myself; but now it was realised.' They remained there for an hour, watching a group of bare-legged children play nearby. Eventually they rose and turned back towards the house, taking a path through a plantation of trees. 'I walked on with Mr L, but without his arm,' wrote Isabella, 'and a slight bitterness seemed to come over his spirit.' They paused near the house: 'I sat to rest in our own meadow,' she wrote, 'and he leaned up against the rails opposite me.'

She and Edward were interrupted by the approach of Mary Lane and the children, with whom they returned to the house for early evening tea. Isabella prepared and poured the tea herself, and 'enjoyed it', she noted in her diary. Perhaps this was a task that in Edinburgh had been carried out by a servant; the customs of the country were more informal, with the hosts often carving and pouring for their guests. 'Mr L sat by me at tea,' wrote Isabella, 'and we talked for an hour on politics, hereditary descent, funds, paupers, emigration, &c.' The week's newspapers had been busy with debate about whether British parishes should finance the emigration of paupers to Australia, where there had been a shortage of labour since the discovery of gold in Victoria in 1851.

'Afterwards, at nine o'clock, dismissing all boys to bed, as it was Sunday, we sat out in the garden,' wrote Isabella. 'Mrs L had cold, and went in at ten.' While Mary warmed herself at the fire inside, Isabella and Edward, now alone, 'talked of Lord Byron, of riding, of courage, of balloons, and of coolness'. Their discussion of balloons may have been prompted by the many advertisements in the Sunday papers for hot-air-balloon launches at London hippodromes and pleasure gardens on the Whit bank holiday. Edward 'smoked and chatted', wrote Isabella, 'and I laughed much'.

As night fell, their banter gave way to a more serious conversation. They discussed 'man's spirit, his life, the grave, immortality, God, the universe, man's reason, and his short fleeting nature'. Isabella told Edward that she had lost her faith, and was alone among her friends in not believing in 'all the illusions of the Christian's creed'. She claimed to be at peace with her new understanding: 'I expressed my gradually acquired calmness of mind,' she wrote. 'I said that the grandeur of truth made up to me for relinquished hopes.' Edward talked to her about a Greek friend who had just died, a fellow medical student. 'He spoke sadly,' wrote Isabella, with 'deep feeling'. Edward confided in her his own religious doubts: 'he longed to pray, longed to believe'.

Together they watched the rise of the moon and listened to the reedy rasp of the landrail. Edward 'seemed entranced by the beauty of the scene', as if the darkening garden were bewitching him, and he told Isabella that he wished to be out all night. The moment inspired her to quote in her journal from Henry Longfellow's epic poem *Evangeline*, first published in 1847 and a bestseller by the early 1850s. As the lovelorn heroine steps outside, 'The calm and the magical moonlight/ Seemed to inundate her soul with indefinable longings.'

At last Isabella thought to comfort Mary Lane. 'Soon after eleven I felt that Mrs L would think us unkind to leave her,' she wrote, 'and we went to the fire. She was still low, and I tried to cheer her.'

In the diary, Isabella replayed the events of the day in her mind's eye, as an observer, the better to enjoy the sensations of being envied and wanted. She had spent so long on the outside of the Lanes' marriage, gazing jealously in, that to be the cause of Mary's discomfort was a secret delight to her now. The journal magically remade the scenes that had passed, no longer dissecting her longings but instead allowing them to infuse her recollections. Being subject to no supervision, tested against no external source, checked by no other perspective, the diary could conjure up a wished-for world, in which memories were coloured with desire. This was an entry to be re-read, for pleasure.

In the late summer of 1852, Henry found his family a villa just outside Reading, Berkshire, from which he could travel the forty miles to London by train in little more than an hour. Reading lay in a fertile valley formed by the River Thames; Berkshire's plentiful produce – corn, beans, cherries, onions, brick-earth, pigs, wool, broomsticks and butter – was carried from the town to London by canal and railroad. An American author who visited Reading that summer remarked on the wild poppies lining the railway track – through the window of a speeding train the scarlet flowers rushed by 'like a river of blood'.

Isabella and the children moved in to Ripon Lodge, a detached house on the hill that rose out of Reading to the west, and she began to take delivery of the furniture that had until then been stored in London. Henry went up to the capital three times a week.

The boys were not enrolled at a school, and Isabella wrote to Combe for his advice on their education. Although her eldest, Alfred, was 'good-humored & sociable', she told him, the seven-year-old Otway was 'of a less amiable & more peculiar disposition'. Like his little brother, the three-year-old Stanley, Doatie had 'a hasty temper, & some amount of obstinacy'. Henry planned to establish a school for middle-class boys in Berkshire, and to send his boys there in due course; his model was the 'secular school' that Combe had founded in Edinburgh, which taught science instead of theology. But Isabella was not sure that a day school would suit her middle son. She wondered whether he might need the discipline of the boarding system.

Her anxieties about her younger children echoed her worries about her own passion and dissatisfaction. Though the family had moved to Edinburgh so that Isabella could keep the boys by her side, she had now started to think of the family home as a place that they might need to escape.

To an extent, Isabella blamed Henry for her sons' unhappiness. 'The children are so dull and dejected when he is with them,' she wrote in her diary, 'nothing goes on but gloom, sullenness, silence, or fault-finding.' On 26 August, Henry was irritated when he came home from London to find that his wife was unpacking and the nursemaid, Eliza, was out on an errand: 'Henry came at 12; much disconcerted to find us out of sorts. E— out; in hurry for dinner. He was cross about potatoes.' At half past three he went on his own to Pangbourne, a village five miles from Reading, to search for a site on which to build a new house. Isabella took Stanley in a chaise to Whiteknights, the grounds of a former country house three miles in the opposite direction: 'a fine park, not now used; the house not inhabited; parties taking tea in it and walking about'. The scene inspired in her the wish 'to possess a quiet spot of earth, and get free from the petty worry and vexation of life'.

She came back in slightly brighter spirits, but Henry spoiled her mood. 'Henry was cross at night, and we had high words after tea. I was thoroughly vexed with the idea of living with him. Very unhappy; miserable day.' Her world had dwindled. There were no more outings with Edward or dinners with novelists and philosophers; just domestic duties, the company of her children, and sour Henry.

In France that summer, Gustave Flaubert completed his draft of the first part of *Madame Bovary*, a work he had started a year earlier. Like Isabella Robinson, the heroine of his novel was succumbing to loneliness and languor: her life was 'cold as a garret whose dormer window looks on the north', wrote Flaubert: 'ennui, the silent spider, was weaving its web in the darkness in every corner of her heart'.

Isabella's discontent stemmed in part from the disparity between her life and the lives of her forebears, especially on her mother's side of the family. Her father, Charles, had met Bridget Curwen at a dinner at her parents' home in Cumberland in about 1808, when he was practising as a barrister on the Northern Circuit. Charles had inherited some land in West Yorkshire, but Bridget's fortune was greater: on their marriage in 1809, £9,500 was settled on her and £5,000 on him.

The Curwens were an ancient and powerful dynasty, with two seats near the Cumbrian coast – Workington Hall and Ewanrigg Hall. Bridget's mother, Isabella, was portrayed by the painter George Romney in the late-eighteenth century as a rosy-lipped, dark-haired beauty. The sole heir to her father's coal-mining fortune, she had eloped with her cousin John Christian when she turned seventeen, reputedly breaking the heart of Fletcher Christian, another cousin, who soon afterwards led the mutiny against Captain Bligh on the *Bounty*. When John Christian married Isabella Curwen, he adopted her surname, gave her an island on Lake Windermere (named Belle Isle or Bella's Isle in her honour), and presented her with a £1,000 diamond ring. John Christian Curwen, as he now was, became a Whig MP for Carlisle and later Cumberland, and earned renown for his social and agricultural reforms. To show his fellow feeling for his countrymen, he once turned up at the House of Commons in the garb of a Cumbrian peasant, a loaf under one arm and a cheese under the other. His wife shared his political convictions, and took a keen interest in the welfare of the people on their land.

Isabella Robinson yearned for such a role. Even her mother had played an active part in her husband's affairs, helping to run his estates and further his connections. Isabella, though, had no more than a house with three or four servants to supervise, and Henry's world of manufacture and commerce was closed to her. He vanished on trains to his factories and iron yards and offices in the City, on steamships to the distant colonies with which he traded.

In Reading, Isabella told George Combe, she had 'many leisure hours'; 'far more leisure than falls to the lot of most women'. Most ladies of her class made and received social calls in the afternoon, but she had no friends in the neighbourhood. Berkshire, she wrote, 'is a pleasant place as far as climate & beauty are concerned, but we have no acquaintance here; nor do I think from the narrow-minded character of the inhabitants, & the way they are mainly led by the clergy that we are very likely to make many agreeable ones.

'You do not know how often I wish I could see & converse with you,' she wrote to Combe, 'or how much I miss the intelligence & earnestness of the little circle I used to meet either in your house, or in those of your friends. *Here* I feel isolated, as one whose views would be condemned almost unheard, if I dared to hint at them.'

She confided to her diary, as she did not to Combe, how much she missed Edward Lane. 'Up late, being stiff and weary,' began her entry of 31 August 1852. 'Boys came to see me and then all went to river; but a thunderstorm drove them in, and the morning was spent in a desultory manner. Wrote to mother.' Isabella received a letter from Mary Lane that day, a friendly note that passed on the news that Lady Drysdale was ill and that Edward had been to the hydropathic spa at Rothesay, on the Isle of Bute, to recover from an injury to his foot. Isabella was disappointed to hear from Mary rather than Edward. 'Ah, thought I, though he is not busy, and cannot even walk now, I am not in all his thoughts.' She had sent him several notes and a gift of studs with which to fasten his shirts, but he had not responded. 'Not one line either of thanks for the studs or of reply to my many notes could he write, though not an hour elapsed but my thoughts did not anxiously and fondly go towards him.' She tried to feel angry with Edward but could summon up only pity – for him and for herself. 'Tears came into my eyes as I thought of him lame and alone, and not the deep bitterness of finding myself so entirely neglected could fortify my heart with pride enough to despise him and forget in my turn. Wayward and deplorable disposition. All that day and several following did the humbling, sorrowful truth of his utter forgetfulness, even of my friendship, follow me, and fill my heart with unspeakable sadness.'

In her lowest moods, Isabella feared that none of her feelings mattered in any case, that her inner life was a matter of supreme indifference. She had come to believe that there was no God and no immortal soul. She was convinced that nothing would succeed death: 'all is dark to me,' she wrote, 'when once I quit this world'. Isabella's loss of faith, said Edward Lane later, 'seems to have given her whole nature such a shock as to have cast a lurid cloud of depression and *malaise* over the rest of her life'. While other discontented beings could take comfort in the idea that this life was merely a preparation for the next, a trial to be endured and to be rewarded with future bliss, Isabella was tortured by the thought that she had only this one, unhappy existence. She sank into a deep and pervasive gloom, her spiritual desolation meshing with her boredom, her heartache and her melancholy. Her religious and romantic disillusions became one.

In an attempt to turn her misery to some account, Isabella suggested to Combe that she publish her views about the myth of immortality. The false expectation of a future life, she argued, fostered spiritual pride and stymied scientific progress; those who believed in Heaven failed to attend to and improve the world in which they lived. She said she knew that Combe had carefully avoided expressing such dangerous opinions in his own work, but since she had no public reputation to protect she had '*no motive* for avoiding blame'.

Combe firmly discouraged her from writing about religion. He tried to persuade her, as he had tried to persuade others over the years, that phrenology need not lead to atheism. To this end, he sent her a clergyman's essay about the relationship between the body and the soul. Isabella was not swayed: the author, she told Combe, 'does away with the usually received opinion that the *soul* & the *body* are separate . . . but then he holds out a hope, that by some mysterious processes of prayer & good works, we *may* become *spirits*, & so live for ever, – a deduction only more complicated but not more probable than the doctrine he discards'. She speculated that human beings would upon death experience 'a revolution into the elements that composed them' – after all, she asked, 'why should human life differ so materially from animal existence?'. At the very least, she said, believers should show humility: 'in the face of so many conflicting religious opinions', she was astonished that 'vain man should in all ages have resolutely & furiously contended for his *own* form – his *own* persuasion, to the total exclusion of all chance of even a hearing for his neighbour's. One would imagine, that the very existence of such *varied* doctrines & opinions would at least teach doubt, & a degree of charity.'

She took Combe's advice, though, and resisted trying to publish her observations. 'There are those living whom my doing so might anger tho' not injure,' she wrote to him, '& perhaps I may merely leave behind me a few remarks to be published or not by my friends, after my death, as they may think fit.' She complied, reluctantly, with the secrecy and self-containment that were required of her.

George Combe was struck by the quality of Isabella's reasoning. 'You are,' he told her in a letter, 'clear-headed, forcible, & intellectually comprehensive in the power of penetrating into the relations of cause & effect, far beyond the average even of educated women.' When he decided in 1853 to write about his own opinions on religion, she was one of the 'very very few' to whom he sent a copy of the manuscript (another was Marian Evans). He impressed upon these favoured readers the importance of keeping its contents a secret. 'I arrive at the conclusion that there is no supernatural religion,' he explained to one correspondent. 'Were the contents of this book known . . . we should find it necessary to leave Edinburgh.' Isabella assured him of her discretion. 'I can safely promise to fulfil the conditions you propose. I shall lock up the book at once among my private papers, & shall mention it to *no one*, unless to Mr Robinson, as you give me permission to do.' She conceded that Henry's 'general opinions are liberal, & he has the utmost respect for your views' – she and her husband did have in common their enthusiasm for scientific progress and secular education – but she could not resist reminding Combe that Henry had only a cursory interest in ideas. 'He has,' she wrote, 'little leisure or inclination for abstract meditations.'

Isabella immersed herself in reading and writing. In 1852 she sent a piece on religion to the newspaper *The Leader*, though she knew that her opinions would probably be considered too extreme even for its radical pages, and *Chambers's Edinburgh Journal* printed another of her poems, 'some lines of mine about some fanciful symbols of immortality that rather pleased me'. In June 1853 the same magazine published an essay about marriage, 'A Woman and Her Master', signed 'A Woman', which Isabella may have written: the predicament of the author, her heightened prose, her intense love for her children and her dissident views all resembled Isabella's own. The essay was indebted to Herbert Spencer's *Social Statics*, a new book that Isabella had read that summer and recommended to Combe as a work of 'deep & thoughtful philosophy'. Marriage, Spencer said, could cause 'the degradation of what should be a free and equal relationship – into one of ruler and subject . . . whatsoever of poetry there is in the passion that unites the sexes, withers up and dies in the cold atmosphere of command'.

Similarly, the author of the *Chambers* piece argued that a husband's inordinate power could ruin his wife, leaving her full of hatred for him and for herself. A woman was not just wronged by a bad marriage, she suggested, but deformed by it. As a feeble satellite to the 'all-controlling planet' of her husband, she became weak, supine, pitifully dependent. As time passed, 'she may strive hard, strive with tears of blood, to be patient, and wise, and strong; but the crippled energies of a life can never be made whole again'. Like a 'white Christian slave', she 'must walk quietly, and with pulses subdued . . . Her face must wear an outward calm, though the fires of Etna boil within her breast.' An unhappy woman, she wrote, often remained in a marriage only because she could not bear to be parted from her offspring. She might feel a 'surpassing tenderness' for her children, but she had no independent right to them, 'none whatever'.

Robert Chambers felt obliged to justify his decision to publish such views. He added a postscript to the essay: 'Our contributor, while perhaps more than sufficiently earnest in depicting what we must believe an exceptive case, is right in looking for a remedy . . . it may in time appear that much less risk is incurred than is now generally supposed, by ruling that a wretched woman may go away with her children from an intolerable husband.'

In the summer of 1853, Edward, Mary and Lady Drysdale visited the Robinsons at Ripon Lodge. Henry was still busy with his sugar mills. He had recently been granted a patent on a coupling disc that could yoke together a new engine and an older mill: the end of the engine's gear shaft was driven into one groove on the iron disc, and the tongue of the mill's top roller into another. Edward had just qualified as a physician – a gentleman doctor, expert in diagnosis rather than surgery – and he and his family were passing through Berkshire on their way to the Continent, where they planned to spend a month's holiday. They asked Isabella, who had been so kind to their children in Edinburgh, if they could leave their sons with her while they were abroad. Arthur and William were five and two. Mary Lane had by now had another son, Sydney Edward

Hamilton, born in 1852, who was dark where his brothers were fair; it may have been in honour of Isabella that he was christened 'Hamilton', as she and Alfred both bore this middle name.

The Lanes and Lady Drysdale travelled to the spa town of Baden in Germany, from which Edward sent several letters to Isabella. He had already visited a hydropathy spa in Scotland and the Bagni di Lucca hot springs in Italy – in a piece he wrote for *Chambers's Edinburgh Journal* in 1851 he praised the Tuscan resort for its 'shady lanes' and 'murmuring river'. Now that he was ready to practise as a doctor, he was making plans for a water-cure retreat of his own, an airy world of glass, water, lawns and sunlight.

On their return to England, Edward Lane and his family stopped at Ripon Lodge to collect the boys, and stayed with the Robinsons for a day and a night.

'I long to know if he thought of me and ever missed me,' Isabella confided in an undated diary entry, 'though in my serious moments I do not at all believe that he does.' She admonished herself: 'How can any one so busy, so beloved, and so admired spare one thought on a plain, awkward-mannered, and distant friend? Good God! I could coin my life's drops if that were possible for his advantage, and ask only to be loved while dying; and he – why should this disparity in affection exist? – he only thinks of me as a quondam acquaintance. Alas!' In moods like this, she valued herself as lowly as she set him high – she was unattractive and graceless, she lamented, where he was loved and prized by all. Her wish to coin her 'life's drops' for Edward was a wish to turn her blood to gold for his gain, to offer herself up for him.

The Robinsons themselves took a trip to Europe in the foggy winter of 1853 – 'cheating November of its gloom', as Henry described it in a letter to Combe. For six or seven weeks the family toured the northern French towns of Calais, St

Omer, Lille and Boulogne. ‘Our stay was chiefly at the last,’ wrote Henry, ‘which Mrs Robinson likes very much.’

The family was back in Ripon Lodge by the end of the year. On the first day of 1854, Isabella got up early (at a quarter to eight), did the accounts, finished her journal for 1853 and began a fresh volume. She strove to be patient and practical with her moody husband and sons. ‘This day was cold, frosty, with east wind,’ she noted, ‘sunny till noon, and cheering. Not well in night, but better on rising, and felt cheerful. Restored good humour to Henry by my sunshine, and greeted the children affectionately, though they seemed rather gloomy.’

Henry had started to build a house for the family at Caversham, a suburb four miles north of Ripon Lodge, and over breakfast he and Isabella discussed what to name it. The two of them then read with the boys. Afterwards, in private, Isabella counted up her letters of the previous year: ‘189 received, and 26 notes; 214 written, and 54 notes’. As she made a tally of her correspondence, she also drew up a list of the acquaintances and relatives who had died, among them her first husband's brother, George Dansey, ‘once a friend but recently a stranger and alienated’; two aunts on her mother's side; and two sons of her eldest brother, John, who lived with his family in Tasmania. This annual stock-taking, which was common in diaries of the time, inspired Isabella at least to try to pray: ‘May the Great Author of the being of all beings here on Earth direct our steps, and lead us to acknowledge and perceive the presence of good and order in the midst of seeming contradiction, pain, and sorrow.’

At half past one Isabella took a walk with Alfred and Stanley. To begin with, her eldest boy was ‘dull and out of sorts’, she said, but all their spirits were lifted by the cold air and the sight of the snowy hills. On their return, Isabella was brought down again by Henry. ‘Dinner good, but Henry sulky and determined to find fault.’ Since she was in charge of the household, his criticisms of the meal were directed at her. 'Read to children after dinner, and then had a long discussion with him as to the causes of his discontent. He railed at the servants, wanted a man-servant (with whom he would disagree in a month); wanted a study; wished I was a more active housekeeper; complained of cold, and planned how to spend less of his time here and more in London.' She responded calmly to his attacks on her domestic management, and to his determination to spend as little time as possible with his family. 'I said all I could think of to bring him to some degree of reason; remarked on the selfishness of complaints, the reasonableness of making the best of things, and pointed out several small things that might be done to make matters better.'

Isabella's behaviour that day seemed designed as a message to herself, a new year's resolution in action. She was trying to act in accordance with such conduct books as Sarah Stickney Ellis's *The Wives of England* (1843), which argued that a woman's mission was to submit to her husband and devote herself to creating a comfortable and serene home. It was, Mrs Ellis wrote, 'unquestionably the inalienable right of all men, whether ill or well, rich or poor, wise or foolish, to be treated with deference, and made much of in their own houses'. To bring a man happiness was a wife's gift and privilege. As Coventry Patmore observed in his narrative poem *The Angel in the House* (1854), 'Man must be pleased, but him to please/ Is woman's pleasure.'

Isabella did her best to suffer Henry's rudeness and bad temper in silence, to wait lovingly for the cloud of his discontent to pass. She stayed with him until he was less vexed, and then went out for another walk with Alfred: 'The wind had sunk, and it was agreeable.' They came in for tea at eight o'clock, after which she and Henry spent another hour discussing the name of their new house. At half past nine she wrote her journal, and completed some exercises in Latin – though no longer able to attend lectures and classes as she had in Edinburgh, she was still trying to correct the deficiencies of her education. By eleven Isabella was in bed: 'and so closed the first day of the year,' she told her diary, 'not unpleasantly, though in some measure spoiled by Henry's ill-humour'. She had been left 'wearied and ruffled', she wrote, by the 'thorough unamiableness of his disposition'.

CHAPTER FOUR

MY IMAGINATION HEATED AS THOUGH WITH REALITIES

Berkshire & Moor Park, 1854

In 1854 a new man entered Isabella's life and the pages of her journal: John Pringle Thom, a Scot of about twenty-four, employed by Henry to be the first teacher at the day school that he planned to set up in Berkshire. Henry's school had not yet got off the ground – he was finding little support for his progressive project among the conservative residents of the district and he was in any case preoccupied by his business in London. In the meantime, John Thom took lodgings in Reading and acted as an English tutor to the Robinson boys.

Thom arrived at Ripon Lodge at half past nine in the morning of 24 March 1854, a dry, cold, gusty day. He gave a lesson to Otway, now nine, while Isabella supervised the studies of Alfred, thirteen, and Stanley, who had just turned five. Until her sons went to school, she was in charge of their education. After Otway's class, she chatted to Thom. 'I was really sorry for the young man,' she wrote in her diary; 'he was lifeless, dispirited, and lonely. Mr Robinson had brought him to Reading and now seemed [to be] deserting him. I resolved to show him that I was conscious of his situation.' She too felt abandoned by Henry to a barren provincial life.

Over the next three months, Isabella's compassionate

attachment to her sons' tutor became febrile and needy. She was by turns caught in a 'storm of passion and excitement' and cast into a 'languid and sorrowful' decline, always hoping that the next encounter with him might answer her desires.

She anticipated her appointments with Thom as anxiously as if he had been her lover. 'My thoughts went often and with somewhat of terror to my planned meeting with Mr Thom,' she wrote in an undated entry, 'and yet an unutterable yearning drove me onward. Tried all I could to reason myself calm, but in vain.' To her dismay, he did not turn up to this meeting. 'Had he possessed or returned a tithe of my real interest in him, he had not so lightly set at nought my invitation. I was crushed, humbled, as I had often been on other occasions, and really cursed the excitable nervousness and clinging emptiness of my heart.

'If I could only live alone,' she wrote, 'if I could only banish all longing for companionship and participation of mental pleasures, I might get on tolerably. As it is, my life is one tissue of excitement, of suffering, of inconsistency. What shall I do?'

Isabella's attraction to Thom had not dispelled her feelings for Edward Lane, to whom she sent a flurry of notes and letters. 'Mr Lane still silent,' ran an undated entry, 'did not even reply to my query, would he like to hear from me? Felt indignant and surprised. I supposed that his personal presence (which is all that is courteous and gracious), is all that his friends can have from him. Absent, they are forgotten.' It seemed not to have occurred to her that Edward's silence might have been deliberate, an attempt to separate himself from an infatuated friend. Once he and Isabella were apart, his prudence reasserted itself. His letters, when they came, were necessarily cautious: he later said that Mary read every word that he and Isabella exchanged.

Isabella did, bleakly, allow that Edward might not reciprocate her feelings. 'Looked at Mr Lane's last two letters,' ran one entry. 'That written at Christmas gave me much pleasure, it is so fresh and clever. But whenever I look at them I feel how widely different is the tame friendship he feels and professes for me and the absorbing regard I feel for him. Would it were otherwise.' This realism did little to stop her daydreams: 'In loneliness and in enjoyment,' she wrote, 'his voice, his look, come freshly back, and I long for his society. I fear time, which takes from my power of attraction, takes away nothing from passionate and uncontrollable feelings.'

In sleep, Isabella was besieged by sensual fantasies, reveries far richer and more beguiling than her dull, empty days. 'Had confused dreams of Mr Lane in night,' she wrote on 24 March 1854, 'and woke with my imagination heated as though with realities. I thought of the subjects that had occupied my sleeping moments all day. I was alternately depressed and excited, and the day was desultory.'

Phrenologists believed that dreams issued from regions of the brain that broke free while reason slept. They 'proceed from some parts of the brain being less at rest than the others,' wrote Catherine Crowe in *The Night Side of Nature*; 'so that, assuming phrenology to be fact, one organ is not in a state to correct the impressions of the other.' Sometimes this correction did not take place even when the dreamer woke. In *Sleep and Dreams* (1851), John Addington Symons explained how, in such cases, a person upon waking 'looks out on a new world projected from his own inner being. By a melancholy power, a fatal gift, of appropriating and assimilating the real objects perceived by his senses, he takes possession of them, nay, disembodies them, and fuses them into his imaginary creation.'

In one dream, Isabella found herself taking flight at night with Edward Lane and her older sons, Alfred and Otway. Mary Lane pursued and overtook them, halting Edward's escape; Isabella, chased by Henry and a figure identified only as 'C', carried on running. 'I never had any dream which took such entire possession of my soul,' she wrote. 'I hurried to finish my morning's avocations, that I might write it down in the form of a story; and all day I could not forget it or hardly realise how much of it was true and how much false. Good God! What puppets of the imagination are we?' She was disturbed and excited by the way that her dreams leaked into her days. The night visions were fragments from an alternate world, intimations of freedom. 'Dreaming all night of absent friends, romantic situations, and Mr Lane,' ran another entry. 'Oh! Why are dreams more blest than waking life?'

Florence Nightingale, in an essay written in the early 1850s, described 'the accumulation of nervous energy' that built up in women such as herself and 'makes them feel . . . when they go to bed, as if they are going mad'. She ascribed the intensity of her dreams to her 'passional nature' – marriage, she thought, might 'at least secure me from the evil of dreaming'. Isabella's dreams, too, were driven by erotic yearnings; and they seemed, in turn, to fire her literary ambitions, waking her in the morning with the urge to set it all down on paper. Her craving for physical contact spilled over into a wish to write. 'Strange, romantic dream at dawn till I rose,' Isabella wrote. 'I have often the plot and groundwork of a novel in my mind during sleep, with names, scenes, and all perfect, yet quite unconnected with aught that has occurred to myself, and I long for the pen of a ready writer to note all down at the time.'

That year, one of the novelists whom Isabella had met in Scotland seemed to cross completely into a world of fantasy. In late February, the sixty-four-year-old Catherine Crowe, who had long since separated from her husband, was found wandering naked through the streets near her home in Darnaway Street, off Moray Place. Charles Dickens reported on Mrs Crowe's strange turn in a letter of 7 March 1854: she 'had gone stark mad – and stark naked . . . She was found t'other day in the street, clothed only in her chastity, a pocket-handkerchief and a visiting-card. She had been informed, it appeared, by the spirits, that if she went in that trim she would be invisible. She is now in a madhouse, and, I fear, hopelessly insane.'

Catherine Crowe was treated briefly at a private asylum in Highgate, just north of London, by the famous alienist – or 'mad doctor' – John Conolly. 'When she came here, her delusions had passed away like a dream,' Dr Conolly told her friend George Combe. 'Is there not some Epidemic influence raging, affecting the brains of multitudes with vain belief, as in the Middle Ages with a propensity to perpetual dancing?' Mrs Crowe moved on from Highgate to the hydropathic spa at Malvern, to take the water cure. In a letter published in the *Daily News* of 29 April, she denied that she was mad, but acknowledged that she had been ill in February with a 'chronic gastric inflammation', and during a period of unconsciousness had fancied that spirits were guiding her.

The story of Mrs Crowe's naked ramble was confirmed by Robert Chambers, who in a letter of 4 March 1854 explained how the novelist's friends, finding her unclothed near her house, had rescued her from her 'terrible condition of mad exposure'. She had thought herself invisible, but had ended up stripped of all dignity and reason, her delusions laid bare to the world.

At the end of May, Henry abandoned his plans to start a school and gave John Thom notice to leave his post as tutor. Isabella was distraught. On Saturday 3 June – a fair day, with gleams of sunlight and a fresh, northerly wind – she sent Alfred to fetch Thom from his lodgings in the London Road, on the eastern edge of Reading. She had not seen the young man in a week, and was engulfed by worry when he did not come at once: 'depressed, anxious, miserable, restless, tears in eyes'. She dressed and ordered dinner, still hoping that he would turn up. At last he came: 'At 12 I heard his voice with boys, but was too much agitated to see him, and ran to room as pale as a ghost, but, recovering a little, descended and saw him in my room.' He seemed as wan and anxious as she. 'He was looking thin, pale, worn, agitated, hopeless. I never saw any one so sadly changed in a week; his great eyes seemed like pale violets, shaded with heavy, drooping lids; his cheeks were hollow, and there was a look of intense dejection about his whole person. He said he had been ill, and in despair at so abrupt a dismissal.' Where he was emptied out, Isabella became over-full with answering emotion, brimming with tears, suffused with heat. 'I could hardly command myself to talk, and had a wretched headache; my cheeks flushed, tears came every second to my eyes, and my voice was choked.'

When she regained her composure, they talked 'long and earnestly'. Isabella criticised Henry for his 'pride and tenacity' in sacking John Thom so suddenly. Thom confessed that he did not know what he could do next. 'He detailed his sufferings, his wretched sufferings; drudgery in Scotland; exclusion from everything, owing to not being an University man.' She sympathised with his plight – like her, he was under-educated, shut out from power, condemned to tedious tasks – and she tried to cheer him with ideas for the future: 'we named plans, most if not all hopeless'.

His distress distracted her from her own: 'We strolled for half an hour in the garden and I became better, and then dined most cheerfully; but the wretched pallor never left his face.' They sat in her room afterwards, discussing sculpture, painting and Italy. Isabella offered Thom some coffee and whisky, which he accepted, and he became 'animated' enough to walk alongside her and her sons when they took a ride on their horses in the afternoon. Alfred went to Thom's lodgings – for 'Dickens, etc.', she wrote; he may have been collecting some books – and then the young man accompanied Isabella and the boys on horseback to Whiteknights Park. They sat by the lake with their books, but 'talked too much to read'. Isabella offered Thom a present of £15, which he turned down, and she made a note of his mother's address, promising that she would write. 'It was nearly our last interview,' wrote Isabella, 'and our feelings were acute though not altogether sad. He was glad, he said, he ever came to Reading; so was I.' They stayed at the park until it was about to close for the day, when they were asked to leave.

Isabella and the boys returned to Ripon Lodge. Henry reached home in time for tea, and was 'civil', Isabella said. They ate together. She wrote for the rest of the evening and went to bed at midnight.

When Thom left the Robinsons' employ that month, Isabella urged him to visit Edward Lane's new water-cure establishment at Moor Park, near Farnham in Surrey, which lay twenty miles south of Reading. The Lanes and Lady Drysdale had moved down from Edinburgh in March to take over the spa from the well-known hydropathist Dr Thomas Smethurst. Thom accepted Isabella's suggestion, hoping that a spell at Moor Park might lessen his dependence on tobacco, alcohol and opium. Edward, as a favour to Isabella, may have agreed to treat the impoverished tutor at a reduced rate.

Moor Park was the health retreat of which Edward had dreamed. He advertised his new clinic among his friends in Scotland and in the classified columns of publications such as the *Athenaeum*, *The Morning Post* and *The Times*. Each Tuesday he went to London to interview prospective patients between 10.30 a.m. and 12.30 p.m. at an office in Mayfair. The consultation fee was a guinea and the basic charge for treatment at the spa was three or four guineas a week, with an extra charge of four shillings for those who wanted a bath attendant to wash and rub them, and five for a fire in the bedroom. Edward hoped that he and his family would themselves benefit from the move to a salubrious site in the south. The doctor was 'always delicate as to health', said Isabella (he suffered from dyspepsia) and Atty continued to be prone to chest complaints.

Hydropathy, which was introduced to Scotland and England in the 1840s, was becoming a popular treatment for the vague, anxiety-related sicknesses of the mid-nineteenth century. Invalids had long 'taken the waters' at spas such as Bath and Buxton, but the new version of the water cure, invented in Silesia by Vincent Priessnitz in the 1830s, aspired to be more scientific and systematic. The theory was that immersion in hot and cold baths and showers could restore health to an unbalanced body. Edward Lane said that many of his patients were the victims of mania, whether an obsession with work (the 'over-toil of the lawyer, the statesman or the mechanic') or with drugs and alcohol ('the suicidal indulgences of the man of fashion'). Charles Darwin sought help from Dr Lane because he was overwhelmed by anxiety about his 'everlasting species-Book', the work that would become *On the Origin of Species*; he suffered from terrible fits of flatulence, as well as nausea, headaches and outbreaks of eczema and boils. 'I have seen many cases of violent indigestion,' said Edward, 'but I cannot recall any where the pain was so truly poignant as in his. When the worst attacks were on he seemed almost crushed with agony, the nervous system being severely shaken and the temporary depression resulting distressingly great.'

Though popular among the intellectual classes, hydropathy was ridiculed in the mainstream press as faddish, comical and self-indulgent. Edward said that, as a hydropath, he had to 'struggle against the whole banded conservatism of the medical profession' in his efforts to be taken seriously. The word 'hydropathy', he argued, was actually a misnomer: Priessnitz had failed to notice how much the success of his treatment owed to diet and environment. Edward preferred to describe his method as the 'nature cure'. Like the hydropath in Charles Reade's novel *It is Never too Late to Mend* (1856), he 'patted Nature on the back' where 'others hit her over the head with bludgeons and brickbats'.

On Tuesday 4 July, a month after her parting from John Thom, Isabella visited Moor Park in the hope of seeing both him and Edward Lane. She caught a train from Reading to the village of Ash, a forty-five-minute journey, and from there a fly took her the last few miles to Moor Park. At 10.30 a.m. she alighted on a gravel drive in front of a wide white house, three storeys high. Above the front door was a plaque bearing the coat of arms of Sir William Temple, the celebrated diplomat and essayist who had lived there in the late-seventeenth century. Temple had bought the 450-acre estate in the 1680s, half a century after the house was built, seeking an escape 'into the ease and freedom of a private scene, where a man may go his own way and his own pace'.

Isabella was greeted by Lady Drysdale, Mary Lane and some of their guests. The doctor was out, but she ran into Thom early in the morning. 'The meeting was a very constrained one,' she wrote in her diary. 'I coloured much, and the eyes of the party were keenly fixed on me. Mr Th— stood about without daring to speak much, and I became nearly silent.'

Inside the house, a billiard table stood to one side of the hall, and a library to the other. Beyond these rose a crinoline staircase, the glory of the building, with iron railings that ballooned out like the skirts of the lady guests. The surrounding walls were decorated with stucco lyres and angels, and illuminated by an oval skylight. Past the stairwell, a door led to the dining room. On one side of this room was a wooden fireplace carved with pastoral figures – a shepherd playing his flute to a shepherdess surrounded by her flock – and on the other side three French windows offered a view down the lawn to a fountain, two canals, and the River Wey. On an island in the river, a summerhouse and a ruined bower nestled in a thicket of trees.

To the right of the terrace outside the dining room were a vinery, an orangery and a greenhouse, and next to those a walled garden, in which gooseberries, raspberries and blackcurrants ripened in the summer. To the left of the terrace a huge cedar spread its boughs over the grass, and a sundial marked the spot at which Sir William Temple's heart, in a silver casket, had been interred after his death. Also beneath the lawn was a deep store room packed with ice that had been harvested in the winter from the canals and river; another icehouse was sunk into the hillside opposite the front door.

It was a warm, intermittently showery day. During a clear, fair spell in the late morning, Isabella walked in the garden with Atty, who was now about six, and a fellow guest, described in her diary as 'Captain D'. Isabella was sharply aware of John Thom, who was strolling on the other side of a hedge with a 'Mr B' (possibly Robert Bell, a Moor Park patient who later gave Mr Thom a job). She exchanged a few words with the gentlemen, but got the impression that Thom was keeping his distance. 'I rather wondered that he avoided me,' wrote Isabella, 'or rather did not seek me.'

Back in the house she changed for dinner, and took her place at the table at about half past one. She sat near two other guests, 'Mrs O' and 'Mrs K': 'Mr T opposite, and never once spoke or looked at me.'

After dinner she spent some time in Lady Drysdale's room, and then went out to the garden, passing Thom at the billiard table. He 'instantly left his game,' she wrote, 'and seeing I was alone, came eagerly out with me. Went to greenhouse, as it rained; sat awhile, and chatted earnestly.' They moved on to the orangery: 'he got me a chair and sat down, but at great distance. We talked very earnestly, but rather hurriedly and confusedly, and not of the things which were uppermost.'

They walked out to the garden. 'I do not know whether he is really more silent than usual,' she wrote, 'but he was certainly strangely quiet; nevertheless, the knowledge that I was understood, and that he really liked to be with me, gave me much interest in the walk.'

When they went back to the house, Isabella learnt that Edward had returned but had already had tea and gone out again. She took her tea with the other guests, and soon afterwards the doctor appeared outside the dining room. He 'came bounding in through the open window to greet me', wrote Isabella, 'with more warmth than I even expected. Very warmly he shook hands; very cordially he sat down quite near me, and asked many questions as to my welfare.' Now she could imagine Thom watching her admirer as well as her, witnessing her gay and easy intimacy with the handsome doctor. Again, she thrilled to the idea that her friendship with Edward Lane might inspire jealousy in others. 'Mr Th— sat opposite,' she wrote, 'and seemed to be reading, but I know watched all that passed.'

Later, the guests gathered in the drawing room on the first floor. 'Dr Lane was in the highest spirits; seated himself on the sofa I had chosen near the piano, and only left me to sing occasionally, and to speak a few words to his guests; but his eyes, his whole attention, his talk, was all mine . . . We spoke of love, of poetry, of his age, and I told him he had never looked better, though he declared he felt quite old; we spoke of music and his songs; he sang sweetly and with enjoyment both a French and a comic song, and several others, including one I asked for, "Oh, the heart is a free and fetterless thing".'

Thom 'had been sitting not far from us all the evening, but had hardly moved, or spoken, or looked up', wrote Isabella, 'and yet I knew that he watched us and felt our presence'. His apparent indifference, she hinted, was a disguise for desire. Only once he came over to her, at first kneeling beside her while they talked – 'as Mr L had just been doing'. They discussed a school that he proposed to set up in Sydenham, a smart London suburb that had seen a surge of business since the Crystal Palace, built for the Great Exhibition, had been reconstructed on Sydenham Hill in 1852. Isabella advised him to write circulars to advertise his plans. 'He looked bright and happy while I spoke,' she wrote. Thom left the house at ten to accompany a clergyman and two other visitors to their homes in the neighbourhood. 'On coming back later in the evening,' said Isabella, 'he seated himself near the door, and was pale, wan, and spiritless as before.'

The company continued to talk and sing into the night. After listening to the refrain of Eurydice in Gluck's opera *Orphée*, Isabella asked Edward to read out Alexander Pope's 'Ode on St Cecilia's Day', 'which he did the last thing, very sweetly, to my no small delight'. Both Gluck's opera and Pope's poem drew on the Greek myth in which Orpheus loses his beloved Eurydice because he cannot resist turning to look at her as they step out of the Underworld.

After the songs and readings, 'and a few more jokes and compliments', the party broke up for the night. 'I know not that I ever more enjoyed an evening,' wrote Isabella. 'All headache was gone, all sense of sorrow; the old enchantment in that fascinating society was coming back upon me, and I felt that no one could compete in attraction with the handsome, graceful, lively, charming L.'

Mary – 'his little wife', 'so sweet, so kind, so unsuspicious' – took Isabella up the billowing staircase to her bedroom, and Edward soon followed: 'and then they left me, but not to sleep; the bed was hard, and my spirits were far too much excited for sleep. I laid and turned till morning, and then it was late.'

As much as Isabella's journal was a place to pledge herself to virtue, it was also a haven for the parts of her that were not accommodated by married life. 'She who is faithfully employed in discharging the various duties of a wife and daughter, a mother and a friend,' according to Thomas

Broadhurst's popular manual *Advice to Young Ladies on the Improvement of the Mind and Conduct of Life* (1810), 'is far more usefully occupied than one who, to the culpable neglect of the most important obligations, is daily absorbed by philosophic and literary speculations, or soaring aloft amidst the enchanted regions of fiction and romance.' In diary entries such as this one, Isabella strayed and soared into the regions that the conduct books condemned.

Back at Ripon Lodge, Isabella rose at seven on Tuesday 11 July to find that it had rained overnight. She had been low since the visit to Moor Park the previous week, but on this morning, she said, she felt 'rather less sad'. After breakfast Henry went to Caversham, where he had chosen a 25-acre hillside site on which to build a house. A 'Miss S' looked after the boys, while Isabella occupied herself with domestic chores. She told the butcher that he had made a mistake in his calculations, and once he had corrected the bill she paid him. At one o'clock she followed Henry to Caversham, where the house was already taking shape. The plot on which Henry was building commanded panoramic views to the south, an aspect that ensured 'extreme healthfulness', according to the estate agents' particulars, but Isabella could muster no enthusiasm. 'Much wearied and did not enjoy it,' she wrote. 'Sat and mused sadly in house. Back after 7. Unpacked and attended to affairs. Henry cross, both then and later.'

A letter from John Thom was waiting for her at home, having been delivered by the carrier at two o'clock. Isabella opened and read it. Thom's purpose in writing, she recorded in her diary, was 'to express his deep regret at my altered looks and illness, and to tell me that he was getting well and had hopes of Sydenham. It was short and somewhat unsatisfactory; not a remark about any former letters of mine; not an acknowledgment for anything. Each letter breathed less interest than the last.' She had imagined, when she visited Moor Park, that the young man stole yearning glimpses of her; but now he claimed only to have noticed that she looked sick. She added, with a hint of martyred pride, 'It was well. I must learn to let him too join the company who could live without me; he would make and find friends, and would never be lonely again.' She envied Thom his freedom.

'It was cool friendship now on his part,' she wrote. 'Had it ever been more? I thought not; and was thus again punished, as oft before, for over-adhesiveness, for love of approbation and excitability. When shall I be calm, cold, tranquil, praiseworthy? Never.'

The next month, Thom took a post as tutor to the fifteen-year-old Maharajah Duleep Singh, with whom he was to travel in Scotland. The Sikh prince was a ward of the East India Company, which had removed him from the Punjabi throne in 1849, and a favourite of Queen Victoria, to whom he had presented the Koh-i-Noor diamond in 1850.

Four days after receiving Thom's letter, Isabella sat in the garden at Ripon Lodge with the latest number of the literary journal the *Athenaeum*, to which the family subscribed. The issue of Saturday 15 July carried an advertisement for Moor Park and pieces about Alexander Pope and Harriet Beecher Stowe, who had published an account of her travels in England (she was 'wholly the heroine of her own book', said the reviewer).

'Wrote out passages from *Athenaeum*,' Isabella noted in her diary, 'and read it at 1 in the garden, under that tree that I never see without thinking of my escapade with Mr Thom.' The nature of the escapade went unexplained.

A month later, Isabella was still dwelling on Thom: he 'clings to my heartstrings', she wrote; 'I cannot divest myself of his image.'

In the summer of 1854, Henry checked Isabella's household accounts and discovered discrepancies that she would not explain. They argued – she resentful of his distrust and surveillance, he angered by her laxity and disobedience. Isabella did not admit that she had been spending money on John Thom. Though he had refused the £15 that she tried to press on him as a leaving gift, she had persuaded him to accept about £55 that year, in money and goods – this amounted to more than a twentieth of the family's expenditure. Isabella believed that Henry had treated Thom shabbily, and she was making up for it. Given her contribution to the household finances, she probably felt entitled to dispense some of the money as she pleased.

That summer Henry also went after his younger brother Albert, demanding reimbursement of the £3,000 that he had repaid their father in 1852. Albert now lived in Westminster with Isabella's sister Julia and their infant daughter, and he was investing in ambitious ventures, among them an expedition to Greenland to discover minerals and a project to build huge steamships to designs by Isambard Kingdom Brunel. Albert refused to pay Henry, claiming that the debt was not his alone, and Henry sued him. When the case came to court in August, the jury found in Henry's favour and Albert was ordered to pay his older brother £3,335.

Isabella said that Henry revelled in the financial misfortunes of others. 'He hates all merit,' she later wrote to Combe, 'he envies all success. I have known him to go into a Bankruptcy court on *purpose* to feast his eyes upon the spectacle of some once-prosperous man in distress.'

CHAPTER FIVE

AND I KNEW THAT I WAS WATCHED

Moor Park, October 1854

Isabella twice visited Moor Park with her sons in the autumn of 1854, once in September and once in October. Alfred was now thirteen, Otway nine and Stanley five. She came partly to take the water cure, partly as a friend of the family. Her passion for Edward was revived in all its intensity.

Lady Drysdale and Edward and Mary Lane conducted a kind of restorative house party at their retreat in the Surrey woodlands. Elizabeth Drysdale, in lace collars and black brocade, 'made the charm of Moor Park', recalled Charles Darwin's daughter Henrietta, who visited in the 1850s. Lady Drysdale's hearing was failing, but her other faculties were undimmed by age. She was 'very Scotch, full of life and character', said Henrietta Darwin, 'and with a most racy twinkle in her eyes before she burst into a hearty peal of laughter; overflowing with kindness and hospitality; so that all waifs were taken under her protection; a great reader, a great whist-player, and the active capable housekeeper of the great establishment'. Charles Darwin was enchanted by the whole family: 'Dr Lane & wife & mother-in-law Lady Drysdale are some of the nicest people I have ever met.' The doctor, he said, 'is too young – that is his only fault – but he is a gentleman &

very well-read man'. He commended Lane for his common sense and modesty. He did not subscribe to 'all the rubbish' spouted by other hydropaths; 'nor does he pretend to explain much, which neither he or any doctor can explain'.

George Combe agreed that Lane was 'a rational well-instructed physician, & not an ignorant quack like many in that line'; his wife was 'a clever little woman', if 'very nervous'; Lady Drysdale was 'the soul and body of Moor Park', 'a big-hearted, active, clever woman, possessed of a good income' who 'manages the household' and 'charms the company by her overflowing good nature & frankness'. At Moor Park as at Royal Circus, Edward was happy to let Lady Drysdale rule the roost. Combe remarked that Dr Lane leant on his wife and mother-in-law: he had 'all his life depended on women'.

Combe identified two flaws in the characters of Mary, Edward and Lady Drysdale. 'Benevolence and Love of Approbation are rampant,' he noted, 'and blind them to the defects of persons who are introduced to them by friends, & recommended to their kindness.'

There were few divisions at Moor Park between the patients and their hosts. Since the water cure was a preventative, health-promoting therapy, its benefits could be enjoyed by the well and the unwell alike. Edward strove to act as a kindly friend to his guests, to allow a spirit of tolerance, openness and possibility to flourish around him. Good company, he wrote, 'lightens and brightens' a patient's path to health: it 'keeps him in spirits', and 'prevents him from brooding over his own ailments'. Edward enjoyed his work and took pride in his successes. 'There are few pleasures in life (if any),' he told Combe, 'like that of being able to afford some real benefit to the health or wellbeing of one's fellow creatures.' If the mind was a part of the body, as the phrenologists and others claimed, a physician could foster happiness and sanity as well as physical health. Edward's powers of persuasion were crucial to the cure.

The patients at the spa formed a 'very intelligent, lively, agreeable, Society', said Combe. The Edinburgh set came, and so did their friends from London. Among the visitors were the logician Alexander Bain, a pioneer of psychological theory, who remarked on the 'kindness and attention' of his hosts; the railway engineer George Hemans, a son of the poet Felicia Hemans; Robert Bell, a friend of Thackeray and Trollope and a well-loved director of the Royal Literary Fund; and the novelists Sydney Lady Morgan, Georgiana Craik and Dinah Mulock, the last of whom wrote her bestseller *John Halifax, Gentleman* (1856) in a room overlooking the sundial in the Moor Park garden.

Mary Lane's brothers, George and Charles Drysdale, were often in residence. Charles gave his address as Moor Park when he became a member of the Institute of Civil Engineers in November 1854 (with a personal recommendation from Henry Robinson's former partner, John Scott Russell). George, though, went to Edinburgh that autumn, to complete his final year of medical training and perhaps to put some distance between himself and his family during the imminent publication of his sex manual.

Each guest at Moor Park was assigned a sitting room and a bedroom, in which a bath stood on end in the corner. Attendants filled the tubs in the morning and rubbed the patients with wet and dry towels until their skin glowed. They then gave them tumblers of cold water to drink. All the residents ate together (dinner at half past one, tea at seven), talked and walked and played games together. 'I have been playing a good deal at Billiards,' Darwin told his son, '& have lately got up to my play & made some splendid strokes!' Edward took them on drives through the rolling heathland to the Bishop's Palace castle at Farnham, to Waverley Abbey and the new military camp at Aldershot. By moving to Moor Park, he had found himself an endlessly social scene, replete with the promise of health, the comforts of family, and the company of clever, sensitive ladies and gentlemen. There were few limits on his access to his guests – as a medical man, he was licensed to visit their bedrooms, listen to their problems, examine their bodies. 'The physician has his patients almost always under his eye,' he wrote.

All the guests were encouraged to walk in the park. 'I strolled a little beyond the glade for an hour & half & enjoyed myself,' reported Charles Darwin in a letter to his wife, '– the fresh yet dark green of the grand Scotch firs, the brown of the catkins of the old Birches with their white stems & a fringe of distant green from the larches, made an excessively pretty view. – At last I fell fast asleep on the grass & awoke with a chorus of birds singing around me, & squirrels running up the trees & some Woodpeckers laughing, & it was as pleasant a rural scene as ever I saw, & I did not care one penny how any of the beasts or birds had been formed.'

Darwin may have felt his preoccupations washed clean away at Moor Park, yet on his walks he found fresh evidence for his theories about the struggle for existence. On the heath near Farnham he discovered among the heather a tiny forest of twenty-six-year-old Scotch firs, tens of thousands of stunted trees no more than three inches high, which had been steadily nibbled down by passing cattle: 'what a play of forces, determining the kinds & proportions of each plant in a square yard of turf! It is to my mind truly wonderful. And yet we are pleased to wonder when some animal or plant becomes extinct.' He was to cite the little firs in the third chapter of *The Origin of Species* as an example of the precariousness and violence of the natural world, how 'the fight goes on'. When examined closely, the pastoral idyll yielded scenes teeming with creative and destructive forces, unresting appetite and strife.

Darwin liked to watch the ants spilling out of their nests in the woods and trailing up and down the hillocks. 'I had such a piece of luck at Moor Park,' he told a friend. 'I found the rare Slave-making Ant, & saw the little black niggers in their Master's nests.' He asked the Moor Park gardener, John Burmingham, to keep an eye on some yellow ants that he had seen in the grounds, and Burmingham later wrote to him with his observations: 'thare whare a grate many eggs b[u]t saw a very few ants either in the nest or on the outside . . . the[y] ceasd to carry eggs in about a week after you left and soon after deserted that Part altogeather.'

When a patient had spent a few days at Moor Park, Edward prescribed stronger treatments. Darwin took a daily shallow bath, a sitz bath (in a tub shaped like a chair) and a douche (a jet of water angled at the afflicted part of the body). For dyspeptics, such as Darwin, the douche was aimed at the abdomen; for women who suffered from hysteria or other diseases of the reproductive organs, it was directed at the pelvis. Some guests submitted themselves to the hot air bath, the dripping sheet and the wet sheet. To take Edward's hot air bath, the patient sat on a piece of cork on a wooden chair fitted with a hooped frame; blankets were laid over the frame and pulled up tight to the chin, while a spirit lamp was lit beneath the seat. After twenty to twenty-five minutes, the bath brought on a heavy sweat said to be beneficial to the liver and abdomen. In the wet-sheet therapy, the patient was wrapped tightly in damp cloth, laid on a bed and covered with a heap of heavy blankets: 'the natural heat of the body acting on the damp linen, vapour is forthwith generated,' explained Edward, 'and the patient is very rapidly in a delightfully comfortable and soothing warm vapour-bath'. John Stuart Blackie – the professor whom Isabella had heard lecture in Edinburgh – described the sensation as 'exactly that of being baked very gently and soothingly in a pie'. Another enthusiast wrote that on emerging from a vapour bath he felt 'as warm as a toast, as fresh as a four-year-old, and as ravenous as an ostrich'.

The treatment was a spiritual and sensual tonic. When taking the water cure, wrote the novelist Edward

Bulwer-Lytton, 'the sense of the present absorbs the past and future: there is a certain freshness and youth which pervade the spirits, and live upon the enjoyment of the actual hour'. The patients' bodies tingled under icy jets of water, sweated in hot clouds of steam, subsided under warm, wet blankets. It was all about temperature, Edward explained: heat soothed the nerves, slowed the blood, softened pain and coaxed poisons out of the body; cold sharpened the appetite, lightened the spirits, strengthened the body's fibre.

The illnesses most responsive to hydropathy were hypochondriasis and hysteria, conditions thought to stem from a disjunction between the body and the mind. The novelist Dinah Mulock attributed the prevalence of hypochondriasis – another term for the dyspepsia that afflicted Darwin and Edward Lane – to 'our present state of high civilisation, where the mind and the body seem cultivated into perpetual warfare one with the other'. The victims were often sensitive, intellectual men; the symptoms could include misanthropy or self-loathing; and the cure, said Miss Mulock, was 'rest, natural living, and an easy mind'.

Hysteria was the female equivalent of this malady. In an influential work of 1853, Robert Brudenell Carter argued that hysteria was a biological disorder caused by emotional trauma: 'the derangements are much more common in the female than in the male – women not only being prone to the emotions, but also more frequently under the necessity of endeavouring to conceal them'. Miss Mulock identified the illness as part of a general female malaise: 'I am afraid it cannot be doubted that there is a large average of unhappiness existent among women: not merely unhappiness of circumstances, but unhappiness of soul.' The cure was a return to nature, she said, aided by the application of water, 'the colder the better': 'some predominant idea . . . otherwise runs in and out of the chambers of the brain like a haunting devil, at last growing into the monomania'.

To distract his patients from their anxieties, Edward encouraged them to read. The family subscribed to journals, made a library available to guests and recited poetry in the evenings. The doctor and his friends gave occasional literary lectures at the Mechanics' Institute in Farnham. Edward Lane spoke on Tennyson, who before becoming Poet Laureate had taken the water cure at Malvern, while Robert Bell discussed the life of William Shakespeare.

When Darwin visited the spa he always brought a stock of books. 'My object here is to think about nothing, bathe much, walk much, eat much & read much novels.' He enjoyed discussing popular fiction with Mary Lane, an avid reader of volumes from Mudie's Lending Library. On one occasion, they debated the authorship of two anonymous novels that both had read, and Mary entered into the discussion with tart, playful self-assurance: 'Mrs Lane agrees with me that the *Betrothed* is by a man,' wrote Darwin. 'She coolly added that *Beneath the Surface* was so poor that it must have been written by a man!' (The author of *Letters of a Betrothed* was in fact a woman, the novelist and poet Marguerite Agnes Power; but Mary was right about *Below the Surface: a Story of English Country Life* – its author was Sir Arthur Hallam Elton, Bt.)

Darwin also engaged in lively debates about evolution with Georgiana Craik, a lady novelist of twenty-three. 'I like Miss Craik very much,' he reported, 'though we have some battles & differ on every subject.'

Edward recalled Darwin's stays at Moor Park with great warmth: 'never was anyone more genial, more considerate, more friendly, more altogether charming . . . he adapted with rare tact and taste to the capacity of his hearer . . . he was as good a listener as a speaker. He never preached nor prosed, but his talk, whether grave or gay (and it was each by turns) was full of life and salt – racy, bright and animated.' These were the same qualities – the delicacy and the spirit – that drew Isabella to Edward.

A water-cure spa was one of the few places in Victorian Britain in which unchaperoned wives and daughters lodged alongside bachelors and married men. Occasionally, this led to trouble: a lady patient at Moor Park reported to a friend of Combe that a gentleman had behaved towards her during her stay in a manner that 'disgusted' her. In 1855, Miss Mulock published a short story, 'The Water-Cure', in which she depicted the sexual undercurrents at the spa as a force for good. The narrator of the story, Alexander, is suffering from writer's block and ill health: 'My body hampers my mind, my mind destroys my body.' He describes himself as 'a self-engrossed, sickly, miserable, hypochondriacal fool'. His cousin, Austin, is similarly afflicted, though where Alexander has overtaxed his brain, Austin has ruined his constitution by smoking and drinking too much. The two young men, Alexander says, are 'mind-murderers and body-murderers'.

The water-cure establishment that the cousins visit is closely modelled on Moor Park: a white building facing a steep wooded hillside, a couple of hours from London by train. 'It was a large, old-fashioned house,' says Alexander, 'baronical-like, with long corridors to pace, and lofty rooms to breathe freely in.' There are about twenty patients, 'of both sexes and all ages, in which the only homogeneity was a general air of pleasantness and pleasure'. Large as the building is, it has 'all the unrestrainedness and cosiness of *home*'.

The doctor in charge of their treatment smilingly confiscates Alexander's manuscript and Austin's cigar, the emblems of their abuses of the mind and the body. He expounds his philosophy: 'For any disorder of the brain, any failure of the mental powers – for each and all of these strange forms in which the body will assuredly, in time, take her revenge upon those who have . . . neglected the common law of nature – that mind and body should work together, and not apart, I know nothing so salutary as going back to a state of nature, and trying the water cure.' Many of his patients come from troubled homes, he observes: 'We want to cure not only the body, but the mind. To do our patients real good, we must make them happy.'

After a spell at the spa, Alexander reports, 'My brain felt clear – my heart throbbed with all the warmth of my youth.' Both he and Austin are so thoroughly rejuvenated that they fall for a lady guest. They eventually discover that she is promised to the doctor himself. The doctor – with his serious, sweet profile, 'so very tender, for all its steadfastness and strength' – turns out to be the romantic hero of the piece. The story's author may have had her own fancies about the gentle, yet commanding, Edward Lane.

A lawyer from Lincoln's Inn (the Inn of Court to which the Walker family was connected) arrived at Moor Park in September 1854. He was welcomed into the house ('comfort and elegance itself,' he noted, 'with a look of cheerful wellbeing quite captivating') and shown to the study. There he and Edward discussed the poet and satirist Jonathan Swift, who in the late-seventeenth century had been employed at Moor Park as a secretary to Sir William Temple. The barrister found Edward 'a perfect master and intelligent appreciator' of the estate's literary history.

In the month that he spent at the spa, the young lawyer threw off the 'crushing tyranny of thought' and regained his delight in his body. 'How keen the pleasure, and how exquisite the delight, which we are sometimes permitted to feel in the bare consciousness of animal existence!' he exulted. 'Call it sensuous! I call it divine.'

In the morning of Sunday 7 October, Edward approached Isabella in the house. 'Dr Lane asked me to walk with him, but I thought he meant only politeness,' she told her diary, 'and I went to the nursery and stayed with my little pets more than an hour.' He sought her out again: 'he reproached me for not coming, and he bade me come away'. Still she lingered with the children 'but at last joined him, and he led me away and alone to our favourite haunts, taking a wider range, and a more secluded path'.

Edward and Isabella crossed the pretty parkland laid out by Sir William Temple and climbed into the woods. It was a sunny, warm day in one of the finest autumns in memory. The main path through the trees on the hill was deep in slippery pine needles and sandy mulch, the light falling through the branches in bright, broad rifts. As the path ploughed east, the valley narrowed and deepened: the river drew close on the right, the hill steepened to the left.

A few hundred yards along the lane, halfway between Moor Park and the ruined Cistercian monastery of Waverley Abbey, a deep cave burrowed into the sandstone, its mouth overhung with trailing roots and weeds, and its floor flooded with a clear rill of water. It was known as Mother Ludwell's – or Ludlam's – Cave or Hole, after a witch who was said once to have lived there. In this cave at the end of the seventeenth century, Jonathan Swift had courted his first love, Esther Johnson, the daughter of Sir William Temple's housekeeper. Swift wrote an ode to the well by which he and Esther used to meet, casting it as the source of an intimate, sensual landscape: 'The meadows interlaced with silver flouds,/ The frizzled thickets, and the taller woods.'

Isabella and Edward took one of the trails that pushed up into the forest on the slopes above the cave, and emerged at the summit of the hill on to moors of bracken, furze and heather. The remains of Waverley Abbey lay to one side, the ripe hop fields and ferny heaths of Farnham to the other. The breeze carried the clean scent of Scotch pine and the marmalade tang of young Douglas firs.

'At last I asked to rest,' wrote Isabella, 'and we sat on a plaid and read *Athenaeum*s, chatting meanwhile. There was something unusual in his manner, something softer than usual in his tone and eye, but I knew not what it proceeded from, and chatted gaily, leading the conversation – talking of Goethe, woman's dress, and of what was becoming and suitable.' Isabella's banter with Edward flitted between the intellectual and the frivolous, matters of the mind and the body, desire and propriety. In alluding to Goethe, she struck a suggestive note. Goethe's most famous novel, *The Sorrows of Young Werther*, was narrated by a young man obsessed with his friend's wife; while his *Elective Affinities*, which had been translated into English earlier in 1854, explored the cross-currents of attraction between two couples on a country estate. The 23 September number of the *Athenaeum* carried an appreciation of Goethe's love poems in which the reviewer imagined that lady readers would judge him 'Guilty – as a *terrible flirt*'.

'We walked on,' Isabella continued, 'and again seated ourselves in a glade of surpassing beauty. The sun shone warmly down upon us, the fern, yellow and brown, was stretched away beneath us, fine old trees in groups adorned the near ground, and far away gleamed the blue hills. I gave myself up to enjoyment. I leaned back against some firm dry heather bushes, and laughed and remarked as I rarely did in that presence.' As she reclined with pleasure on the shrubby ground, the natural world seemed to conspire with her: the sun warmed her skin, the trees and the hills decorated her view, the heather yielded to her body.

And then something extraordinary happened: the fantasies that Isabella had nurtured in her diary crossed into life. 'All at once,' she wrote, 'just as I was joking my companion on his want of memory, he leaned over me, and exclaimed "If you say that again I will kiss you." You may believe I made no opposition, for had I not dreamed of him and of this full many a time before?' With the doctor's kiss, the suspense and the teasing fell away, and Isabella entered a rapturous daze. She had passed into a world in which dreams had become facts, and the facts correspondingly dreamlike. 'What followed I hardly remember – passionate kisses, whispered words, confessions of the past. Oh, God! I had never hoped to see this hour, or to have my part of love returned. But so it was. He was nervous, and confused, and eager as myself.

'At last we roused ourselves,' she wrote, 'and walked on happy, fearful, almost silent. We sauntered not heeding where, to a grove of pines, and there looked over another view beautiful as that on this side, but wilder.'

As they descended into the park they caught sight of the Brown sisters, acquaintances from Edinburgh who were staying at the house. Isabella and Edward 'thought it necessary slowly to join them. They had observed nothing – we were safe. Constraining ourselves to converse, we succeeded in disarming all suspicion, and reached the house together, but late for dinner.'

Isabella went to her room to ready herself for the meal. She was 'flushed and excited' on going down to the dining room, she said, 'and neither I nor Dr L, fairly met one another's eyes or spoke'. To her relief, a fellow patient – 'Mr S' – sat and talked to her at the table, and afterwards she and the children, along with Edward and Mary Lane, accompanied him in a carriage to the railway station. She hugged her secret to her. 'We were a little crowded in going, but a sense of hidden happiness and satisfaction was glowing at my heart. We chatted in returning, but of indifferent matters, and dear little innocent Mrs L— sat behind with her fine baby asleep and laid under her cloak.'

In the afternoon Isabella found herself in the stable yard with Mary Lane and Otway, and soon afterwards 'lost sight of everyone' except Stanley, whose nurse was out. Her youngest son ran about her room till dusk. She then 'lay down and dozed, quite overpowered with remembrance and memories'. She was brought a candle to dress for the evening meal, for which she chose a gown of pale blue silk. 'I looked well', she wrote. 'I met his glance as I came (at the sound of the gong) to the dining room, and I knew that I was watched.'

After tea, 'some time passed in a desultory manner'. Most of the guests had gone up to the drawing room on the first floor, but Isabella hung back. 'I walked with Alfred in the hall, unwilling to go upstairs lest I might see him no more alone.' Eventually Lady Drysdale invited her into the library, where Edward found her when he came in to the house from the stable yard. He was 'cold, shivering, nervous, ill', said Isabella. Alfred headed upstairs to listen to one of the Misses Brown read a ghost story. Edward and Isabella went into his study.

The doctor's study was a corner room, adjacent to the dining room, with windows that looked out to the river on one side and to Sir William Temple's sundial on another. In the evening, with the shutters and doors closed and a fire burning in the hearth, it was snug and warm. The walls and doors were covered with horizontal panels of red, rich-grained wood, so smooth and continuous that the doors when shut seemed to disappear, their presence betrayed only by the thin grooves cut into the panels and the rubbed shine of the doorknobs. A couple of feet behind each half-hidden door lay another door, the space between them a narrow chamber the size of a cupboard. This sealed off the study from the sounds of the house, and the house from the sounds of the study.

Edward and Isabella drew near the fire. 'How the evening passed I know not,' wrote Isabella, as if she had lost all sense of time and self. 'It was full of passionate excitement, long and clinging kisses, and nervous sensations, not unaccompanied with dread of intrusion. Yet bliss predominated.' Edward, she wrote, 'was particularly gentle, soothing my agitation, and never for an instant forgetting the gentleman and the kindly friend.' At one point Alfred knocked at the study door, interrupting their love-making. He told the doctor that one of his sons had asked if he would go to see him in bed. Edward went upstairs – 'reluctantly', said Isabella. When he came back down she had fallen into a languid swoon. He 'softly kissed my closed eyes', she wrote. 'I tried to raise my drooping head, but in vain.' He became anxious: 'at last,' she wrote, 'absolute dread of anyone breaking in, he advised me to go. I smoothed my tumbled hair and in a few moments found myself in the drawing room, at half past nine. Fortunately, only a few of the guests were there. No one had a right to question my absence or appearance.'

In the drawing room, Isabella busied herself by examining a book of autographs and chatting with a fellow guest. Edward and Mary came in together, and Lady Drysdale followed soon after. 'What an escape I had had! What a calm appearance I could now make! General conversation followed. I turned to listen, and Dr Lane reported to Miss B— some of the finest odes of Byron. When they went I rose too, and was gliding away, when Dr L— gave me a warm shake, so warm that it crushed my fingers with the rings, so that I felt it for an hour.' Edward pressed the rings into her flesh as if to awaken her to the force of his desire, the reality of their new compact. She was overcharged again by the memory of what had happened, her euphoria touched with fear.

'Alas!' ended the entry of 7 October. 'I slept little that night, waking, rising, dreaming – and slowly came the morn.'

The next morning, Isabella was exhausted. From her bedroom, she overheard Edward talking to his wife. Later he came in to her apartment to show her a long letter he had written to a prospective patient in Edinburgh. 'It was a nicely written letter,' she noted. She went back to bed. 'I lay down, wearied, exhausted, nervous. He tapped at half past twelve, and bade me come down and walk: but I refused, and dozed on.' Soon afterwards Mary came up to see her, and she decided to dress.

Isabella 'slowly went out' to join Edward. They met at the

foot of the stairs, and then 'sauntered out together, walking all round the grounds and by the water, yet saying little to one another, for both were weary and feeble. I named my not having slept; he said he was in pain, and could hardly get on at all. Both were agitated, confused, and nervous, and I asked him how it was he acted as he did on Sunday.' Isabella suggested that they climb out of the still, close valley. 'I proposed leaving the grounds (as the air was hot and moist) and getting a breeze on the hill. We climbed it slowly, and I rested among the dry fern. I shall not state what followed.'

In declining to describe her most intimate moments, Isabella was adhering to a well-worn literary convention. The newly betrothed heroine of Fanny Burney's novel *Evelina* (1778) protests: 'I cannot write the scene that followed, though every word is engraved in my heart.' The formula implied that there were acts and feelings too sacred – or indelicate – to be committed to paper; it elided sensuality and propriety, performing a kind of trick whereby the coy heroine was enabled by silence to be at once passionate and polite – jealous of her own and her lover's privacy, respectful of her reader's finer feelings.

Isabella and Edward 'rose soon more composed and cheerful', and went back to the house 'quickly, fearful of being too late'. Over dinner, Isabella again avoided conversation with Edward: 'I talked all I could to Lady Drysdale, for there were few persons present, and turned from him, leaving him to talk to Miss T—.' Afterwards, she took 'a nice long ride' with Edward in a carriage to the abandoned abbey at Waverley, the Brown sisters both sitting behind.

Two days later – on Wednesday 10 October 1854, Edward Lane's thirty-first birthday – Isabella was due to depart. She and Edward walked around the grounds. The doctor stopped to talk to another patient, and then joined Isabella and her eldest son 'near the bounding fence'. They set out for the wood, 'taking the usual circuit, walking through paths that I had never seen before of the greatest beauty, reaching the outer pine wood, and finally returning by Swift's cottage, and lower walk'. The building known as Swift's cottage was the former home of his inamorata Esther, which lay on the main path between Moor Park and Waverley Abbey. By 1854, the cottage was surrounded by rose trees and covered with moss, clematis and Virginia creeper; a sign outside read 'Ginger beer for sale'.

'We talked with the utmost confidence, but somewhat more calmly,' wrote Isabella. 'I entreated him to believe that since my marriage I had never before once in the smallest degree transgressed. He consoled me for what I had done now, and conjured me to forgive myself. He said he had always liked me, and had thought with pity of my being thrown away, as my husband was evidently unsuited to me, and was, as he could plainly see, violent tempered and unamiable.'

Edward reminded Isabella of the vulnerability of his own position: 'we spoke of his early age, thirty-one, the sweet unsuspicious character of his wife, rather than pain whom he would cut off his right hand.' They were moving on to the subject of Isabella's unhappiness – 'my often bitter misery and wish for death' – when Lady Drysdale and Mary Lane appeared. They had come to ask Isabella if she wanted them to book a fly to take her to the railway station. The doctor's wife and mother-in-law were as warm and trusting as ever: 'they kindly received my determination to go away about 7, and went off again without one cold or displeased look, and yet we were walking arm-in-arm through those lonely woods and talking how earnestly'.

At seven o'clock that evening, Isabella set out with Edward for Ash station in a covered cab drawn by a single horse: she and Edward sat inside the narrow carriage, and Alfred perched with the driver on top. Her younger boys were not with them – they may have gone ahead with their nurse.

'I never spent so blessed an hour as the one that followed,' wrote Isabella, 'full of such bliss that I could willingly have died not to wake out of it again. I shall not relate ALL that passed, suffice it to say I leaned back at last in silent joy in those arms I had so often dreamed of and kissed the curls and smooth face, so radiant with beauty, that had dazzled my outward and inward vision since the first interview, November 15, 1850.' Edward seemed as he kissed her to melt into a dazzle of soft curls and skin, the flesh-and-blood man merging with the idol of her dreams.

Between kisses, they confided in one another. 'All former times were adverted to and explained,' Isabella wrote. Edward told her that he had hidden his true feelings, 'from prudential motives', and that the suppression had caused him 'much pain'. Isabella reminded him of some lines from the French novel *Paul and Virginia* that she had read out to the guests at Moor Park, and confessed to having chosen them as a message to him. Jacques-Henri Bernardin de Saint-Pierre's novel of 1787 described a great love between a girl and boy brought up together on the island of Mauritius, one of whom dies of grief at the death of the other.

Edward 'had always known I had liked him,' continued Isabella, 'but not the full extent of the feeling, and owned it had never been indelicately expressed. This relieved me. Heaven itself could not be more blessed than those moments. While life itself shall endure their remembrance shall not pass away from a memory charged with much suffering and little bliss; how gentle, how gentlemanly he was – how little selfish!'

Though Isabella painted a romantic, tender scene, the setting was distinctly louche. The late-eighteenth-century guide to prostitution *Harris's List of Covent Garden Ladies: Or a Man of Pleasure's Kalender for the Year* recommended coaches for illicit trysts: 'the undulating motion of the coach, with the pretty little occasional jolts, contribute greatly to enhance the pleasure of the critical moment, if all matters are rightly placed'. By 1838, reported the *Crim Con Gazette*, the London hackney cab commissioners were so disturbed by the immorality conducted in their vehicles that they proposed to curtail both the pleasure and the privacy by banning coach blinds and coach cushions altogether. Isabella's conduct in the carriage was especially shameless: a child, her son, was sitting on the roof while she and Edward Lane whispered and touched inside.

As Isabella sat demurely writing up these scenes in her diary, perhaps in plain view of her children or her husband, none could guess at the images swarming through her head and the journal's pages. By recording her encounters in her secret book, she recreated the thrill of transgression, of pleasures sharpened by the danger of discovery.

CHAPTER SIX

THE FUTURE HORRIBLE

Boulogne & Moor Park, 1854–56

In late October 1854, within weeks of her trysts with Edward Lane, Isabella and her family left England for the French fishing port of Boulogne-sur-Mer, where they had rented a house for the winter. At Boulogne harbour, the passengers from the steam ferry were hustled into the customs house to have their passports checked, and then greeted on the quay by a surge of noisy agents from the hotels and boarding houses: 'Hôtel de l'Europe! Hôtel des Bains! Hôtel du Londres!' Just past them on the wooden jetty, the fishermen sorted their fish and wove their nets.

Isabella took up residence with Henry, their sons and their servants in a three-storey house at 21 rue du Jeu de Paume. The building formed part of a steep terrace along the northern side of the Tintelleries gardens, an elegant hillside park in which fashionable English expatriates promenaded, in silk and satin, each afternoon. 'We have established ourselves in a very pleasant square in Boulogne for the winter,' Isabella wrote to George Combe, '& the boys go to school regularly in the principal College of the town.' Alfred and Otway had briefly attended a day school in Berkshire after John Thom's dismissal. Now they joined a sizeable band of British boys at the town's

Municipal College, a liberal establishment, where their parents intended that they would become proficient in French.

More than 7,000 British people lived in Boulogne, a quarter of the total population, and another 100,000 crossed from Folkestone on visits each year. By comparison with other towns in northern France, Boulogne was lively, even cosmopolitan, and the cost of living on the Continent was lower than it was in England. The height of the season was the autumn, when the sky seemed bluer on this side of the Channel. There were two English chapels in Boulogne, two English clubs (with billiard and card tables and British newspapers) and two English reading rooms and circulating libraries. Some of the British visitors were raffish types, intent on escaping debt or scandal; some came to recuperate from illness. By moving his family here while the new house in Berkshire was completed, Henry Robinson could hope to see an improvement in his wife's wellbeing, his sons' education and his own finances.

Charles Dickens was staying in Boulogne in the month before the Robinsons arrived. He explained the resort's appeal in his magazine *Household Words* in November. 'It is a bright, airy, pleasant cheerful town; and if you were to walk down either of its three well-paved main streets, towards five o'clock in the afternoon, when delicate odours of cookery fill the air, and its hotel windows (it is full of hotels) give glimpses of long tables set out for dinner, and made to look sumptuous by the aid of napkins folded fan-wise, you would rightly judge it to be an uncommonly good town to eat and drink in.' On the esplanade, visitors peered through telescopes at the chalky English cliffs across the water. When the weather was fine, they were wheeled out to sea from the beach in wooden bathing machines. Dickens was charmed by Boulogne's fishing quarter, 'hung with great brown nets across the narrow up-hill streets'. Seagulls cried on the rooftops and the smell of fish gusted up the lanes.

The Robinsons' street climbed to the old, walled town on the hilltop, which Dickens compared to a fairytale castle, the surrounding houses rooted in the deep streets like beanstalks. The place seemed full of children, he observed: 'English children, with governesses reading novels as they walk down the shady lanes of trees, or nursemaids interchanging gossip on the seats; French children with their smiling *bonnes* in snow-white caps.' Alfred, Otway and Stanley joined their ranks.

That November a series of storms battered the coast of northern France, marking the start of a bitter winter. Henry returned to England, where he spent most of the next few months supervising the business in London and the construction of the house in Caversham. The weather was even crueller on that side of the Channel: the Thames froze over, and the frosts in Berkshire slowed progress on the house. When Henry visited Boulogne for a few days in February 1855, he told his wife that their new home would not be ready to move into until June.

Isabella may have hoped to escape in Boulogne from the petty restrictions of Berkshire society, but she felt horribly isolated. Edward rarely wrote to her, and in her diary she bemoaned her 'unhappy turn of mind in clinging to shadows and delusions'. In her letters to George Combe, she attributed her low spirits to spiritual despair. With no belief in God to sustain her, she told him, she did not know where to find comfort or meaning – she had 'nothing bright, glorious, or consolatory' to put in place of a hope of Heaven. There was a hint of rebuke in her plea: by following Combe's rational principles, she had found only emptiness. Those such as he, who achieved great things, could 'console themselves with the feeling of not having lived in vain', she wrote, but she and countless other women, 'who merely exist quietly, who bring up families (it may be), to tread in the purposeless steps of those who went before them – what motive – what hope may be found *strong* enough to enable them to bear up against trials, separations, old age & death itself?' She did not specify the immediate causes of her distress, but the 'trials' and 'separations' of which she wrote were veiled references to her parting from Edward. She added: 'Better, it seems to me, never to have lived at all than to advance through *ignorance* & perplexities to the land of annihilation.'

She apologised for her bleakness: 'dear Mr Combe, I must entreat your pardon for all this. I think you will tell me that I am ill – & am therefore, an indifferent judge of these things; – or, that other minds, better constituted, feel not as I feel.' But she had no one else to ask for help: 'it is from you alone that I seek information, or reproof'.

Combe wrote back promptly: 'Is your physical health sound?' he asked. 'An eye under the influence of jaundice sees all objects yellow, and a low-toned organism finds all creation dark & unconsolatory. This affects the orthodox believer as well as you. You may read in their diaries how, in this state of health, they despair of salvation; & become more miserable than you, for hell then yawns for them; & *its gates* at least, in your case are closed.' Combe insisted that the believer's fear of Hell was worse than her dread of the 'land of annihilation'. He recommended that she stop thinking so much: 'intellect alone does not fill up the vacuum of unsatisfied desire'. Pragmatically, if piously, he recommended that she sublimate her energies in charity work. To divert herself, he said, she must do something useful – like the nuns who worked in hospitals. 'To be happy, we must love disinterestedly, and we must act out our love in good deeds.'

Combe may have had in mind the example of Florence Nightingale, an acquaintance of his great friend Sir James Clark, who in 1853 had escaped her constrained existence by training as a nurse with the Sisters of Charity in Paris. Miss Nightingale shared Edward Lane's philosophy on medicine: 'Nature alone cures,' she said; 'what nursing has to do . . . is put the patient in the best condition for nature to act upon him.' On 10 October 1854 – the day that Isabella's diary recorded the kisses in the carriage – Nightingale set out from home on the first leg of her mission to the Crimea, where England, France and Turkey had been at war with Russia since the spring. The fighting was intensifying, and by the time she reached Constantinople the British troops had suffered a humiliating defeat at Balaclava. News of her work among the wounded reached England in early November.

A closer acquaintance of George Combe's, however, had given way to her amorous feelings. In July 1854, Marian Evans eloped to Germany with George Henry Lewes, a married man long estranged from his wife. She and Lewes were figureheads of secular and progressive thought in Britain, and their behaviour threatened to discredit the philosophy of their circle. Combe was 'deeply mortified and distressed' when he learnt of the elopement. He was also surprised, since an examination of Miss Evans's cranium in the 1840s had not indicated an excess of Amativeness (as she had herself expected), but of Adhesiveness. In November, the same month that he replied to Isabella's letter, Combe wrote to a mutual friend: 'I should like to know whether there is insanity in Miss Evans's family; for her conduct, with *her* brain, seems to me like morbid mental aberration.' She and Lewes had, 'in my opinion, by their practical conduct, inflicted a great injury on the cause of religious freedom'. Their behaviour seemed to suggest that progressive thought led to moral anarchy.

George Drysdale, meanwhile, finally completed his book *Physical, Sexual, and Natural Religion*, on which he had been working for four years. This work not only confirmed but celebrated the connection between free thought and free love. A 450-page guide to contraception, sexual diseases and population control, it was printed in December 1854 by the radical publisher Edward Truelove. The book was welcomed in the *People's Paper* as a 'Bible of the Body', and condemned in the mainstream press as a 'Bible of the Brothel'. To protect his family, George kept his authorship a secret: he was billed on the title page as 'A Student of Medicine'. Concealed within the work was a memoir of George's own tortured youth, told in the third person and presented as a case study.

Having been crippled by shame as a young man, George had now thrown off his inhibitions. He argued that sexual desire was natural, in men and women, and ought to be satisfied. 'Every individual,' he wrote, 'should make it his conscientious aim, that he or she should have sufficiency of love to satisfy the sexual demands of his nature, and that others around him should have the same.' He said that many women became ill because they did not have enough sexual intercourse: 'unless we can supply to the female organs their proper natural stimulus, and a healthy and natural amount of exercise, female disease will spring up on every side around us'. George argued that in women, as in men, 'strong sexual appetites are a very great virtue . . . If chastity must continue to be regarded as the highest female virtue; it is impossible to give any woman real liberty.'

Masturbation, George said, was as common among women as men, and as harmful. He noted the 'pernicious effect' of keeping the natural passions 'pent up in the gloomy caverns of the mind'. He urged his readers to adopt contraceptive techniques, so that they could enjoy frequent intercourse instead of resorting to onanism. To prevent pregnancy, he recommended having intercourse eight days after menstruation (here he accidentally identified a highly fertile phase); or withdrawing the penis before ejaculation (though he warned that this method entailed the same health risks as masturbation); or rinsing out the vagina with warm water immediately after intercourse; or (his favoured procedure) blocking the neck of the womb with a sponge beforehand. He also advocated the sheep-gut condom, 'an artificial sheath for the penis, made of very delicate membrane'.

To use any such device was to defy the Christian teaching that procreation, rather than pleasure, was the primary purpose of sex. George Drysdale defended contraception by reference to *An Essay on the Principle of Population* (1798), an influential work by the Rev. Thomas Malthus, which warned that only positive checks on reproduction would avert a disastrous overpopulation of the Earth. Contraceptives, George argued, could eradicate poverty and venereal disease as well as erotic frustration. Malthus had recommended abstention from intercourse, but many Victorian liberals adapted his arguments to justify contraception. Among the neo-Malthusians who gathered at Moor Park in the 1850s were George Combe, the psychologist Alexander Bain and James Stuart Laurie, a schools inspector who had recommended John Thom to the Robinsons.

George Drysdale had composed an astonishingly frank and joyful manifesto for sexual freedom, unparalleled in Victorian literature, even if its premise was the evil of onanism. But it was of limited use to a middle-class married woman such as Isabella: she could not do as George had done, and pay others to satisfy her sexual needs.

Isabella rose at eight on 29 January 1855, 'not very well', having had an unsettling dream in which she found herself walking in a garden as a child with her mother, her father and one of her brothers. The dream reminded her that she was now 'in middle life myself, my mother old and broken, my father in the grave, my own children growing up, it was my turn to go next, a few more suns would see me decrepit and dying'. She would 'never fathom life's great mystery', she feared, but would only 'become as though I had never been – my thoughts, my love, my dreamings, turned to clay! O God! What hollow mockery seemed the gift of life – how I wished that my work were done and that I could lay it down; it had not been to me a blessing.'

She blamed others for her bad start – 'my youth was blighted by the bigotry and ignorance and want of thought of those who had the charge of my bringing up' – but admitted that her own conduct had sealed her fate: 'alas! Late in the day, I mourn over errors that I am unable to overcome; my soul is clouded by remorse and bitterness. I strive with but faint hopes of success to bring up my three sons, who (with all my love for them) ought to be in better hands.' The diary could lure Isabella into morbid self-absorption, draw her into its dark reflections, so that she could see nothing but emptiness ahead and behind: 'The past a desert, the present thorny, the future horrible; eternity a blank.'

Isabella's birthdays often brought on maudlin thoughts. 'Youth is well nigh gone,' she had written as she turned thirty-nine: 'I shudder at old age, which I must face!' On 28 February 1855, the day after her forty-second birthday, she 'dreamt very painfully of a final walk with Dr Lane, of an anguished parting, of a *discovery* and *wandering* in shame and wretchedness in the world'. This was the first diary entry in which she alluded to the fear of being discovered – she imagined herself cast out from her home to wander the Earth as a fallen woman. 'Woke (1st of March) alarmed and miserable,' she added, 'and had headache all day.'

Ten years earlier, a sexual scandal had threatened to disgrace the Curwen branch of Isabella's family. Isabella's first cousin Isabella Curwen, also named after their rich and beautiful grandmother, was married in 1830 to the Rev. John Wordsworth, rector of Moresby, Cumberland, and the eldest son of the poet William Wordsworth. She was 'a treasure, pure-minded and amiable', according to her new aunt Dorothy Wordsworth, 'painfully shy . . . and always remarkably modest'. In 1843, after giving birth to her sixth child, Isabella Wordsworth fell ill and, on the advice of two obstetricians, she repaired to Rome. She asked her husband to bring their children to her, which he did in the summer of 1845. In December that year their four-year-old son contracted a fever and died. John accused his wife of causing the boy's death, and removed the remaining children from her. She wrote in despair to her parents in Cumberland, revealing to them that her husband had been sharing a house in Rome with a sixteen-year-old Italian girl. John had given the girl a pledge, in writing, that he would marry her upon the death of his sick wife, and that he would settle his estate on her and their future children.

Henry Curwen was appalled by the 'brutal manner' in which his daughter was being treated. He wrote to his son-in-law insisting that he restore the children to their mother and return at once to Cumberland. If not, he threatened, he would expose the story of John's sexual delinquency to his bishop. Curwen also wrote to William Wordsworth – 'the poor old poet', as he described him – to tell him of his son's infamous behaviour. Both Henry Curwen and William Wordsworth altered their wills to settle their money directly on their grandchildren instead of on the errant John, and Curwen made arrangements to buy from the Italian girl the pledge of marriage that John had given her. In effect, he was paying off the woman who had it in her power to bring shame on the family, while blackmailing his son-in-law into behaving himself. John Wordsworth complied with most of Curwen's demands and not a whisper of the scandal reached the public. Isabella Wordsworth stayed in Italy, while her children were dispersed to various schools. She died at Bagni di Lucca in 1848. John Wordsworth remarried three times. His misconduct remained a secret: he has been remembered, by his father's biographers, as a dutiful dullard.

The containment of adultery – for the sake of the adulterer's children, spouse, parents and wider family – was standard practice among the gentry. Within circles such as these, where reputation counted for so much, the families of a betrayed wife and her husband would work furiously to hush up any misdemeanours. The standards were different when the transgressor was the wife, but the principle remained: if the story was kept within the family, the crime could be overcome. Only an overt sign of sin – a written pledge or confession – might prove impossible to hide.

Isabella continued to correspond with John Thom and with Edward Lane. Though she endured a long period of silence from the doctor, she told her diary that a 'sweet, mournful little note' in April 'quite made amends' for his neglect. She replied to this note with a 'nice, long, but rather sad letter'. She imagined that she and he were confiding, in muted messages, how much they missed each other.

She told Combe that she was following his advice by occupying herself with her children's education. 'I have found more employment in actively superintending the progress & conduct of my sons than when they were at school in England,' she wrote; '& I am much more cheerful in consequence. They have several masters during leisure hours, for whom I assist them to prepare.' Among these new masters was a young French tutor called Eugene Le Petit. Despite his indifferent looks, Isabella found him beguiling. She arranged to take lessons from him herself.

In the morning of 9 April, Monsieur Le Petit corrected some translations that he had set Isabella. He 'did not leave me till 12,' she wrote; 'there was something very gentle and almost cheerful in his manner, and he said they had enjoyed yesterday afternoon: He looked better than usual, and I found that with my usual clingingness of disposition I was beginning to think more of his presence and approbation than conduced to my peace.' She tried to knock some sense into herself: 'Foolish heart, ever thus giving away its interest and regard for those who care not one iota about thee further than their interest is concerned.'

Two months later, shortly before the Robinsons were due to return to England, Le Petit gave a lesson to the boys and then helped Isabella with a translation. He stayed late to finish it, she noted on 9 June, and 'the time flew by' as they had so much to say about religion, music and a new book by Frederick Gretton, a translator of Latin. Le Petit 'was very gay and friendly', wrote Isabella, 'and owned that he should miss us sadly'. She added, 'I felt this was more likely to be my case than his. The utter frigidity of his conduct rather surprises me: others (handsomer than he is) have found attraction in my company, and where I have shown so much and unvarying kindness as I have to him, and where gratitude is evidently felt, it is a marvel that a warmer feeling does not sometimes come uppermost.' Unknown to Henry, Isabella had presented Le Petit with a piano worth £30, among other gifts. She told herself that the tutor's coolness was for the best: 'Temperaments most widely differ,' she wrote, 'and after all it is happy every way that he has got the moderation.'

Isabella and the boys returned to England in June to move in to Balmore House, the huge white villa that Henry had built at Caversham. The name 'Balmore' carried a tinge of grandeur by association with Balmoral, Aberdeenshire, where the castle that Queen Victoria and the Prince Consort had commissioned in 1853 was still under construction. Henry's house was Italianate in design, and equipped with a greenhouse, an ornate conservatory, wrought-iron balconies and terraces, a coach house and stables. It was bedded on a foundation of concrete on chalk rock, with internal double walls and a ventilating shaft. The ground floor contained three reception rooms, as well as a study and a boudoir (a private room for Isabella); on the upper floors were eight bedrooms, two dressing rooms and a bathroom; in the basement the servants' hall and a kitchen.

As soon as Isabella reached the house, Henry went to see Edward Lane at Moor Park to arrange for her to visit the spa as a patient. Perhaps she was suffering from a recurrence of the 'uterine disease' with which she had been diagnosed in Blackheath in 1849; or was claiming as much in order to see Edward again. Henry paid the doctor £10 10 shillings to give Isabella a fortnight's water therapy.

Isabella and her eldest son, Alfred, arrived at Moor Park in time for tea on Thursday 21 June, and were warmly welcomed by Lady Drysdale and Mary Lane. Edward got home later. He 'looked pleased to see me', said Isabella, but she noticed that he seemed uneasy in her company, only half-heartedly taking up where they had left off the previous autumn. 'I went with him to see sunset, and reached the hill in time to see it. How often had I wished to see it with him, but now he was ill, cold, low, and sad, and could not enjoy it; into garden, sat in bower, renewed the love of old times, but not so excitingly.' Back at the house, they conversed sedately in his study until ten.

'I value his beauty and prize his accomplishments,' she wrote in an undated entry. 'Yet, having none of those gifts myself, I must be content to be disregarded – overlooked, if not disliked. I should do the same in the case of a plain or unattractive person who might be even fond of me. 'Tis only human nature to do so.'

As ever, Isabella could not control herself in sleep: 'the night in happy dreams united me to my soul's idol. I was with him as of old, and even more tenderly united, for my love was in great measure returned. I had sacrificed everything for him, and could so have died. Hour after hour I thus dreamed, and, on awaking, I lay in a delicious state of semi-consciousness, half-realising all that I wished to enjoy, and with the latter lines of Shelley's *Epipsychidion* floating in my ears – true and false – my hopes, wishes, and the past half-realised bliss, blended in one sweet picture. Ah! Why not wholly realised?'

Percy Bysshe Shelley's notorious poem culminated in a

fusion between the poet and his mistress – 'Our breath shall intermix, our bosoms bound,/ And our veins beat together' – but Isabella's enigmatic reference to her 'half-realised', or half-enacted, bliss seemed to indicate an incompleteness in her physical union with the doctor: something short of orgasm, perhaps, or consummation. Although her diary entries of October 1854 had implied that she and Edward had intercourse – in the glade, the study, the carriage – they could equally well have described intense kisses and caresses. 'All day,' she wrote, 'this dream haunted my brain. "I never loved any one as I did thee, both mind and body," I had said in my dream, and in my waking moments the same idea was breathed still in my ear.'

On Sunday 24 June, Isabella and Edward took a walk to Mother Ludlam's Cave, and sat talking on a bench near the well. 'At length,' she wrote, he 'took me alone up the very valley where we had first enjoyed the happiness of loving', but the landscape was 'changed now and so was he'. They 'talked only commonplace'.

The next day, the doctor sat by her in the house, 'and at length brought a book of old songs and sat very near me looking them over'. They went out to walk together, and in 'our private bower' they read a song by the radical and licentious French poet Pierre-Jean de Béranger. Edward 'talked of his health and prospects', wrote Isabella, 'but he was cold and mentally sad. It was the shrine of the idol I had once worshiped that was left to me.' None the less, she claimed, 'it was enough for my woman's heart'. They walked until dark and then looked at some prints in his study. Here, at last, some of the old feeling was rekindled. After 'one long, passionate, clinging embrace', Isabella went late to bed. She was 'much excited', she wrote. 'Dreamed of him all night, and longed and mused and glowed.'

In a further, undated entry, Edward was remote again. He 'smoked a cigar', Isabella recorded, 'and we talked of man's destiny in the future and the pre-Adamite world'. This was a contemporary debate about how to reconcile the claims of geology and of Christianity: if there had once been a world without human inhabitants, as geological findings indicated, there was reason to expect that the race would one day die out. But as Isabella talked to Edward of an empty past and an empty future, she noticed that he was erasing her from his past and future too. 'There was romance in the circumstances in which we walked,' she wrote, 'but none in his manner. Never had he been colder. He forgot times and places in which I had been with him. He talked coldly, jestingly, almost selfishly; and the evening, that might have almost crazed me with its sweetness, that might have made me dream on for months on one image, was fated to chill at once, and I believe for ever, every lingering thought of my having in the least the power to interest him. I walked on by his side tired and crushed in spirit, but he knew it not.'

Isabella left Moor Park in early July. Two months later she visited again to take the Lanes' three boys to the coast with her own children. Atty was 'painfully delicate' with a chest complaint, she wrote, and Edward and Mary were too busy with their guests to take him to the seaside themselves. Isabella returned the Lane children to their parents on 10 October, Edward's thirty-third birthday, and stayed on at the spa for a few days. Mary had just given birth to a fourth son, Walter Temple, presumably named after Sir William Temple of Moor Park.

When Isabella caught Edward by himself in the evening of 10 October, she apologised for having written him an indiscreet letter. 'I begged a thousand pardons and said how much I regretted it; I must have written it in a perverse mood, I said.' He was forgiving: 'It was all over now, he replied, and we parted with one of those long, caressing kisses that shake my very soul, and make me dream and long for hours.'

On the fourth day of Isabella's visit – 14 October – she and Edward chatted in the drawing room until eleven in the evening. An elderly female patient sat behind them on the sofa, 'too deaf' to hear their conversation but loath to leave. Finally the old lady took herself up to bed. Edward, said Isabella, 'after talking some little time appeared to return to his former kind feeling for me, caressed me, and tempted me, and finally, after some delay, we adjourned to the next room and spent a quarter of an hour in blissful excitement'. The experience – which again took place in the doctor's study – was so intense, so pleasurable and unsettling, that Isabella came close to collapse. 'I became nearly helpless with the effects of his presence, could hardly let him depart, wept when he bade me try to obviate consequences, and finally bade him a passionate farewell. I was alone, passion wasted and sorrowful, sleep was far from me that night; I tossed and dreamed and burned till morning, too weary and weak to rise.'

Isabella's abject submission to Edward that evening, her delirious excitement in his arms and the exhausted melancholy that ensued, suggested that something new had happened between them – perhaps that they had for the first time consummated their relationship. By urging Isabella to 'obviate consequences', Edward seemed to be telling her to take steps to prevent a pregnancy; the most common post-coital safeguard, as described in George Drysdale's manual, among others, was to douche the vagina with a syringe.

The next day, as if suddenly awakened to the dangers of his situation, Edward told Isabella that their sexual relationship was over. 'The Dr came to my room,' she wrote, 'and sat a long while talking coldly of life, reputation, chances, caution, and my partner.' She tried to appeal to his romanticism. 'I cut a lock off his fine hair, said how much I had always loved him, spoke of his love-telling eyes and fine face and mouth; still he moved not; the interview closed without even a kiss.' It was a humiliating scene, in which Isabella wooed the doctor as a man might a woman, and failed to win him. She concluded, with wounded pride, that Edward cared more for comfort and respectability than he cared for her. 'I saw that, though I might have caused momentary passion, I was not wholly beloved, but that regard for reputation and ease were the moving springs of his conduct.' Her words betrayed how much she had wanted from him: not just an affair, but all of his love.

In November 1855 the Robinsons again decamped to Boulogne, handing over Balmore House to the decorators for the winter. 'It is very far from being finished, not being yet painted or papered; so that we must again leave it, to have it completed,' Isabella explained to Combe; 'indeed we shd have removed much sooner, but that Mr Robinson was anxious to get some necessary planting done, & that has delayed us till now.'

The fourteen-year-old Alfred had started to board at Queenwood School, Hampshire, a progressive college that specialised in the practical teaching of science. 'We have every reason to be satisfied with it, on his account,' reported Isabella to Combe, who had recommended the school. 'He is much interested in Chemistry, & in several branches of physical science; & is learning singing & gymnastics; besides being permitted to amuse himself in the workshop, with carpenters' tools, at leisure hours.' The headmaster, she said, 'speaks well of our boy's general conduct; tho' he is by no means forward in booklearning'. Otway and Stanley continued to be educated in Boulogne.

The Robinsons were together in France for the Christmas of 1855, during another winter of heavy rain and snow. As much as Isabella still thought of Edward, her dreams of him were no longer a refuge. For years he had allowed an air of ambiguity to attend their relationship, but now it was clear that he would always put his wife and family before her. The spell had been broken.

Isabella resumed her flirtation with Eugene Le Petit. This

time she received more encouragement from the young tutor, and their closeness caught Henry's attention. On 30 December he confronted her. 'After tea Henry commenced a most unpleasant discussion,' she recorded; 'accused me of some intimacy with the Le P— family, of which he could not ascertain the extent; said he was aware of my writing and posting and receiving letters that he knew nothing about.' He showed such 'suspicion and ill-feeling', she wrote, 'that I was alarmed and truly distressed'. She admitted to her diary that the blame was 'deserved, as I could not help feeling it', and yet she believed that her wrongdoing was 'excused by the harsh, narrow spirit of my partner'. She said what she could to disarm her husband's suspicions, and tried to stand firm in the face of his accusations. They continued to argue until after midnight, by which time Isabella 'had headache and nervous agitation'. Henry 'seemed sorry at the consequence of this stormy altercation,' she wrote, 'and said many conciliatory things'.

Fleetingly, Isabella portrayed Henry as a vulnerable figure: worried, regretful, capable of compassion. She closed the diary entry on a note of defensive certainty: 'It was too late then. Love, respect, complacency, friendship, patience, were all gone; nothing on my part remained but dread, weariness, disgust, and constraint. It is my children alone that keep me; once they leave the parental roof, and I will quit him.'

Isabella's desire to escape had grown stronger over the years. She and Henry had 'long been on the worst of terms', she later told Combe in a letter, and she often pleaded with her husband to release her, 'to let the frequent separations between us become a permanent one' and to let her live with her sons elsewhere. But he 'would not hear me', she said, 'because he would have thereby lost my income'. On questions of property and self-interest, Henry was 'utterly without probity', Isabella said; he was 'not what may be called sane'.

She felt paralysed, caught between her attachment to her sons and her longing for freedom.

Isabella had come to believe that the institution of marriage was arbitrary and unjust, and early in 1856 she sent Combe a letter in which she described the marital bond as a 'superstition'. Marriage was the subject of much contemporary debate. A Royal Commission had been set up to investigate divorce law in 1850, and reformists such as Caroline Norton were campaigning to improve the lot of married women. Mrs Norton set out the injustices of wedlock in a 'Letter to the Queen' in 1855. 'A married woman in England has *no legal existence*,' she reminded the sovereign: 'her being is absorbed in that of her husband.' A wife could not undertake legal proceedings, or keep her own earnings, or spend her own money as she wished. She 'has no legal right even to her clothes or ornaments; her husband may take them and sell them if he pleases'. A wife's identity was subsumed in that of her husband, even when the couple were in truth 'about as much "one" as those ingenious twisted groups of animal death we sometimes see in sculpture; one creature wild to resist, and the other fierce to destroy'. Caroline Norton spoke from experience: when she had left her unfaithful, bullying, profligate husband in 1836, he had kept her children from her and had confiscated the money that she earned through her writing. 'I exist and I suffer,' she said; 'but the law denies my existence.'

George Drysdale considered marriage 'one of the chief instruments for the degradation of women', as well as an unhealthy curb on sexual exercise. 'A great proportion of the marriages we see around us,' he wrote, 'did not take place from love at all, but from some interested motive, such as wealth, social position, or other advantages . . . Such marriages are in reality cases of *legalised prostitution*.'

That spring Isabella fell seriously ill. She may have been suffering from diphtheria, which was rife in Boulogne between 1855 and 1857. The longest and gravest diphtheria epidemic on record, the disease took the lives of 366 people in the town, 341 of them children. *The Lancet* reported that English visitors to Boulogne were particularly affected by the outbreak of the mid-1850s, to the extent that the disease became known in England as 'Boulogne sore throat'. Its symptoms were intensely swollen airways and high fever.

One day in May, Henry looked in on Isabella in her sickroom to find that she had become delirious. As she lay in her bed, restless and raving, he heard her muttering the names of other men. His suspicions again aroused, he went to her desk and lifted out the journal that she had brought with her from England. She had always kept her diary 'private' from him, he said later. Perhaps in her feverish distraction she had left her desk unlocked; perhaps she half-wanted him to find her secrets and blow their life apart. Henry opened her journal and read.

Henry read of his wife's infatuations with John Thom and Eugene Le Petit. He read of the bliss that she experienced in the arms of Edward Lane. He read that in his own company she felt only contempt, disgust and dread, and that when Otway and Stanley were of age she would leave him.

The scene echoed the moment in Anne Brontë's *The Tenant of Wildfell Hall* in which Arthur Huntingdon discovers his wife's diary. The dissolute, unfaithful Mr Huntingdon wrests Helen's journal from her: 'I HATE him!' he reads. 'The word stares me in the face like a guilty confession but it is true: I hate him – I hate him!' Huntingdon responds with glee to the evidence of his wife's unhappiness and hatred. Having learnt from the journal that she plans to flee with their son and make a living as an artist, he confiscates her jewels and burns her paintbrushes and easels. 'It's well you couldn't keep your own secret – ha, ha!' he sneers. 'It's well these women must be blabbing – if they haven't a friend to talk to, they must whisper their secrets to the fishes, or write them on the sand or something.'

Henry Robinson was horrorstruck by the diary's revelations, but his shock swiftly resolved into an icy rage. As soon as Isabella was in a state to understand what was said to her, he informed her that he had taken possession of her diaries and letters. He was also removing Otway and Stanley from her, he said, and returning with them to England. He sailed for Folkestone with his sons, leaving Alfred in France with his mother. In Isabella's desk at Balmore House, Henry found further diaries and other papers: essays, letters, notes and poems. He took them all.

BOOK II

OUT FLEW THE WEB

Out flew the web and floated wide;
The mirror crack'd from side to side;
'The curse is come upon me,' cried
The Lady of Shalott

From Alfred Tennyson's *The Lady of Shalott* (1842)

CHAPTER SEVEN

IMPURE PROCEEDINGS

Westminster Hall, 14 June 1858

Henry's counsel was the first to address the bench.

'The Robinsons married in 1844,' said Montagu Chambers QC, 'Mrs Robinson being then the widow of a Mr Dansey, and possessed of between £400 and £500 a year, which was settled upon her to her separate use. After their marriage the Robinsons resided at Blackheath, Edinburgh, Boulogne, and in the neighbourhood of Reading. During their residence at Edinburgh in 1850 they became acquainted with Mr Lane, then studying for the law, who afterwards married a daughter of Lady Drysdale. He set up a hydropathic establishment at Moor Park, which is probably well known to your Lordships as having formerly been the residence of Sir William Temple.'

The three judges in the new Court of Divorce and Matrimonial Causes sat on a raised platform beneath a canopy hung with red curtains. Sir Cresswell Cresswell, a spindly sixty-four-year-old bachelor who wielded a lorgnette, was the Judge Ordinary, the official in charge of the court. Sir Alexander Cockburn, a short man of fifty-five with sharp, pouchy blue eyes, was Chief Justice of the Court of Common Pleas, the third highest-ranking judge in the land; he too was a bachelor but, as was widely known among his peers, he had two children (aged twelve and nineteen) by an unmarried woman. Though he cut a dignified figure at the bench, Cockburn was a renowned socialite who often scrambled into court just in time for the start of the proceedings at eleven. Sir William Wightman was the least senior of the three in the court but the most experienced in law and in wedlock: at seventy-two, he had served as a judge for twenty-seven years and been married for thirty-nine. The judges had decided to hear the Robinson case without a jury: they would arrive at a verdict themselves. They wore horsehair wigs and red robes trimmed with ermine, heavy in the heat.

The sun funnelled in to the courtroom through a glass turret and a ring of round skylights in its dome, bathing the long desks and benches below. The stench of the city was pushing in, too. In the heat wave that laid siege to London that June, a 'Great Stink' of sewage lifted off the fat banks of the Thames and sifted into the Houses of Parliament and the adjoining courts at Westminster Hall. The temperature climbed, to eighty-five degrees Fahrenheit by noon and ninety degrees by three o'clock.

Mr Chambers – a former Grenadier Guardsman and parliamentarian of fifty-eight, with thick, dark eyebrows and a genial, knowing manner – continued: 'Mr Robinson was a civil engineer, and necessarily a good deal from town. He had commenced building a house for himself in the neighbourhood of Reading. When they went thither they renewed their acquaintanceship with the Lanes, and they used often to visit Moor Park together. Still more frequently Mrs Robinson went there alone; and it will be proved that the intimacy between the respondents attracted the attention of some of the patients and servants of the establishment. Mr Robinson, however, remained perfectly convinced of the fidelity of his wife, until at last, in the year 1857, during an illness of Mrs Robinson, he made an accidental discovery of an extraordinary narrative that at once opened his eyes to the impurity and infidelity of Mrs Robinson.'

Chambers and the other Queen's Counsel wore black silk gowns, white shirts, white collar-bands, and bristly white wigs that lapped over their sideburns. They sat facing the judges' bench, with their juniors behind them in gowns of coarse black cloth. A crowd of spectators filled the rest of the courtroom and the gallery that ran round the inside of the dome, the men in jackets, waistcoats and cravats, hats in their hands; the women in lace collars and wide, sprung skirts, their hair parted beneath flaring bonnets. Henry may have been among the spectators, though it is unlikely that either Isabella or Edward attended the trial; they would be kept informed by their lawyers of how the case unfolded. None of the chief protagonists was allowed to appear as a witness.

'Mrs Robinson had been unwell,' said Chambers, 'and her husband then found several diaries in her handwriting which gave a most extravagant narrative of his wife's impure proceeding. It would seem after Mrs Robinson became acquainted with Mr Lane at Edinburgh she, according to the diary, did not like him very much at first, but in a short time she admired him greatly. She even went into a detailed statement as to how he looked and how he was dressed. There were certain accounts of subsequent meetings at Moor Park, in 1854, which led to the conclusive inference that adultery had been committed.'

A few of the facts in Chambers's synopsis were wrong. Edward Lane was already married when the Robinsons met him in 1850, and he was by then studying medicine, having qualified as a lawyer three years earlier. Isabella was attracted to him immediately, according to the diary; only later, in pique, did she write sharply about him. And Henry read Isabella's diary in 1856, not 1857. Mistakes were often introduced in the relay of information before a trial – Henry had given his story to his solicitor, who had then instructed the barristers – but the error about the date on which he read the diary may have been deliberate. A husband was expected to act swiftly on discovering his wife's infidelity, and a delay in seeking legal redress could count against him. 'The first thing which the Court looks to when a charge of adultery is preferred,' advised a divorce guide of 1860, 'is the date of the charge relatively to the date of the criminal fact charged, and the date of its becoming known by the party alleging it.' Any lapse of time would give rise to the possibility that Henry had condoned Isabella's adultery, or connived with her to undo their marriage. Either would be a bar to divorce.

'I propose,' said Chambers, 'to put in evidence certain diaries written by Mrs Robinson. They will establish Mrs Robinson's guilt, but I am bound to confess that I entertain some doubt whether your Lordships will consider it sufficient as against Dr Lane.'

At this, Edward Lane's counsel, William Forsyth QC, got to his feet. He said that he objected to the admission of the diaries as evidence against either of the respondents. 'If Mrs Robinson is found guilty of adultery, it can only be with Dr Lane,' argued Forsyth, a long-faced Scot of forty-five, 'but her admissions or confessions, if the diary is so taken, can be no evidence against him, and therefore ought not to be used at all.'

The issue of the diary's status as evidence was to vex the court throughout the trial. The rules suggested that it could be used against Mrs Robinson (as a confession) but not against Dr Lane (as an accusation).

The judges conferred, and announced that they considered the diaries admissible, against her if not him. Cresswell explained: 'If several persons are indicted for burglary or conspiracy, and one of them makes a confession inculpating the rest, against whom there is no other evidence, it is quite true that his statement would not be evidence against anybody else, but could not the man himself be convicted?'

'No,' said Forsyth.

In moments of impatience, Cresswell twiddled his spectacles on their stick. Before delivering a crushing put-down he often adopted an expression of unusually attentive politeness. He addressed Forsyth: 'I would be glad to see any authority for that statement from the learned counsel.'

Forsyth took his point no further and Isabella's counsel, Dr Robert Phillimore, quickly abandoned his own plan to contest the introduction of the diary. He rose to say that he had been about to object to it on Mrs Robinson's behalf, 'but after the expression of opinion I have just heard from the court I will not proceed'. The defence lawyers' first strategy – to destroy the main evidence against their clients by eliminating the diary – had collapsed.

Chambers called for Isabella's journals to be produced for the court. He asked the clerk to read from them, but first warned that their contents might embarrass innocent parties. 'The diary contains the names of two young men whom Mrs Robinson apparently endeavoured to corrupt,' he said, deftly introducing an image of his client's wife as a predatory and ageing seductress. 'My impression is that her endeavours did not prove successful, although I will admit that it is quite possible they did. She accused them of coldness and restraint, and a desire to escape from her; and therefore I will not, if I can avoid it, introduce their names, especially as they seem to have been young men.'

With this, Chambers indicated to the clerk of the court the relevant passages in the three volumes of the diary dating from 1850, 1854 and 1855. At a long table just below the judges' bench, the clerk read aloud a short extract about Isabella Robinson's first encounter with Edward Lane in 1850, another about a poem that she had written under the title of 'Spirit Discord', and another about the 'preponderance of Amativeness' that she identified in her character.

Then he turned to the entries on which Henry's case rested.

The first was that of 7 October 1854, in which Isabella and Edward first kissed among the ferns: 'Oh, God! I had never hoped to see this hour, or to have any part of my part of love returned. But so it was.' The clerk moved on to the extract of 10 October, which described the 'bliss' Isabella experienced with Edward in a carriage taking her from Moor Park to Ash railway station. 'I leaned back at last in silent joy,' read the clerk, 'in those arms I had so often dreamed of.' The final words from this entry, about the doctor's 'unselfish' love-making, were omitted. Since the passage was read out at the behest of Henry's lawyers, perhaps it was Henry who chose to delete this last clause, which implied that his own sexual technique was less satisfactory than that of Edward Lane. There may have been a limit to how far he would humiliate himself in his efforts to get rid of his wife.

The last entry the clerk read that day was from 14 October (in fact, the passage was written in October 1855, though this was not made clear in court) and described how Edward seduced Isabella in the house at Moor Park. 'The doctor . . . caressed me, and tempted me, and finally, after some delay, we adjourned to the next room and spent a quarter of an hour in blissful excitement.' This entry included the line in which Edward advised Isabella to 'try to obviate consequences', a suggestion that had moved her to tears.

The Sunday newspaper the *Observer* declined to publish the diary extracts, not just because they were lewd, but also because they were written vividly enough to excite a reader: 'it would be quite improper to print them in a family newspaper', explained the editor. 'They contain admissions in all but the plainest terms of the criminality imputed to the unfortunate lady in question, and they are moreover penned with a degree of descriptive ability which renders them most dangerous reading. Under such circumstances it has been considered the wiser course to omit them altogether.' The idea that certain kinds of writing were dangerous – especially to young women – was commonplace: usually the culprits were French novels, but Isabella Robinson's diary showed that a middle-class Englishwoman could assault her own decency in prose.

The Divorce Court investigated adultery from the perspective of the injured party, giving the spectators in the courtroom and the readers of newspapers a cuckold's quick glimpses of a woman's forbidden liaisons. But Isabella's diary complicated the perspective: to hear of Henry's discovery of the journal may have put the court in the position of the horrified husband; yet to hear the diary extracts was to inhabit his wife's consciousness, to imagine adultery as an adulteress.

Once the readings were over, Chambers took the floor again. 'I am really quite at a loss,' he said, 'to know what will be the defence set up on the other side. I have been given to understand that it will be contended that what this lady wrote were mere hallucinations, and have no reference to facts.' Chambers claimed that his witnesses would confirm the diary's accuracy: 'the parole evidence I will call before your Lordships will be found to corroborate the diary in many important particulars, and to show what she had written was not unlikely to have occurred.'

Henry Robinson had gathered seven witnesses to testify on his behalf: his father, his brother-in-law, a nursemaid to his sons, and a guest and three servants from Moor Park. They waited to be called in the great vault of Westminster Hall, a fourteenth-century law court that now served as an extravagant antechamber to the newer courtrooms along its west flank. The witnesses stood beneath a high hammer-beam roof, the finest of its kind in England, in which each oak beam tapered to a carving of an angel clutching a shield.

Chambers called James Jay to the witness box. Mr Jay, a forty-nine-year-old magistrate and alderman who was married to Henry Robinson's sister Sarah, made his way into the courtroom through the furthest arched doorway on the right-hand side of Westminster Hall. He walked over to the bench and climbed the steps to a railed pen alongside the judges. After taking the oath, he confirmed that in February 1844 he had been present at Henry and Isabella's wedding in St Peter's, Hereford, a medieval church at the end of the Jays' street. He testified that when Henry married Isabella, she was a widow with one child. For several years after the marriage, he said, the Robinsons lived at Blackheath, and when he had visited them there they always seemed to be on good terms. Henry, in his view, was a kind and affectionate husband.

James Jay was shown the three relevant volumes of the journal, and was asked whether they were written in Isabella's hand. He said that they were.

Forsyth asked Jay whether he knew Mrs Robinson's age. Jay replied that he did not – she looked about fifty, he said. This completed his evidence.

The next witness was Henry's father, who had moved to London with his wife and sons in the late 1830s. An usher led the seventy-two-year-old James Robinson to the bench, where he took the oath. He simply testified that Henry and Isabella seemed to live on good terms.

Then came Eliza Power, now in her late forties, the Irish-born nurse who had looked after the Robinson children for eight years. She confirmed that Henry was kind to his wife and that when the family lived in Edinburgh his business engagements had sometimes taken him away from home.

The law required that a husband petitioning for divorce on the grounds of adultery establish that he had taken care of his wife and treated her with propriety. Henry's first three witnesses had testified to this effect.

The next to be called was Frances Brown, an Edinburgh resident of about forty-four. An usher led her to the witness box. She climbed the steps, and he let down the rail.

In reply to Chambers's questions, Miss Brown explained that she had become acquainted with Mr and Mrs Robinson in Edinburgh towards the end of 1850, and that she and her sister frequently met them at social events. In 1854 the sisters took the water cure together at Dr Lane's establishment in Surrey.

'I stayed with Dr and Mrs Lane at Moor Park in October 1854,' she said, 'and was there when Mrs Robinson came on a visit of about three days that month.'

Were Dr Lane and Mrs Robinson intimate? asked Chambers.

'They had been intimate from the time I knew them,' said Miss Brown, 'but I did not notice that they were then more intimate than on former occasions.'

Chambers asked her about the incident described in the diary in which Edward and Isabella, returning to the house after an amorous tryst on 7 October 1854, stopped to talk to the Brown sisters. Miss Brown confirmed all the incidents in which she played a part. 'One Sunday afternoon, pretty late, my sister and I met Dr Lane and Mrs Robinson coming from a walk. They seemed to be coming from the moors. The ground in the neighbourhood of Moor Park was thinly wooded. They approached and talked to us.'

Chambers asked whether she remembered telling a ghost story to one of Mrs Robinson's sons that evening, as mentioned in the diary. She said that she did. He asked whether she remembered the manner of Mrs Robinson's departure from Moor Park, which in the diary was the occasion of the sexual encounter in the carriage.

'When Mrs Robinson left Moor Park, she went in a carriage at night,' said Miss Brown, 'and Dr Lane went with her to the station.'

Under cross-examination, Miss Brown agreed that Dr Lane 'paid great attention to all the ladies under his care' at the Moor Park hydropathic establishment. Had it ever occurred to her that there was an improper attachment between the doctor and Mrs Robinson? No, she said, it had not. How many married ladies were staying at Moor Park that October, asked the defence lawyer, and did Dr Lane walk in the grounds with any of them?

'I can remember seven ladies there,' said Miss Brown, 'some married, some single. Dr Lane was in the habit of walking out with different ladies in the grounds.'

She answered a series of questions about the landscape around the house at Moor Park: there were many trees nearby, she confirmed; the moorland was about a mile away. She was asked whether Mrs Robinson took her eldest son, Alfred, with her when she drove off to the station with Dr Lane. Yes, said Miss Brown, she probably did.

Miss Brown was dismissed, and in her place the clerk of the court summoned Levi Warren, a stable boy who had been employed by Dr Lane at Moor Park in 1854. Warren agreed that Mrs Robinson usually came to Moor Park with her son 'Master Alfred' and that she and Dr Lane often walked together in the grounds. Then he dropped his bombshell.

'I have also seen them in the summerhouse,' said Warren; 'him sitting with his arm around her waist.' The summerhouse, he added, was on an island on the river running through Moor Park, and he had seen the two of them alone there more than once.

Warren was the first witness to allege anything improper between Edward and Isabella. In legal terms, the scene that he described was a 'proximate act', an event that fell short of catching a couple *in flagrante* but was strongly suggestive of an improper liaison. Proximate acts might include a married lady keeping a secret correspondence with a gentleman; or visiting a single man at his house, and closing the shutters; or letting a man into her house at night in a clandestine fashion – or, as in this case, sitting in a summerhouse with a man's hand at her waist.

When cross-examined, though, Levi Warren revealed his bias. It emerged that the stable boy had a long association with Henry Robinson, on whose behalf he was testifying. He had worked for him in 1851 and had secured the position at Moor Park on his recommendation. When he subsequently left Dr Lane's employ (he found the place 'hard', he said; he 'did not like it') Henry again helped out, recommending him for another job.

The defence lawyers, led by Phillimore and Forsyth, established that Henry had interviewed Warren about the events at Moor Park with the help of a private investigator, the former police detective Charles Frederick Field. Charley Field was a cheerful, astute fellow, plump and unscrupulous – the inspiration for Inspector Bucket in Dickens's *Bleak House* (1853) – who since leaving the police force had been frequently employed by men seeking to gather evidence of their wives' adultery. The lawyers asked Warren whether it was true that after this meeting with ex-Inspector Field he had confessed to the butler at Moor Park that he had in fact not seen Dr Lane with his arm around Mrs Robinson. They insinuated that Warren had lied to the court, having been bribed by Henry's agent to give false evidence.

Warren denied it. He said that he had talked to the Moor Park butler about meeting Mr Field and Mr Robinson, but had not confided any intention to lie about what he had seen in the summerhouse.

Divorce suits often hinged on the evidence of servants and hotel staff, they being the likeliest witnesses to acts of illicit intimacy among the middle and upper classes, but judges were on their guard against corrupt or vengeful employees. 'The testimony of discarded domestics should be received with great caution, and the most sifting,' warned a legal handbook, 'otherwise our position is fearful, our tables and beds would be surrounded with snares, and our comforts converted into instruments of terror and alarm.'

Two further Moor Park servants were called. John Thomas Jenkins testified that he thought that Dr Lane used to pay more attention to Mrs Robinson than to any of the other ladies.

Did he ever see any familiarity between them? asked a defence lawyer.

No, conceded John Jenkins, he did not.

Sarah Burmingham, the sister of the Moor Park gardener who corresponded with Darwin, gave similar evidence about the closeness between Dr Lane and Mrs Robinson. She added that Mrs Robinson had spoken to her of the doctor as a 'very handsome' and 'fascinating' person.

The court heard testimony – the newspaper reports did not specify from which servant – that Dr Lane had been seen emerging from Mrs Robinson's room; that she had been seen in his study; and that they whispered together at the dinner table.

The petitioner's case, said Chambers, rested here.

It now fell to counsel for Edward and Isabella to present the case for the defence. But when Isabella's counsel, Dr Phillimore, began to outline his arguments, Cockburn stopped him. In his clear, melodious voice, the Chief Justice said that the material being introduced was unfit for the ears of ladies. He suggested that the court adjourn for a short time, and that on its reassembly all women should be excluded from the room. The other judges agreed. On the same grounds, it seems that the reporters in the courtroom were discouraged or forbidden from printing the exchanges that ensued, as no further details of that day's hearing appeared in the press.

Most of the petitioners to the divorce court, which had opened in January, were men accusing their wives of adultery. The new law stipulated that to secure a divorce, a husband needed to establish just his wife's infidelity, whereas a woman needed to prove that her husband was not only unfaithful but also guilty of desertion, cruelty, bigamy, incest, rape, sodomy or bestiality. This double standard was based on the social danger posed by the adulteress. Because she might bear her husband another man's child, the unfaithful wife threatened certainties about paternity, kinship, succession and inheritance, the underpinnings of bourgeois society. The archetypal English adulteress was Queen Guinevere, a woman whose infidelity ushered in the ruin of her husband's realm. 'The shadow of another cleaves to me,' says Guinevere in Tennyson's *Idylls of the King* (1859), 'And makes me one pollution.'

The most notorious adulteress in contemporary literature was Madame Bovary, the bored provincial wife in Flaubert's novel of 1857. Emma Bovary is restless, sensual, melancholic, steeped in romantic fiction – one of her favourite books is St Pierre's *Paul and Virginia*, the novel that Isabella quoted to Edward in October 1854. She becomes infatuated with a young clerk, whom she plies with presents, and in the book's most scandalous episode – edited out of the original serialisation but reinstated by Flaubert in the published novel – she and he commit adultery in a carriage.

Though not published in English for many years, the novel immediately provoked comment in the British press. An essay in the *Saturday Review* in 1857 described Emma Bovary as 'one of the most essentially disgusting' characters in literature; the essayist claimed that women of her kind threatened to destroy society from within. He reassured his readers that there was no danger that 'our novelists' would outrage public decency as Flaubert had done, but he warned that English propriety carried its own risks. The national reticence about sex might end by inflaming desire: 'a light literature entirely based upon love, and absolutely and systematically silent as to one most important side of it,' he observed, might 'have some tendency to stimulate passions to which it is far too proper ever to allude.'

A fortnight before the Robinson trial began, a painting of an adulteress had been put on show in the summer exhibition of the Royal Academy, a mile west of the Divorce Court. The central panel of Augustus Leopold Egg's triptych showed a middle-class family in their living room, the husband having just learnt that his wife has betrayed him. Like Henry Robinson, this husband has not found his wife's transgression in the flesh but in writing: he has uncovered her crime by reading a letter. The husband is slumped in a chair, dead-eyed, a leaf of the letter in his hand. Beneath his foot is a portrait of his wife's lover. The wife lies flung across the richly carpeted floor of the room, her face hidden in shame. Their children, two girls, are momentarily distracted from the house of cards that they are building in the corner, a fragile tower balanced on a book by the French novelist Honoré de Balzac. Half of an apple lies next to the wife on the floor, an emblem of the apple with which Eve tempted Adam. The other half of the apple, stabbed through with a knife, sits on the table by the husband.

The panels on either side of this central scene show the family's fate. The mother and children are divided by the moment of discovery. On the left are the two girls, living together in melancholy poverty; on the right is the adulteress, huddled with a baby under Waterloo Bridge, a mile north of the Divorce Court, a notorious haunt of prostitutes and suicides. Two playbills on the brick arches under the bridge advertise farces about miserable marriages. The more recent of these, Tom Taylor's *Victims,* which opened at the Haymarket in London in July 1857, featured an intellectually pretentious woman who despised her businessman husband and flirted with a pale young poet.

Egg's painting plunged the viewer into a collapsing marriage, a terrible turning moment. Instead of a title, the triptych was labelled with a fictional diary entry, intensifying the realism and immediacy and incompleteness of its story. 'August the 4th. Have just heard that B— has been dead more than a fortnight, so his poor children have now lost both parents. I hear *she* was seen on Friday last near the Strand, evidently without a place to lay her head. What a fall hers has been!' Like most representations of adultery – and unlike Isabella Robinson's diary – the painting did not depict the wife's excited transgression, but her dismal disgrace.

Yet the message of the painting was equivocal: on the one hand it was a moral work about the awful consequences of adultery; on the other a work of pathos, in which the adulteress and her children were tragic figures. *The Times* observed that the painting 'is not easy to read'. The *Athenaeum* judged it 'an impure thing': 'there must be a line drawn as to where the horrors that should be painted for public and innocent sight begin, and we think Mr Egg has put one foot at least beyond this line'. By giving voice to both sides of the Robinsons' story, the new court was negotiating the same treacherous boundary.

CHAPTER EIGHT

I HAVE LOST EVERY THING

1856–58

In May 1856, Isabella's version of her story had fallen almost silent. The diary stopped at the point at which it was seized. But in a series of letters to George Combe in 1858, she, Edward, Henry and Lady Drysdale outlined the events of the two years between Henry's discovery and his petition for divorce. In the course of the correspondence, Combe took on the role of a kind of judge, a moral arbiter of the case. The letters that he sent and received, which are held in an archive in the National Library of Scotland, hover between the private and public realms, the world of the diary and the world of the court. They reveal how and why the case came to trial, in spite of the potentially terrible consequences for all concerned.

In June 1856, Isabella recovered from her illness and returned from France with her eldest son. Henry refused to allow her back into the family home, so she and Alfred, who was now fifteen, stayed briefly in Albion Street, a small, smart terrace north of Hyde Park, and then moved twenty miles south, to a cottage in the market town of Reigate, Surrey. In the 'gloom & solitude' of their two rented rooms, wrote Isabella, she descended into a 'deep & continued sorrow'. She had been cast out of society and separated from her beloved Otway and Stanley. Her younger sons, she said, had been 'dragged' from her side as she lay shattered by illness. Henry retained all of the furniture and other goods that she had brought to the marriage, as well as her diaries, poems, essays and correspondence, among them her letters from Edward Lane.

'I have lost every thing,' she wrote, 'but I was careless & thoughtless, & so deserved to suffer.' For many months, she was 'in a state bordering on distraction, & seriously contemplated self-destruction'. She said that only the hope of one day being reunited with her children saved her from suicide.

In the autumn she visited Moor Park and told Edward about what had happened in Boulogne, warning him that Henry was intent on revenge: having taken almost everything that she held dear, he now wanted to bring about her public disgrace and the destruction of the family she admired. And he wanted money.

Henry hated and envied Edward Lane, Isabella explained to Combe. 'He resolved if possible to ruin him. He said publicly that he would shut up Moor Pk.' He also believed, she said, that if he blackened Isabella's name he would be able to retain much of her property and keep her as 'a poor pensioner on his bounty'. Henry told her that he intended to allow her only £100 a year on which to live.

Henry consulted solicitors. His first plan was to sue Edward for damages on the grounds of his 'criminal conversation' with Isabella, who by law was her husband's chattel, but his lawyers advised him not to commence proceedings straight away. They presumably told him that he had no chance of winning with only the diary as evidence, since the law then required two witnesses to prove adultery. In December 1856 he hired ex-Inspector Charley Field to gather further evidence against his wife.

Edward was still running the spa at Moor Park, while suffering from renewed attacks of dyspepsia. When he discovered that Henry's agent had been questioning his servants, he wrote to Isabella. He sent his letter via a lawyer called Gregg, a former patient at Moor Park, and Isabella replied in the same way. This system concealed the correspondence between the pair, cloaking their exchanges in envelopes addressed to or penned by a third party, and so eluding – for instance – the attention of curious servants, or the inquiries of a wife or mother-in-law. Edward hoped to keep the story from Mary and Lady Drysdale. He arranged to meet Isabella to discuss their situation.

Edward and Isabella suspected that Henry intended to obtain a judicial separation. Isabella assured Edward that if Henry sued for a separation, she would accept the charge of adultery. By this means, she would spare Edward from being involved in the case, making it possible that his part in the story would remain a secret. Edward's last words to her, she later said, were that 'come what would, he should know that he suffered unjustly'. As the author of the incriminating diary, she accepted that the fault was all hers.

Neither Edward nor Isabella expected Henry to seek a full divorce, which under the system then in place was extraordinarily complicated and expensive. A cuckolded husband had to be granted a separation in the Consistory Court in Doctors' Commons; to be awarded damages in the Court of the King's Bench; and then to secure a private Act of Parliament to end the marriage. The cost could run to thousands of pounds. Only 325 such divorces had been granted between 1670 and 1857, an average of fewer than two a year.

Since the early 1850s, though, Parliament had been debating how to change the law to make the procedure fairer, cheaper, more consistent and transparent. This would entail a transfer of power from the ecclesiastical court in Doctors' Commons – described by Dickens as a 'cosey, dosey, old-fashioned, time-forgotten, sleepy-headed little family party' – to a new secular court. Henry's lawyers advised him that if he secured a separation under the existing ecclesiastical system, he would be well placed to win a full divorce if a secular court were established by Parliament.

In April, Henry petitioned for a formal separation from his wife, and the citation was served on Isabella at the end of the month.

George and Cecy Combe were staying at Moor Park in July 1857, when Edward Lane learnt about Henry's petition and finally revealed to his wife and mother-in-law the disaster that might descend on them all. They hid their distress from their guests. Combe merely noted in his diary that both his hostesses had fallen ill. 'Mrs Lane is still in bed from a Sun-stroke received at the zoological gardens on 14th July,' he wrote on 25 July. 'Lady Drysdale is taken ill, her pulse 120, with great derangement of the digestive system.' The women's ailments, he wrote, 'make us sad'.

This was the Combes' second visit to Moor Park. George suffered from digestive problems, and Cecy from nervous depression and anxiety. They enjoyed their month at the spa. The wheat and rye in the neighbourhood were under the sickle, George noted, and the brambleberries and lime trees in blossom. The guests picked huge figs from the espaliered trees in the walled garden, and at night gathered glowworms from the paths. 'Cecy & I walked in the Dell,' George wrote on 25 July, '& enjoyed the balmy zephyrs & beautiful landscape. We reposed long on the dry turf, & she sung old English melodies which are my delight.'

The occasional despatch from the outside world intruded on the Combes' peace. On 9 July, George observed that the papers were full of the trial of Madeleine Smith, a Glaswegian architect's daughter accused of poisoning a lover who had refused to return her incriminating love letters. In these letters

Miss Smith had seemed to rejoice in her sexual transgression, noted the judge, 'alluding to it, in one passage in particular, in terms which I will not read, for perhaps they were never committed to paper as having passed between a man and a woman'. Her conduct was shocking enough, but far worse was the pleasure that she took in recalling it. Combe wrote: 'the base of the brain must have been generally large & the coronal region deficient'. These were the same characteristics – the large organ of Amativeness and the small organ of Veneration – that he had identified in Isabella.

By 3 August, the day of the Combes' departure, Mary and her mother seemed to have recovered. The Lanes and Lady Drysdale gathered with their guests to see off their eminent friends. One patient, a sixty-year-old widow from Aberdeenshire, begged a lock of hair from Combe. Cecy was amused by the request, especially when George struggled to supply his admirer with a strand: 'one could scarcely be found,' he wrote, 'the locks are so scanty and short'. On this comic note, the affectionate old couple took their leave of the residents of Moor Park, and set off in a carriage for the railway station.

Edward's family had succeeded so far in concealing their plight, but Henry Robinson was working against them. Within a few days of the Combes' departure from Moor Park, Henry called on Robert Chambers in Edinburgh and produced Isabella's diary, explaining that he had come upon it by accident while fetching something for her from her writing desk. '9 August', recorded Chambers in his own journal. 'Mr H. O. Robinson called in the evening, and read me extracts from his wife's journal, revealing the progress of her guilty affection for —— ——. A singular expose, which kept me up for three hours with unabated interest.' Even in his own diary, Chambers blanked out Edward Lane's name, alive to the possibility that this private record too might become public. Though Henry asked Chambers to keep the matter a secret for the time being, he confided the story to other acquaintances in Edinburgh.

Later that month, as Henry had hoped, Parliament passed an Act to establish a secular divorce court, with procedures that put a full dissolution of marriage within his reach. By making divorce more widely available, Lord Palmerston's government aimed to reduce the number of 'irregular unions' in the country, enabling women legitimately to escape violent husbands and men to rid themselves of unfaithful wives. The court was scheduled to open in 1858.

In the meantime, Henry proceeded with his suit in Doctors' Commons and enrolled Otway and Stanley as boarders at Tonbridge School in Kent; he gave his name in the register as the Rev. Henry Oliver Robinson, perhaps in the hope that this would disguise his identity when the separation case came to court. Tonbridge was a traditional boys' public school, with about 160 pupils. The head was 'a strict master', according to a contemporary: 'the cane was always within reach.' Otway was selected for the thirteen-a-side football team, which played an unusually ferocious form of the game: 'anyone running with the ball may be collared, charged, hacked over, or tripped up', read Rule 13.

On 3 December 1857, the Consistory Court at Doctors' Commons, an ancient yard next to St Paul's Cathedral, was presented with Henry Robinson's petition for a divorce *a mensa et thoro* – a divorce from bed and board, or a judicial separation. His evidence, which was heard in private, consisted of the diary extracts and the testimony of two Moor Park servants. Henry's petition was one of the last, perhaps the very last, to be heard under the old system. Isabella, as she had promised Edward, did not resist the suit. Her counsel rose to say that he felt that he could offer no opposition on her behalf. The court granted Henry his separation and *The Times* reported the case in a few lines the next day, making no mention of the circumstances of the adultery or the name of the alleged adulterer.

Under the terms of her marriage settlement, Isabella kept her private income after the separation, though she no longer accrued as much interest on her funds. An economic crisis in late 1857 had reduced the value of many investments. She now received about £390 a year, which after Alfred's expenses of £150 left her, she said, with 'scarcely enough to live as a gentlewoman' – £300 a year was considered the minimum required to run a middle-class household with one servant. While living with Henry, Isabella had been among the most affluent of her class; now she had almost dropped out of it altogether. Henry hoped to reduce her income still further.

Henry was staying in Balmore House that month, with Otway and Stanley, who were home for the holidays, and with one of his two illegitimate daughters, whom he planned to introduce to society in Reading. On 12 December, nine days after securing his separation from Isabella, he wrote to Robert Chambers to give him permission to divulge the details of the diary to their friends in Edinburgh. Chambers told the story of Isabella's 'impassioned and disgusting' escapades to George Combe, who relayed it to his friend Sir James Clark.

Clark, who had treated Keats in Rome during his final illness, was one of Queen Victoria's favourite physicians; it was he who had arranged for Combe to read the heads of the Royal children. Combe apologised profusely to him for having introduced him to the inhabitants of Moor Park, adding that though he had no doubt that Isabella was to blame for the affair, the doctor would 'pay a sad penalty'. Combe noted that Henry Robinson was said not to have 'reverenced the conjugal vow' himself.

Edward was in London for Christmas, in a six-storey Georgian house in Devonshire Place, Marylebone. With him were his wife, his mother-in-law, his children and his three brothers-in-law. George Drysdale was now a practising physician, having received his medical degree in Edinburgh in 1855, and Charles was a medical student at University College London, having abandoned his career as an engineer in the same year.

On 28 December 1857, Edward learnt that the rumour of his misconduct was abroad, and he wrote to Combe the next day with a 'full, flat, peremptory, & indignant denial' of the affair with Isabella. He claimed that he could not account for the diary entries about him – Isabella must have been 'half out of her mind', he said. She had not resisted the judicial separation, he told Combe, because 'she had done *me* an incalculable injury, & she determined that, at whatever cost, she wd not add to it by mixing up my name publicly with such a scandal'. Two days later – on 1 January 1858 – Lady Drysdale followed this up with her own letter to the Combes: 'You will believe my solemn words when I declare that Lane is most perfectly innocent – nay that when Mary and I often urged the necessity of having the unfortunate woman . . . as she had such an unhappy home, Lane was always loath to yield to our entreaties considering her a bore.'

Edward went to Edinburgh to defend himself in person, catching the express train that left London at 9.15 a.m. on Saturday 2 January, and reached the Scottish capital at about 10 p.m. The next morning, he spent two and a half hours talking to George Combe at his house in Melville Street. Edward fiercely protested his innocence. Isabella's diary entries were fantasies, he said: her religious doubts had thrown her 'clean off the rails of common sense & common propriety'. In her journal's pages 'fact and fiction were recklessly jumbled together' and 'a loose rein was too frequently given to a prurient & diseased imagination'. He claimed that he had not flirted with Isabella in Edinburgh; in fact, he had always taken a book with him on their carriage rides to the coast in order to have a means of escape from her 'facile' conversation. 'I never wrote a line to Mrs R,' he said, 'which might not be proclaimed at the market cross.' The doctor said that he was eager to sue Henry for defamation, but his solicitor had advised him against doing anything that would publicise the story, since his reputation 'would be ruined equally by success as by failure'.

Edward's indignation was genuine. Isabella's experience of their relationship probably bore little resemblance to his own. The sentimental terms in which she recounted their trysts, the passion and longing that she attributed to him, may indeed have struck him as fantasies, derived more from romantic literature than reality. In the rhapsodic rhetoric of some of her diary entries she may even have implied that they had sexual intercourse when they did not. She had also been careless: by writing her diary and leaving it lying around, she seemed to have wantonly inflicted pain on him and his family. Edward's only recourse was to pit his word against the diary's words, to insist that Isabella had made it all up. He turned on his former friend. She was 'a rhapsodical & vaporing fool', he wrote, 'a vile & crazy woman' given to 'moonshine lucubrations'.

Edward was enraged by the contrast between his position and that of Henry Robinson. Henry emerged from the journal as 'the consummation of human meanness, paltriness, rascality & cruelty', Edward told Combe; his behaviour had left Isabella 'anxious to escape, almost at any price, from the bondage of a union that had made her life well-nigh intolerable'. Yet this horrible husband, who was known to have a mistress and illegitimate children, was perfectly innocent in the eyes of the law.

George Combe was won over. 'I was deeply moved by poor Lane's distress,' he reported to Sir James Clark. 'Lane is broken down, & Lady Drysdale & Mrs Lane are living in agonising terror of publicity.' Having so enthusiastically recommended Moor Park to his friends, Combe felt personally responsible for the doctor's honour. He worked to distance himself from Isabella. She 'professed a great interest in the new Philosophy,' he told Clark, 'but Mrs Combe & I never liked her'. Though she was 'a clever intellectual woman', her 'deficient coronal region gave a cold low tone to her intellectual manifestations, that deprived her of all interest for us'.

Combe's friends were astonished by the story. Isabella Robinson was 'an extraordinary woman', said Sir James Clark, 'the first . . . that ever kept a record of her own infamy'. Marmaduke Blake Sampson, City editor of *The Times* and a keen supporter of phrenology, thought that Edward should take some of the blame even if he were innocent of adultery: 'by devoting himself to her morning rides & allowing a mutual intercourse with the children he . . . paid her the greatest attention that it was in the power of a grave man enjoying a position in society to allow. He has touched pitch and has been defiled. Were he to recognise the consequences that have taken place as the legitimate results of his own want of perception, dignity, and prudence I should have more confidence in any representations he might make than can be felt while he represents himself a victim.'

Two days after Edward's visit to Edinburgh, Henry Robinson wrote to Combe with his own account of the affair. Disingenuously, he claimed that he had not wished to inflict the painful story on Combe, but had just learnt from Robert Chambers that it had reached his ears – now 'my pen is set free, and I obey the natural impulse to communicate to a kind and honored acquaintance the sad tale'. He told Combe that he was eager to correct any misrepresentations that Isabella might have circulated. He described the dismay, grief, surprise and horror he had felt upon reading the diary and making the 'dread discovery' that Isabella was conducting an 'amour' with Eugene Le Petit, 'although there was room to hope that it had not reached a criminal extent'. He said that he had been even more horrified to find that his wife had since 1850 been 'the slave of a passion for Dr E. L.', which evolved in 1854 into a 'criminal intimacy'. Henry offered to show Combe the corroborative evidence against Edward, as long as he treated it as 'strictly private and confidential'.

Combe declined: 'Now, your offer to lay before me, *confidentially*, the evidence of his criminality, would only complicate our difficulties; for I could not ask Dr Lane for any explanations, and we must condemn him unheard in his defence.'

Both Henry and Isabella had violated the boundary between the private and the public: Isabella by writing about Edward in her journal; Henry by reading and disseminating her secret words. Combe responded by working urgently to re-establish the distinctions between confidential and free information. He scrupulously separated out the public statements from the whispered allegations, matters of record from matters of rumour. By refusing to read the diary, he also made it easier for himself to believe in Edward's innocence.

Edward thanked Combe for his protection: 'you have acted towards me not only as a kind friend but as a man of honour – determined that at any rate, so far as in you lay, I shd not be stabbed in the dark'. Henry, by contrast, was behaving in a 'furtive', 'under-hand & malignant' manner.

Edward persisted in hoping that he could contain the scandal. 'I speak to you,' he wrote to Combe, 'with all the . . . fullness of a son to a father', an appeal that invoked the honesty but also the confidentiality of the family circle. He reminded Combe of 'the peculiar circumstances of my position, which renders the avoidance of all publicity a matter of so much moment'. Lady Drysdale made the same point. 'May I . . . entreat that you and Mrs Combe will consider this letter as *strictly confidential*,' she wrote, 'for every day I feel more sure that *silence* is our only safety.'

A scandal involving another Mrs Robinson had blown up in 1857, and with it a controversy about the printing of private gossip. In March, the novelist Elizabeth Gaskell published a biography of Charlotte Brontë, who had died in 1855, in which she described a love affair between Charlotte's brother Branwell and Lydia Robinson, a 'mature and wicked' married woman who employed him in the 1840s as a tutor to her sons. 'The case presents the reverse of the usual features,' wrote Mrs Gaskell; 'the man became the victim; the man's life was blighted, and crushed out of him by suffering, and guilt entailed by guilt; the man's family were stung by keenest shame.' The woman in question, now Lady Scott, threatened legal action against Mrs Gaskell's publishers in May 1857, with the result that the book was withdrawn and altered.

When the Court of Divorce and Matrimonial Causes opened at the beginning of 1858, Henry Robinson became the eleventh person to lodge a petition for a divorce *a vinculo matrimonii* – from the bonds of marriage. This form of divorce would have the same effect as the death of a spouse: if Henry won his suit, he would, like a widower, be free to take another wife.

The new court conducted its proceedings in public. It aspired to be seen to protect and to punish, defining what was allowed within marriage while demonstrating the very visible disgrace that awaited those who transgressed. Among the key components of the Divorce Act were a provision for the protection of married women's property, which entitled wronged wives to keep their own earnings, and a relaxation of the standard of proof required to prove adultery. Most importantly, the process was simpler. Henry Robinson and others like him would not have been able to afford a full divorce before 1858.

Having already convinced the church court of Isabella's adultery, Henry had reason to feel confident that the new court would grant his petition. Where Doctors' Commons had required two witnesses to adultery, this court needed just one. A guide of 1860 explained: 'To require absolutely evidence of two witnesses to facts scarcely ever otherwise than secret, is, in most cases, to ensure a defeat of the suit and a denial of justice.' Nor did Henry's counsel need to establish adultery beyond a reasonable doubt; since this was a common law rather than a criminal trial, he had only to persuade the judges that his case was more probable than Isabella's.

Henry's solicitors advised him that though his case against Edward Lane was comparatively slight, a man petitioning for divorce was now obliged to name his wife's alleged lover as co-respondent. This might work to Henry's financial advantage: if his petition was successful, Edward could be ordered by the court to pay him costs and damages. In February 1858, Henry served papers on both Edward and Isabella.

In the Consistory Court, Isabella had shielded Edward by letting Henry's suit go through unopposed, but there was no way of keeping the doctor out of the secular proceedings. To protect Edward now, she would have to deny adultery.

Isabella and Edward's barristers met to formulate their case. On 22 April, Isabella denied adultery via her solicitor, and the next day Edward did the same. Edward organised for the diary to be transcribed by copyists, at a cost of £150, so that his counsel could use it in his defence.

In the first five months of 1858, 180 petitions were brought before the Divorce Court judges. It was not until Monday 10 May that the court granted its first divorce, but the dissolutions then came apace: by lunchtime the next day, the court had divorced eight couples. 'I cannot help expressing my satisfaction at the manner in which the new Act works,' said Lord Campbell, the Lord Chancellor, who had helped to formulate the Divorce Act. 'Now all classes are placed upon the same footing.'

Several of the earliest petitioners to the court were solicitors. As lawyers, they were quick to see the possibilities of the new Act; and, like Henry Robinson, they were modern middle-class men, more interested in revenge than reputation, more eager to secure their freedom than to preserve their families' honour. The evidence was necessarily tawdry. On 12 May, a solicitor called Tourle accused his wife of seducing their neighbour's son. His witnesses were his nephew, who had happened upon Mrs Tourle and the neighbour's son in her drawing room, 'red and confused'; his servant, who claimed to have seen the young man with his arm around Mrs Tourle's waist in her dining room one afternoon in November 1856; a coachman, who said he saw the pair kissing in the woods in the summer of 1857; and the staff of a hotel in Albermarle Street, London, who testified that they had shared a room. On the basis of these sightings of a couple on the edge of sex, the divorce was granted.

As the judges rattled through their roster, they were setting out what constituted cruelty, how to prove adultery, the limits of a man's dominion over his wife and children. In doing so, they besieged the public with tales of domestic misery. 'Everybody with whom one speaks of any wretched marriage,' ran an editorial in the *Daily News* at the end of May, 'at once matches the case with another, which brings up the mention of a third; so that the imagination becomes haunted with images of cursed homes.' Even Queen Victoria seemed suddenly worried about the institution: 'I think people marry far too much,' she wrote to her newlywed daughter Vicky in May; 'it is such a lottery after all, and to a poor woman a very doubtful happiness.' Charles Dickens, whose novels had done much to glorify the middle-class Victorian home, had himself slipped into domestic crisis. On Friday 11 June, three days before the Robinson case began, he issued a statement in which he announced that he and his wife, Catherine, had signed a deed of separation. By drawing up a private agreement, Dickens at least avoided the publicity of the courtroom. In the newspapers, he denied rumours that he had committed adultery, either with a young actress or with his wife's sister. The 'breath of these slanders,' he said, had assailed his readers 'like an unwholesome air'.

CHAPTER NINE

BURN THAT BOOK, AND BE HAPPY!

Westminster Hall, 15 June 1858

By Tuesday 15 June, news of the Robinson trial had spread. When the court convened at 11 a.m., several eminent lawyers pressed into the stifling courtroom to watch the proceedings. Among them was the former Lord Chancellor Henry Brougham, famous for successfully defending Queen Caroline on a charge of adultery when George IV tried to divorce her in the 1820s. Lord Brougham may have been aware of Isabella's ancestry, which was not mentioned in the course of the trial: in the 1820s he had sat in the House of Commons alongside her grandfather John Christian Curwen, a fellow landowner in the north-west of England. The first reports of *Robinson v Robinson & Lane* appeared in that day's press.

Of the three judges at the bench, Sir Cresswell Cresswell was the most au fait with the intricacies of the new law, having been in charge of the Divorce Court since January, but Sir Alexander Cockburn was to dominate the proceedings. He enjoyed the limelight, and the Robinson trial was already attracting more attention than any yet heard by the court. He also had a special interest in allegations of madness, having made his name at the bar in 1843 by securing an acquittal on the grounds of insanity: he had called nine doctors to the Old

Bailey to testify that his client, Daniel M'Naghten, had been in thrall to 'a fierce and fearful delusion' when he tried to assassinate the Prime Minister, Robert Peel. The verdict revolutionised ideas on mental delusion and criminal responsibility, making the insanity plea commonplace in the criminal courts. A lawyer could now argue that his apparently sane client had committed a crime in a moment of madness – or, as the barristers in Isabella's case would suggest, had falsely confessed to a crime while prey to insanity.

Forsyth, for Edward Lane, began. Usually, it was counsel for the respondent rather than for the co-respondent who addressed the judges first, but Isabella had agreed to let Edward's counsel lead; this meant that his lawyers would be able to cross-examine her witnesses, but hers could not cross-examine his. Their hope was that the case against Edward would quickly collapse, and with it the case against Isabella.

'My learned friend has admitted,' said Forsyth, 'that he has not sufficient evidence to fix the co-respondent, but the consequences of suspicion are so serious to Dr Lane that I would not feel justified in foregoing the opportunity of addressing your Lordships and calling evidence. Dr Lane's honour, reputation, domestic happiness, and means of existence are all at stake in the inquiry.'

The court, he noted, had deemed the journal admissible against Isabella but not against Edward: 'As against that gentleman it must be taken to be non-existent, as if it had never been written. I will, therefore, dismiss all consideration and allusion to that journal.'

Without the evidence of the diary, said Forsyth, 'could any case be more meagre upon which to charge adultery against a co-respondent than the present? Here is Dr Lane, a young man with a wife and family, accused of adultery with a woman fifty years of age, because he has been seen walking with her in his own grounds and whispering to her at the dinner table, and because she has been seen in his study, which was an open thoroughfare to all the household; and he has been once met coming out of her rooms.'

He reminded the court that the doctor consorted with all the lady patients at Moor Park. 'Dr Lane had been urged by Mrs Lane's mother to show every attention to Mrs Robinson – to drive with her, and ride and walk with her in the park. Lady patients will be called to prove that they have never seen anything to justify them in supposing there was the slightest shade of suspicion against the parties. I say fearlessly that, with the exception of the evidence of the witness Warren, there is nothing whatever in the case to raise suspicion. The opposite side has not dared to produce one letter from Dr Lane to Mrs Robinson, although many passed between them. It is said that Dr Lane was once seen coming out of Mrs Robinson's chamber; but the fact is, that gentleman is in the habit of visiting all the lady patients' chambers. Mrs Robinson might have been unwell, and nothing is more likely that under such circumstances Dr Lane should have extended his visits as far as her room.' He assured the court: 'I will get rid of every rag or shred of suspicion against Dr Lane.'

Forsyth's first witness was Auguste Giet, a former butler at Moor Park whose duties had included the supervision of the pantry near the doctor's study.

Giet testified that Levi Warren, the stable boy who had given evidence the previous day, made a trip from Moor Park to London in 1856. Afterwards, Giet said, the boy told him that he had had a meeting with ex-Inspector Field and Henry Robinson, whom he had told 'that he had never seen Dr Lane with his arm around Mrs Robinson's waist'. Giet added: 'He also told me that he had never seen them in that position.'

Forsyth produced two letters that Warren had written to Giet and he showed them to the butler, asking him to confirm that the letters were in Warren's hand. Giet said that they were. Forsyth showed the court one of these letters, in which

Warren asked the butler to keep quiet about what he had confided in him.

The lawyer enquired whether Giet remembered seeing Mrs Robinson at Moor Park. Yes, the butler replied, but he had never noticed her walking with Dr Lane.

Forsyth asked about the location of the study in which Isabella and Edward were alleged to have committed adultery. Giet confirmed that the servants used the study as a shortcut from the pantry to the dining room.

The butler was told that he could step down from the witness box. Even without his evidence, it had been easy enough to dismiss the testimony of a disaffected stable boy; the judges could now disregard it altogether.

Forsyth called Caroline Suckling, the fifty-three-year-old wife of Captain William Suckling, a distant relative of Lord Nelson. The Sucklings were regular guests at Moor Park. George Combe had met them there in 1856, and taken a dislike to their eight-year-old daughter, Florence Horatia Nelson Suckling; Combe described her in his journal as 'a spoiled only child & heiress, about whom I gave her mother advice'.

Mrs Suckling testified that she was staying at Moor Park in September 1854, and had a clear recollection of Mrs Robinson's presence there.

'I never saw any communication between the doctor and that lady. I saw Mrs Robinson in conversation with him, in which conversations I myself often joined; but there was no difference in the treatment by Dr Lane of Mrs Robinson and any other lady there.'

Forsyth asked Mrs Suckling about Mary Lane.

'Dr and Mrs Lane were on the most excellent terms,' said Mrs Suckling. 'She was about twenty-five years of age, and was a friend of Mrs Robinson.'

Questioned further about the intimacy between the doctor and Isabella, Mrs Suckling said that she had once seen Dr Lane walking with her on the public terrace outside the house. 'But he was in the habit of walking with every lady patient and every gentleman patient by turns on the terrace and in the park.'

Mrs Suckling stepped down, and Forsyth summoned Lady Drysdale to the witness box. Edward, as the co-respondent, was not entitled to testify in court; nor, as his wife, was Mary. But Lady Drysdale was able to appear as a witness in her son-in-law's defence.

In answer to Forsyth's questions, Elizabeth Drysdale told the court that she had lived with her daughter and Edward Lane ever since their marriage. The Lanes, she said, had long been very intimate with the Robinson family. Forsyth asked her about Dr Lane's behaviour towards Mrs Robinson.

'His conduct was always exactly the same to Mrs Robinson as to the other ladies in the house,' Lady Drysdale said. 'I often urged Dr Lane to pay kind attention to Mrs Robinson.'

Why was that? asked Forsyth.

'Because I thought that Mrs Robinson's home was an unhappy one,' she replied.

Forsyth asked Lady Drysdale whether she was aware of the doctor's walks with Mrs Robinson.

'Mrs Lane and I always knew when the doctor drove or walked out with Mrs Robinson,' she said. 'He was accustomed to walk about the grounds with different ladies living in the establishment.'

Did she ever notice any improper familiarities pass between Dr Lane and Mrs Robinson?

No, said Lady Drysdale, she did not.

Forsyth had no further questions.

Jesse Addams, who was assisting Montagu Chambers with Henry's case, rose to cross-examine Lady Drysdale.

Dr Addams had represented Henry the previous December when he had secured his judicial separation in the Consistory Court. Isabella, too, brought with her to the new court her representative from December's trial, Dr Phillimore, while a

James Deane had been assigned to Edward Lane's defence. As former practitioners in Doctors' Commons, they were Doctors of Civil Law, and as Queen's Counsel they were also qualified to practise in the new court.

Addams asked Lady Drysdale to describe Mary Lane's temperament.

'My daughter is a very sweet-tempered person,' said Lady Drysdale.

And how old was she at the time of the alleged affair?

'About twenty-seven years of age,' said Lady Drysdale.

'And very unsuspicious?' asked Addams.

'She had no suspicions of her husband,' said Lady Drysdale. 'She had no cause.'

The barrister asked her the age of Mrs Robinson.

'The age of most of the lady patients is about fifty,' replied Lady Drysdale, 'or perhaps fifty-five. I should say that Mrs Robinson was fifty-five but I am afraid of saying too much.' At this, some of the spectators in the courtroom laughed.

Isabella had in fact been forty-one at the time of the alleged adultery. Even if Lady Drysdale did not know this, she surely knew that her own daughter, Mary, was thirty-one rather than twenty-seven when her husband was said to have strayed.

One of the judges asked Lady Drysdale how the Robinsons and the Lanes had become so close.

'Mrs Robinson was remarkably kind to Dr Lane's children, my little grandchildren,' said Lady Drysdale, 'and that led to the intimacy.'

Lady Drysdale was dismissed. Her account of the mutual confidence that existed between her son-in-law, her daughter and herself, said *The Morning Post*, had been 'most effective and touching'.

Forsyth's next witness was Mr Reed, a surveyor, who produced a plan of the Moor Park grounds. He pointed out on the plan the location of a summerhouse. He testified that a person standing in the position that Levi Warren had described could not have seen into the summerhouse at all, let alone have observed Dr Lane's arm encircling Mrs Robinson's waist.

The last witness for Edward Lane was Dr Mark Richardson, a former surgeon in the Bengal Army, who had been at Moor Park when Mrs Robinson visited in 1856. Like all the Moor Park patients before him, he testified that Dr Lane had behaved towards her in exactly the same way as towards the other female guests.

For the summing-up, Forsyth handed over to his junior, John Duke Coleridge, a great-nephew of the poet. Coleridge repeated to the court that there was no evidence to inculpate Edward Lane.

Phillimore then rose to put forward Isabella's case. It seemed a tall order, not least because he had offered no defence at all when he represented her in Doctors' Commons. But the rules had changed – in particular the rule that required the petitioner to publicly identify his wife's alleged lover.

'This is one of the most remarkable cases I have ever heard of,' said Phillimore. 'It seems admitted that the case against Dr Lane rests on nothing but Mrs Robinson's diary, which can not be admitted against him; and it might, therefore, happen that Dr Lane will be dismissed on the ground that no adultery was proved against him; and Mrs Robinson will be divorced on the ground that her adultery with Dr Lane has been proved. I need hardly say what a state of jurisprudence such a state of things would represent.' To find Mrs Robinson guilty and Dr Lane innocent, as he pointed out, would render the moment of their intimacy at once real and unreal, a fact and a fiction. She might be proven to have had sexual intercourse with him, while he was cleared of having had sexual intercourse with her.

The jowly, confident Robert Phillimore had more than fifteen years' experience in both church and common law: through the church courts he had acquired a deep knowledge of the precedents of marital law; and he was equally familiar with the procedures and personalities of the secular system. He was well connected and well liked: a former MP, the son and brother of eminent academic lawyers, and a good friend of the former Chancellor (and future Prime Minister) William Gladstone. Phillimore was probably unaware that Gladstone kept a private diary in the 1850s in which he recorded his 'rescue work' with prostitutes and his subsequent episodes of repentant self-flagellation.

Cockburn took issue with Phillimore's argument that the Robinson case had become absurd. Suppose a wife had confessed to adultery, the judge said, but concealed her lover's identity by substituting someone else's name for his – the court could not convict the man whom she had falsely accused, but it could still convict her. He asked: 'You would not compel a husband to keep such a wife?'

'Mr Robinson must stand or fall by his own plea,' replied Phillimore. 'He has not charged his wife with adultery with any "person unknown", or with any of the other individuals of whom in her monstrous journal she has spoken with such levity. He has charged her specifically with adultery with Dr Lane; and therefore, if the adultery with Dr Lane cannot be proved, the plea altogether fails. By Dr Lane's innocence or guilt she must stand or fall.'

Phillimore moved to his next stratagem: an attack on the diary's veracity. 'Here is a case in which there is no proximate act leading up to adultery of any sort or kind proved,' he said. 'Then we must fall back on what is called the confession of the wife, and that confession, it must be admitted, presents itself in an entirely novel shape – a confession to be gathered from certain expressions in a diary kept by the lady. Journals are proverbially untrue. Everybody associated with literature knows that Horace Walpole, for instance, deliberately put down in his diary things which were false.' Walpole's mid-eighteenth-century diaries about the courts of George II and George III had been published in the 1840s.

'Things false and disgraceful to himself?' asked Cresswell.

'On the contrary,' Phillimore admitted, 'he generally sought to give a good colouring to his own acts. But instances are not wanting of persons who have a morbid disposition to write evil of themselves as well as good. I might, for instance, mention the *Confessions* of Rousseau, in which many things were recorded which were most disgraceful to the writer.' The 'disgraceful' elements in the autobiography of Jean Jacques Rousseau, published four years after the author's death in 1782, included his admissions that he had fathered several illegitimate children and that he masturbated.

'Yes,' said Cockburn, 'but we must not assume that they were untrue.'

'I might also instance the entry in Pepys's diary,' Phillimore persevered: '"Have made £500 this year by cheating. God forgive me therefore."'

'I am afraid we must not say that that was untrue,' repeated Cockburn, provoking laughter in the courtroom. Samuel Pepys's diary was famous for its frankness. The edition of 1848 omitted many passages that were, the editor explained, 'of so indelicate a character that no one with a well-regulated mind will regret their loss'. Pepys had been edited not for falsehood but for excessive honesty.

To establish that Isabella's diary dealt in distortions, Phillimore drew the court's attention to its frequent allusions to her vivid dreams. 'All day I could not forget it or hardly realise how much of it was true and how much false', she wrote, and, 'Good God! What puppets of the imagination are we?' Phillimore invited the court to adopt Isabella's scepticism about her perceptions as its own. In the diary, he suggested, she was tapping into a region of sexual and imaginative anarchy, giving herself over to mirage and hallucination. According to Henry Holland's *Chapters on Mental Physiology* (1852), dreams were close cousins of insanity: both displayed 'the loss, partial or complete, of power to distinguish between unreal images created within the sensorium and the actual perceptions drawn from the external senses, thereby giving to the former the semblance and influence of realities'.

Phillimore argued that it was not Isabella and Edward who had transgressed; rather, it was the diary that had crossed a boundary, and mutated into fiction. 'I must contend,' he said, 'that the diary is not corroborated by one tittle of positive evidence. The passages relied on by the other side are not a narrative of anything that really occurred, but they are the merest illusions.'

No one could read the diary, he said, without the impression that it was 'the product of extravagance, of excitement, and of irritability, bordering on, if not actually in, the domain of madness. There never was a document which bore on the face of it the marks of so flighty, extravagant, excitable, romantic, irritable, foolish and disordered a mind as this diary of Mrs Robinson.'

If Phillimore, who himself kept a diary, had struggled to find examples of false confessions in journals, it may have been because his reading was limited to the journals of famous men. But he was touching upon an incipient, barely articulated sense of unease about diaries in mid-nineteenth-century England. Of all the written life stories that fascinated the Victorians – biographies, autobiographies, memoirs, journals of health and travel and politics – the personal diary was the most subjective and raw, the most revealing of the problems of writing and reading about the self.

Although people had kept records of their domestic and spiritual lives for hundreds of years, the practice spread dramatically in the early-nineteenth century. Before then, most journals had been household books, private to the family rather than to the individual, and secret thoughts were enclosed in letters to trusted friends. The fashion for private diaries was fuelled by the popularity of Romantic poetry, which prized introspection, and by the first publications of personal journals: the seventeenth-century diaries of John Evelyn originally appeared in 1818 and those of Pepys in 1825. The number of diaries published each year doubled in the 1820s, and in the 1830s reached a peak that was maintained into the 1850s. In most cases, the authors of these journals had not imagined that their words would one day be read by strangers. An eighteenth-century diary by Isabella's ancestor Samuel Curwen, whose branch of the family had emigrated to the United States from Cumberland, was published in 1842. The preface quoted Curwen's plea: 'may [these papers] prove an entertainment to my friends, to whom I commend them, requesting their care to keep them from the inspection of all others, they being negligently written and but for the eye of candor and friendship'. The promise of openness drew in the reader, while the editor insisted that publication of Curwen's diary was 'in no wise a violation of his injunction', but 'due to his memory'.

Made-up diaries had also become commonplace by the 1850s. The epistolary novel of the eighteenth century, in which a story was told through letters, had gradually given way to the diary novel, in which the heroine wrote missives to herself. The beginnings of this shift could be traced to Samuel Richardson's hugely popular *Pamela* (1740), in which the narrator's letters to her parents are replaced, as she becomes more isolated, with something closer to a journal. In Frances Sheridan's *The Memoirs of Miss Sidney Bidulph, Extracted from her Own Journal* (1761) the heroine writes a series of letters to a confidante, but the terms in which she describes her enterprise anticipate the deeper secrecy of the private diarist: 'to you only, my second self . . . to you I am bound by solemn promise, and reciprocal confidence, to disclose the inmost secrets of my soul, and with you they are as safe as in my own breast'.

Some of the first diary novels of the nineteenth century purported to be real. *The Diary of an Ennuyée*, published anonymously in 1826, was described by its publisher as a journal discovered among the effects of a young woman who had died of tuberculosis. Soon afterwards it was exposed as a fictional work by Anna Brownell Jameson. In a preface to a subsequent edition, Mrs Jameson apologised for having pretended that the journal was genuine: 'the intention was not to create an illusion, by giving to fiction the appearance of truth; but, in fact, to conceal truth by throwing over it the veil of fiction'. Also originally taken to be authentic was *So much of the Diary of Lady Willoughby, as Relates to Her Domestic History, and to the Eventful Period of the Reign of Charles the First*, published in 1844 in mock-seventeenth-century trappings: the text was printed in antique type on wide, creamy, ribbed leaves of paper, their gilded edges indented with a pattern of diamonds. The author, Hannah Mary Rathbone, published *Some Further Portions . . .* from the same imaginary work in 1848, with a preface in which she admitted to 'personating' a historical figure. The success of her pastiche inspired a string of imitations through the 1850s, novels in the guise of newly discovered journals by forgotten women, most of them only lightly masquerading as fact. These published diaries, real and imaginary, exploited the idea that the diary was the purest of literary narratives; and simultaneously undermined it.

Both Emily Brontë in *Wuthering Heights* (1847) and her sister Anne in *The Tenant of Wildfell Hall* used journals as the scaffolds for the plots of their novels. Dinah Mulock, a regular at Moor Park, in 1852 wrote a novel in the shape of the secret journal of a governess, and Wilkie Collins in 1856 published two tales in the guise of journals by women. By now, the *Athenaeum* observed: 'The Diary seems to have superseded Letters as the means by which persons are made to relate their own stories.' The thrill of the form lay precisely in its verisimilitude, its semblance of reality. The reader of a diary could feel the naughty pleasure of scanning pages not meant for her eyes; or accept the role of the trusted friend for whom the narrator longed. Whether as a spy or a confidante, or both, she experienced a sharp sensation of proximity.

To cash in on the craze for writing as well as reading journals, the publisher John Letts printed the first large formatted diaries in the 1820s. By 1850 the Letts company was selling several thousand diaries a year, in dozens of different formats. These were the books in which Isabella wrote; they came bound in cloth or in red Russian calf hide, which gave off a faint scent of birch bark, and could be fitted with protective covers and spring locks. 'Use your diary with the utmost familiarity and confidence,' Letts counselled the novice diarist, 'conceal nothing from its pages nor suffer any other eye than your own to scan them.' The word 'diarist' was first recorded in 1818 and 'diarise' in 1842 (these were equivalents to the more established 'journaliser' or 'journalist', for someone who kept a journal, and 'journalising' or 'journalism', for the activity of keeping it).

Women, in particular, took to diarising with a passion. *Punch* magazine satirised the trend in 1849 in its column 'My Wife's Diary', which affected to be a series of excerpts from a lady's diary that an outraged husband had read, transcribed, and secretly submitted to the editor of the magazine. The wife's concerns are mercenary and banal: she plots to hide the port from her husband and to sweet-talk him into giving her pretty shawls and sewing boxes. He '*contradicted* me about the horse-radish', she complains, 'when I *knew* I was right'. Diaries were often dismissed as receptacles for women's silliness: 'the young lady may get a bound volume of any size to hold her twelvemonth's superfluity of thought,' observed a review of Letts diaries in the *Examiner* in 1856, 'bound neatly and printed on good paper'.

Yet even ladies' diaries were finding their way into print. At the time that Isabella began her journal, the most recent published diaries by a woman were those of the novelist Fanny Burney, which appeared in three volumes after her death in 1840. Following her example, an ambitious female diarist might hope that she was composing her journal as a form of apprenticeship, a rehearsal for novel-writing; and she might even wonder whether the journal itself would one day find an audience. Burney's diary illuminated the artful artlessness of the best journals: they could aim for complete honesty ('a Journal in which I must confess my *every* thought must open my whole Heart!') while also aspiring to dramatic excitement ('Alas, alas! My poor Journal! – how dull, unentertaining, uninteresting thou art! – oh what would I give for some adventure worth reciting – for something which would surprise – astonish you!)' To satisfy a diary's hunger for stories, its author might be driven to live more interestingly; or to imagine doing so. Burney had edited her journals for publication, and then destroyed the originals.

Diaries (from the Latin *dies*) and journals (from the French *jour*) were by definition daily records, yet their air of immediacy could be misleading. Isabella's entries were often written up a day or more after the events they described. A diary could only approximate real time, as it could only shadow and catch at the feelings that it sought to pin down. It worked upon its author, tending to intensify her emotions and alter her perceptions. Jane Carlyle, the wife of the historian Thomas Carlyle, described this process in an entry in her private diary of 21 October 1855: 'Your journal all about feelings aggravates whatever is factitious and morbid in you; that I have made experience of.' The act of diary-keeping honoured many of the values of Victorian society – self-reliance, autonomy, the capacity to keep secrets. But if taken too far, these same virtues could turn to vices. Self-reliance could become a radical disconnection from society, its codes and rules and restraints; secrecy could curdle into deceit;

self-monitoring into solipsism; and introspection into monomania.

In *Mr Nightingale's Diary*, a one-act farce set in a water-cure spa, Charles Dickens and his friend Mark Lemon explored the idea that a journal could pander to and promote its writer's fantasies. Dickens was inspired to write the piece after accompanying his wife to the celebrated hydropathic establishment at Malvern in 1851 (Catherine was 'seriously ill with some kind of nervous trouble', he wrote). The play was staged before the Queen and the Prince Consort in Piccadilly that May, with Dickens, Lemon, Wilkie Collins and the painter Augustus Egg among the cast.

Mr Nightingale hides a real secret in his diary – he is paying his wife to pretend to be dead – but most of his entries record anxieties about his body. The play parodied the fashion for self-diagnostic 'diaries of health'. 'Dyspeptic', runs one entry. 'Feel as if kitten at play within me.' By dwelling on his body, Mr Nightingale has riddled it with imagined sicknesses, acquiring a morbid sensitivity to every twinge and shiver, much as keeping a diary encouraged Isabella to interpret every detail of others' behaviour in the light of her own preoccupations. 'You *are* ill, if you only knew it,' he tells a servant at the hydropathy spa. 'If you were as intimate with your own interior as I am with mine, your hair would stand on end.'

Mr Nightingale describes the diary as his 'only comfort', but it has become a symptom of his sickness, even a cause. When it is stolen and read by others, the journal betrays him: instead of helping him to look into himself, it enables others to read him; instead of cleansing him of his sin, it delivers him up for punishment. Its passivity is an illusion. At the end of the play Mr Nightingale is given the advice: 'Burn that book, and be happy!'

CHAPTER TEN

AN INSANE TENDERNESS

Westminster Hall, 15 June 1858

At lunchtime the judges withdrew for refreshment – typically a meat chop and a glass of sherry – and then took up their places on the bench for the afternoon.

Dr Phillimore, having raised the possibility that parts of Isabella's diary were fictional, still needed to explain to the court what had driven her to invent such degrading scenes. He told the judges that the journal was the product of uterine disease.

'I will be able to prove,' said Phillimore, 'that it is a characteristic of this disease that it produces sexual delusions of a most extravagant character', making a woman 'suppose herself guilty of the most horrible, and, indeed, the most impossible crimes'. The illness, he said, sometimes arose from a pressure on the brain, sometimes from malfunction in the uterus itself. To establish this, he said, he would call a number of medical witnesses.

Joseph Kidd was sworn. He was an Irish Quaker, tall, fine-featured and blue-eyed, who had been admitted a Fellow of the Royal College of Surgeons in 1847 and had taken his medical degree at Aberdeen in 1853. No mention was made in court of the unconventional branch of medicine in which he had trained: he was a homeopathic doctor, like John Drysdale, and had returned to Ireland in 1847, during the Great Hunger, to try to alleviate his countrymen's suffering with his alternative remedies. When Isabella had first consulted Dr Kidd in Blackheath, he had been twenty-five years old. He was her type: young, handsome, clever, idealistic, open to new ideas.

Kidd testified that Mrs Robinson had been his patient between 1849 and 1856, especially 1849 and the three or four years after that. In 1849, he said, he had treated her for a disorder of the womb. He based his diagnosis on the headaches, depression and irregular menstruation that she suffered after Stanley's birth, all of which he believed to be manifestations of post-natal uterine disease.

Kidd was asked to describe Mrs Robinson's temperament.

'Her general tendency was a morbid excitement,' he said, an allusion to Isabella's heightened sexuality. 'I regarded her as of a naturally morbid and depressed condition. Her mind alternated between excitement and depression.'

Might her uterine disease have produced such symptoms? asked Phillimore.

'I did not refer them to it at the time,' said Kidd, 'but from the statements in the diary, I think they might be attributed to this cause.'

Phillimore asked Kidd whether he was prepared to state that Mrs Robinson had suffered from nymphomania or erotomania since 1852.

He could not testify to that, he said, as she had not been so directly his patient during this period.

Phillimore dismissed Kidd and proceeded to call three more physicians as witnesses. Their task was to confirm that uterine disease, the condition that Kidd had diagnosed, could cause erotomania or nymphomania, the conditions from which Isabella's counsel claimed that she was suffering.

The first of the specialists was James Henry Bennet,

forty-one, a cherubic man with lustrous eyes and luxuriant black hair. Dr Bennet, of the Royal Free Hospital in London, represented the modern school of gynaecology. He was an authority on uterine inflammation and a pioneer of vaginal examination with a speculum – a practice from which most doctors then recoiled. The speculum was controversial, in part, because of the possibility that its use might excite female patients.

The second was Sir Charles Locock, fifty-nine, a slight, grey-haired man with a dry, decisive manner. Having been Queen Victoria's obstetrician since 1840, Dr Locock was granted a baronetcy in 1857 after delivering her ninth child. He was the author of nearly all of the entries on female disease in the standard manual *The Cyclopaedia of Practical Medicine*, and he took a particular interest in hypersexuality. Like Bennet, he was an advocate of the speculum. He had experience as a medical witness: in 1854 he was asked by the Consistory Court at Doctors' Commons to conduct a physical examination of Euphemia Ruskin who, after six years as the wife of the celebrated art critic John Ruskin, had petitioned for an annulment on the grounds that her marriage had never been consummated. Locock had confirmed to the judge that Mrs Ruskin was a virgin.

The last medical witness for Isabella's defence was Benignus Forbes Winslow, aged forty-seven, an alienist and asylum keeper. As the founder and editor of the *Journal of Psychological Medicine and Mental Pathology*, he was a well-known and combative pioneer of the mental sciences. Dr Forbes Winslow, shiny-pated and self-assured, had appeared as one of Alexander Cockburn's expert witnesses in the M'Naghten trial and his publications included a defence of the insanity plea.

The judges ordered the court to be cleared of women during the medical evidence, and most newspapers did not repeat the ensuing testimony – *The Times* pronounced it 'obviously not of a fit nature for a detailed report'. Even the fullest account, in a legal digest published in 1860, provided only a sketch: Bennet, Locock and Forbes Winslow testified that uterine disease could give rise to a 'morbid condition of the mind on sexual subjects', provoking women to accuse themselves, 'without the slightest foundation, of the most flagrant acts of unchastity'. They said that it was common for such women to have 'strong and extravagant mental delusions' about sex while remaining perfectly sane on all other subjects. After hearing the doctors' testimony, Cockburn adjourned the case until the following day.

Though the press reported sparingly on the physicians' evidence, the medical literature of the time expounded in detail the conditions that they had described.

Gynaecology was a new specialism, and the diagnosis of 'uterine disease' encompassed all manner of female complaints, emotional and physical. Since a woman's reproductive system was believed to exert a strong influence on her mental health, a gynaecological disorder implied mental illness, and vice versa – about ten per cent of sufferers from uterine disease were said to end up in asylums. Any change in a woman's sexual or reproductive life was seen as an opportunity for emotional derangements such as the sexual mania attributed to Isabella. After giving birth, wrote Dr Bennet, a woman usually lost all erotic appetite, but 'in some exceptional cases, so far from inertia being the result of uterine inflammation, the sexual feelings are exaggerated. Indeed, I have known this exaggeration carried so far as to constitute a kind of nymphomania. When this is the case there is often clitoric enlargement, and its sequela, local irritation.' Alternatively, the trigger for hysterical nymphomania could be the menopause: the eminent gynaecologist E. J. Tilt (a colleague of Bennet) identified the 'change of life', or 'dodging-time', as the most common cause. Forbes Winslow, too, observed that women sometimes experienced erotic mania when they stopped menstruating. Then again, an amative woman could be unbalanced simply by a sudden reduction in the frequency with which she had intercourse: as a result of widowhood, for instance, or a husband's prolonged absences on business. Tilt argued that 'sub-acute ovaritis' (which accounted for a third of uterine diseases) was usually caused by sexual privation. When Euphemia Ruskin petitioned for an annulment of her marriage on the grounds of non-consummation, John Ruskin wanted to justify his reluctance to have intercourse with his wife by bringing the court's attention to her 'slight nervous affection of the brain'. His lawyer dissuaded him, pointing out that the court was likely to see Euphemia's supposed derangement as a result of sexual frustration, rather than a justification for her husband's distaste.

Female sexual mania took two forms: erotomania and nymphomania. These were distinct illnesses, according to J. E. D. Esquirol's influential *Mental Maladies: a Treatise on Insanity*: erotomania was a disorder of the brain, while nymphomania had its origin in the reproductive organs. Erotomaniacs, Esquirol wrote, were 'restless, thoughtful, greatly depressed in mind, agitated, irritable and passionate'. He gave as an example a thirty-two-year-old married woman who developed an obsession with a young man of higher rank than her husband. She suffered from 'insane tenderness', nervous pains and changeable moods. 'She is now, gay and full of laughter; now, melancholic and weeps; and is now angry, in her solitary conversations . . . She sleeps little, and her rest is troubled by dreams, and even nightmare.' In her dreams, said Esquirol, she copulated with succubi and incubi, male and female demons.

Nymphomaniacs were less prone than erotomaniacs to mood swings and obsessions, and more given to indiscriminate sexual hunger. The American physician Horatio Storer reported in 1856 on a nymphomaniac patient aged twenty-four whose much older husband was having difficulty in achieving an erection: she felt overwhelmed with desire every time she met a man. In effect, any woman who reported a powerful impulse to have intercourse with a man other than her husband could be classified as a sexual maniac.

Erotomania and nymphomania were hard to distinguish. 'The two may exist together,' noted Daniel H. Tuke in 1857. 'Patients may most completely exceed the limits of propriety without our having any evidence that the primary disease is in the reproductive organs. It is difficult, in not a few instances, to determine whether the origin of the malady is there, or in the head.' In any case, it suited Isabella's counsel to be vague about which of the two conditions afflicted her. They required her to be suffering from symptoms of both: the romantic delusion of the stalker, who imagined that her love was reciprocated, and the lascivious heat of the sex maniac. To accommodate all possibilities, Isabella's witnesses included a specialist in the brain, Forbes Winslow, and two specialists in the reproductive organs, Locock and Bennet.

The rise in the diagnosis of sexual mania in women corresponded to an intense contemporary anxiety about unsatisfied female desire. It had recently come to light that there was an excess of spinsters in Britain. According to the census of 1851, the country contained half a million more women than men, chiefly because men died younger and migrated more often. For every 100 males, there were 104 females. Older women were especially likely to live alone: forty-two per cent of those aged between forty and sixty were widows or spinsters. The 'redundant women' or 'involuntary nuns' revealed by the census had become the object of sociological and medical concern. Though Dr William Acton famously announced in 1857 that 'the majority of women (happily for them) are not very much troubled by sexual feeling of any kind', many physicians feared that single women might in fact be driven mad by suppressed and unsatisfied sexual urges.

The treatments for sexual monomania were various. Some physicians, following the phrenologists, targeted the cerebellum: the Scottish alienist Sir Alexander Morison claimed to have cured an erotomaniac governess aged twenty-two by applying leeches to her shaven head, then douching the back of her skull with cold water. Bennet recommended injecting the vagina with a pump syringe, and subjecting the whole body to hip baths, deep baths and showers. Storer suggested that the sufferer should be treated with sponge baths, cold enemas and borax douches, refrain from sexual intercourse and literary pursuits, sleep on mattresses and pillows stuffed with hair, and abstain from meat and brandy. Locock advised the application of electricity to the pelvis of the afflicted woman, or of leeches to her groin, labia, uterus or feet. A London surgeon relieved at least one patient of her sexual feelings by removing her 'enlarged' clitoris, an operation reported in *The Lancet* in 1853.

The chief symptom of nymphomania – implied but probably not named in the courtroom that Tuesday – was masturbation. The French doctor M. D. T. Bienville, who popularised the term nymphomania in a treatise published in English in 1775, identified 'secret pollutions' as the key to the disease. 'Nymphomania,' as Tilt spelt out, 'is the almost irresistible desire to relieve the irritation of the pudenda by friction.' This would explain why Isabella had written the erotic scenes in her journal – they were pieces of personalised pornography – and why she had been reckless enough to do so: her 'self-abuse' or 'self-pollution' had weakened her grip on sanity. In some cases, Tilt noted, a woman could stimulate herself with words alone. He quoted a French doctor who observed that 'fictional tableaux can excite the generative organs more effectively than the presence of men' and had 'many times seen the genitals inflame in this way without any external action or being touched'. The solitary acts of reading and writing, in which most middle-class women indulged, might mask and incite more carnal pleasures.

This was especially true of diaries. Everything that distinguished masturbation as a sexual practice also distinguished diary-writing as a literary practice. If masturbation was a sexual communion with the self, diary-writing was an emotional communion of the same kind. Both required a person to imaginatively divide, to become the subject and the object of a story. Both were private, self-sufficient activities. The medical witnesses in the Divorce Court suggested that Isabella had become mired in a circle of desire and excitement, recorded and created by her diary: her lascivious thoughts, translated to paper, took on an apparent reality that gratified her erotic impulses. Her journal did not only echo her secret life, but abetted it. It was both symptom and cause of her sickness. In their efforts to save Edward while condemning Isabella, the lawyers had come up with a sex act in which she had been able to indulge without the participation of any man.

Isabella's defence was far more degrading than a confession of adultery would have been. The story of how she came to claim that she was a sexual maniac emerges in a series of letters that she exchanged with George Combe in February 1858.

On 14 February, just before Henry filed his petition for a full divorce, Isabella sent a letter to Lady Drysdale, her first communication with any of Edward's family. 'My dear Lady Drysdale,' she wrote from her cottage in Reigate, 'I deeply regret that so much importance has been attached to the loose and unguarded expressions in my journal, which I considered as sacred as my own thoughts, & I deplore it the more, since they have been used as the means of accusing another so unjustly. I can only solemnly declare that he is perfectly innocent of the slightest participation in any thought, word or act, therein expressed!' The references to Edward, she said, were the 'lax and purely imaginative recitals of a Lady's thoughts, unwisely committed to a journal, and never intended to see the light'.

Lady Drysdale forwarded the letter to Combe, who had by now decided to do all he could to support Edward. He was not convinced that Isabella's denial would help their cause. The tone was 'too light & flippant', he told Lady Drysdale. Anyone reading it would think: 'Oh, she sees that she has injured Lane by betraying their secret, & now she thinks to save him by denying everything.' To protect the doctor, Combe said, they needed 'to destroy the credibility of the Journal as a record of actual occurrences'.

A week later, on 21 February, Isabella wrote to Combe himself. She said that she knew that Henry had been in touch with him (someone seemed to be keeping her informed of how the story was breaking in Edinburgh). She begged him: 'assist me, if you can, to clear a mutual friend from blame, who, with his family, is implicated by my unguarded & thoughtless conduct; & whose generous concern & sympathy for my wretched social position has drawn them into this sorrow'. Isabella said that she had regarded the journal 'as my inalienable property, & as my sole confidant', and was horrified that it might be used to hurt those who had shown her kindness. She assured Combe that she had 'the ardent wish to make all the reparation in my power to a family who have been annoyed & injured by certain careless, unguarded, private writings of mine – writings which a too lively imagination caused me to compose, & which the almost entire absence of caution & secretiveness occasioned me to retain'.

Combe seized the chance to help the doctor. In his reply of 23 February, he began by reminding Isabella of what was at stake: '*if* your Journal contains the descriptions now mentioned, & be *true*, Dr Lane is ruined as a professional man; for no woman of reputation could venture under his roof, with such a stain attaching to him. His poor wife is robbed of his affections, & Lady Drysdale, in her old age, sees the dearest objects of her affections disgraced & ruined.'

He told Isabella that he was perplexed by the diary entries that had been described to him. He could not believe that they were factual, as it was impossible to imagine that she would have been reckless enough to keep a record of her sins. 'You knew that you were mortal, & might be killed in a railway train, drowned in a storm, or die of spasm of the heart or apoplexy in a moment, or as actually happened fall ill of fever and become delirious. In any one of such cases your records of your own shame & your friend's destruction would be certain to see the light. I tell you freely, therefore, that all my knowledge of human nature is baffled to account for your conduct in writing down such descriptions *if they were true*.'

He suggested that Isabella could dismiss the diary entries as 'a safety valve to an excited brain', 'the wildest speculations on all subjects sacred & profane, & the most fervid and passionate longings'. Yet he told her that Robert Chambers, who had read the diary, had scoffed at the idea that the incriminating entries were fantasies. The difficulty, Combe said, lay in the journal's realism: 'your antics, as described to me, are not of fancies & speculations, but of downright facts, with places, dates, & all the adjuncts of reality'. To illustrate the problem he fabricated a diary entry of his own. 'Suppose that I should enter in my Journal "21st Feby 1854, I called on Mrs Robinson in Moray Place; we sat on the sofa together, & talked of many topics in philosophy & religion. On looking to know the hour, I found my watch gone. I had looked at it when I entered, having only half an hour to spare, & nobody but she could have taken it. I charged her with the theft, & she gave me back the watch, saying that she had taken it as a joke." Suppose this entry to have fallen into the hands of my wife or my executors, would it be possible for them to believe that in making this entry I was merely disporting my fancy?' He summed up: how was it possible to account for the diary entries so as 'to enable minds of ordinary sagacity and experience to believe them *to be fictions*?'.

By pointing out to her how incredible the diary seemed, Combe was hinting, opaquely, at how Isabella could explain it away: since to keep the journal was an act verging on madness, the contents of the journal could be ascribed to madness too. Perhaps the entries were so precise because they were not dreams but hallucinations.

Combe told Isabella that he was glad of the opportunity to 'lay the case this clearly before you, in the earnest hope that you will be able to clear up the mystery in a way that will vindicate yourself & Dr Lane'. On the same day he wrote a letter to the doctor in which he more directly named the solution to which he was pointing Isabella: she 'writes like a very clever woman', he said, but 'the only explanation is insanity'. In a letter to Henry Robinson, Combe had also observed: 'It looks like insanity.' To Sir James Clark he wrote: 'The woman was not mad in the usual sense', but 'she must have been labouring under excitement of the sexual propensity, & finding no outlet for it *de facto*, for she was not attractive, she indulged it in impure imaginations & to enhance the pleasure wrote these down as facts'.

On 26 February 1858, three days after Combe wrote to her, Isabella sent her answer. 'I will make my reply as clear & as satisfactory to you as I can,' she said, 'but I fear I must do so at some *length*, as writing is, after all, an irksome & roundabout way of expressing ourselves.' The letter ran to nearly two thousand words, almost half of which were taken up with an impassioned denunciation of Henry, as a husband and as a man. She named his insensitivity, his unpoetic soul, his meanness, his underhand raids on her money, the immorality of his private life. She ran through the sorry story of their marriage. She blamed herself for her naivety and impulsiveness – 'In looking back on my life, I see nothing but a series of erroneous steps, as far as worldliness & prudence are concerned' – and claimed to be reconciled to her lot. 'I have been sad so long that sorrow finds me patient & resigned; & perhaps, I have even learned useful lessons.'

Yet Isabella's contrition kept giving way to fury and pride. The letter was suffused with her rage at the injury done to her by all those who had read her diary. The unauthorised reading of her journal, she wrote, was 'an *injustice*, a *meanness*, a *robbery*'. 'That men, mere strangers, no ways authorised, should have considered themselves at liberty to pry into, to peruse, to censure, to select from, my private writings, with curious, unchivalrous, ignoble hands, I cannot understand. I could no more have done so than I could have listened meanly to their prayers, their midnight whisperings in sleep, or their accents of delirium; I should have considered myself insulted by bare proposition to read papers not meant for my eyes but the writer's.'

By conjuring up the intrusive, clumsy hands of the men who read her words, the eager eavesdropping at her bedside, Isabella depicted the illicit reading of her diary as an almost sexual assault. The secret spaces of her diary were aligned with the secret spaces of her body. Gustave Freytag's *Debit and Credit*, published in English in 1857, played on the same parallel. The heroine of the novel slips her diary – 'a small thin book bound in red silk' – beneath her corset before a ball: 'No stranger was allowed to look into this precious book – no one must see or touch this sanctuary.' When a rakish gentleman steals the diary from beneath her underclothes, her beau proves his own honour by recovering the volume and handing it back to her unread.

Isabella's hatred of Henry burned bright. 'Could I dream that the man who called himself my husband; who had smiled from his lofty pedestal of worldly prudence at my poetic outbursts, would cruelly enter my sick chamber (actually in search of *money*) & deprive me of my papers – those poor little treasures of a disappointed nature; & keep them too, in spite of the *immutable laws* of *real* justice.' By English law, a woman's papers were the property of her husband – as the reformer Caroline Norton complained, 'the copyrights of my works are *his*; my very soul and brains are not my own!'. Isabella remarked that her brother Frederick, 'whom no one can blame for being either poetic or enthusiastic', agreed with her that Henry had been barbaric to force her writings from her when she was ill, and then to use them against her. 'It is only on a *woman* that this indignity would be inflicted,' she wrote. '*Man* would resist, & make the cowards who had dared to insult his privacy, recoil & tremble.'

In the loneliness of her marriage, 'What was my resource?' she asked. 'What my consolation? Solitude & my pen. Here I lived in a world of my own, one that scarcely any one ever entered. I felt that in my study, at least, I was a ruler; & that all I wrote was *my own*.'

She dismissed the diary as a fanciful literary work, though even as she did so she could not resist casting her writing in a romantic light: 'I dipped my pen but too often in the fairy ink of poesy; – the true & actual, the shadowy & the visionary were too often blended – I had the fatal gift – more curse than boon – of giving "to airy nothings, a local habitation & a name".' Her apparent composure, she said, belied an intense and desperate imaginative world: 'If I have appeared calm, it was because a seething poetic life was sternly repressed into the precincts of solitude, there to be indulged with perchance twofold alacrity, in that it was a preeminently essential fact of my individuality, & that it had no outer food.'

As to why she had preserved her journals, 'I can only reply that I have almost no Caution – that I thought if I died, no evil to any one could result from what would then be waste paper; that if I lived, *no one would take them from me*; besides, I always promised myself to put them to rights, compare, destroy & sift them.'

Isabella claimed that she was at a loss to know what more she could do to help the doctor. 'I must say,' she wrote, 'that it rather surprised me that you should eagerly look for my explanations regarding my journal, as tho' I could even yet do something towards removing the impression they have made, & the evil they have done. I see not *how* this can be.'

This letter was no more effective in discrediting the diary than the previous two that she had written. Though she was by turns angry and remorseful, Isabella sounded like a perfectly rational woman. She had ignored Combe's veiled instructions to declare herself insane. Over the next few days, though, she discovered that Henry had initiated proceedings for a divorce in the new court. She reread Combe's letter. On Sunday 28 February, the day after her forty-fifth birthday, Isabella wrote to Combe for the last time.

'I have been reconsidering your letter & my reply to it, & it occurs to me that the latter may have appeared to you somewhat vague & inconclusive. Will you allow me to make a few definite & final remarks upon the subject.' The incriminating diary entries, she said, were written while 'I was the victim temporarily of my own fancies & delusions . . . I constantly put down for facts what were the wildest imaginings of a mind exhausted with the tyranny of long years, & given up to seek in imaginative writings for the only solace of my daily lot.' In these entries she had given 'free vent to the suggestions of my imagination': 'each & all of them as regards the friend now specially referred to, are purely & entirely imaginative & fictitious'.

Isabella expressed humility and sorrow: her regrets were 'of a deeper kind than can well be imagined by any other human being than myself. I have not, & cannot have another word to add.' Her words had brought nothing but pain to Edward and his family; her best recourse, now, was a denunciation of her own sanity, and then silence.

At last she had provided George Combe with the answer that he needed. She had submitted to his guidance, as she had when she was tormented by the contradictions of her nature. He passed on the good news to Edward. Isabella's latest letter, Combe said, was 'written in a calm, earnest tone, indicating a sense of the injury she has done you, and declaring most solemnly that every one of the entries in her Journal in relation to you are pure fictions'. The diary, he said, was 'the invention of a brain either insane or on the brink of insanity'. In a letter to Lady Drysdale, he explained that Isabella had failed to give a '*rational* account' of her diary entries, but had at least provided 'an *insane* account'.

George Combe believed, or endeavoured to believe, that Isabella had been crazed by unsatisfied desire. His own books had helped to establish the idea that one part of the brain could be disordered while all the others remained sound: an individual could even house a 'double' or 'divided' consciousness, in which one self was unaware of the actions of the other (Forbes Winslow quoted Combe on this subject in his *Obscure Diseases of the Brain and Mind*). Over the next few weeks, Combe showed Isabella's letters to his friends in Edinburgh and consulted doctors and lawyers about how to establish that she was insane. To this end, he wrote to his nephew Dr James Cox, a commissioner of the Board of Lunacy in Scotland; to his friend William Ivory, an advocate whose father, Lord Ivory, ruled on divorce cases in Scotland; and to Professor John Hughes Bennett, who had in 1851 published an essay about the physiological causes of the craze for mesmerism in Edinburgh.

The Drysdale family, given George's troubled history, may also have found it possible to believe that Isabella had a hidden streak of insanity. Edward readily adopted the argument that she was mad. In his reply to Combe he described her as 'a fantastical, vain, egotistical being half-crazed through misery, & goaded on by wild hallucinations to put down as facts all the fancies & desires of a much-diseased & most corrupt imagination'.

He and the Drysdale brothers, all of them now students or practitioners of medicine, were well placed to help put together a medical defence. The physicians who appeared in Westminster Hall on 15 June were closely connected to their circle. Locock, as an *accoucheur* to Queen Victoria, was a colleague of Combe's great friend Sir James Clark; Bennet, as a progressive gynaecologist, was known to George Drysdale and to the Drysdales' friend James Young Simpson (all three were 'speculumisers'); Forbes Winslow was an early phrenologist and admirer of Combe; and Kidd was a former patient of the homeopath John Drysdale.

Robert Chambers remained sceptical that the diary was a product of insanity. It read like 'a history of events as well as a journal of thoughts,' he told Combe, 'and I must ever deem it one of the strangest things ever presented to my notice, that a woman shd have deliberately committed to paper through a space of months and years the particulars of a criminal intrigue which had no basis but her fancy, and which involved the possible infamy of another innocent person'. After Combe had showed him Isabella's letters, Chambers claimed to accept her denial of adultery, but his tone remained incredulous. 'Had you only seen the Journal,' he wrote to Combe, 'how amusing it would have been to you to hear it described as a work of imagination – daydreams . . . I do not believe that Lane was guilty; but that the lady was an adulteress in her heart, and willing or wishful to be one in reality, it were lunacy to doubt after what I have seen.'

Edward still hoped to stop Henry's suit. Even on 16 March he told Combe that he did not know 'whether peace is to be the order of the day or war to the knife': 'All is a sea of uncertainty.' But on 25 March he realised that the trial was inevitable. Robert Chambers had just been to London to try to talk Henry out of the action, Edward reported to Combe, and had found him 'perfectly impassable & determined': he 'evidently does not *wish* to be convinced. He has a bad wife and he wants to be rid of her at any price.' The more that Edward's friends in Edinburgh tried to play down the evidence of the diary, the more Henry craved a public vindication. In a courtroom four years earlier, he had experienced the pleasure of triumphing over his younger brother. He now sought the same unequivocal victory over his wife, and over the educated gentlemen whom she so valued. Henry's hatred of Isabella, said Edward, seemed 'to have become so intent, as to have bereft him of reason on all subjects connected with her, and turned him into a complete fanatic'.

CHAPTER ELEVEN

A GREAT DITCH OF POISON

16 June–20 August 1858

The heat of London peaked on Wednesday 16 June 1858. As the temperature rose to a hundred degrees Fahrenheit, the highest ever recorded in the city, the Thames's thickening stew of smells filtered further in to the Houses of Parliament and the courts at Westminster Hall. The heavy river lay dark, low and rank in the sun. It was 'pestiferous, degraded, a mere sewer', said *The Morning Post*, and 'a powerful shock to the nose'. Huge quantities of excrement were emptied into its waters each day, releasing vapours that were believed to contaminate those who inhaled them. 'A great ditch of poison,' complained the *Illustrated London News*, 'is allowed to crawl, day by day and night by night, through the grandest city in the world.'

In the Westminster courts, the judges performed their duties under a sense of danger, dealing with the business brought before them as quickly as possible. The Divorce Court opened, as usual, at eleven, but Cockburn began by announcing that he was going to suspend the Robinson trial. The judges, he said, were baffled by Edward Lane's position in the case. They had decided to adjourn to discuss whether they could take the unprecedented step of dismissing the doctor from the suit so that Isabella's lawyers could call him as a witness. 'That question,' said Cockburn, 'involves such grave consequences and such serious principles as regards the administration of justice under the Divorce Act, that we are anxious to have the assistance of all the members of the Court before making a precedent. We adjourn the case till Monday, when we hope to be able to state the conclusion at which we may have arrived.'

The case had exposed a lacuna in the law. When a wife sued for divorce, she did not need to name her husband's lover – this was partly because her petition never rested solely on adultery; partly because the man's lover, being a woman, could not be called on to pay the court costs; and partly, as a guide to divorce explained, 'to protect the character of perhaps an innocent third party from being blasted behind her back'. When a man tried to divorce his wife, though, he was compelled to name the paramour. For many Victorian men, an allegation of adultery would not be disastrous, but for Edward Lane, whose livelihood rested on his being trusted with the care of ladies, it would. He was as vulnerable to disgrace as a woman, and he stood to be ruined by a woman's words.

Before the judges adjourned to consider the problem, Isabella's counsel asked to call John Thom as their final witness. Cockburn agreed to hear his testimony.

Thom introduced himself as a gentleman 'connected with literature' who knew Mr and Mrs Robinson, 'the latter intimately'. 'I became acquainted with them at Reading in 1854,' he testified, 'and afterwards met Mrs Robinson at Moor Park.'

Phillimore asked him to describe Mrs Robinson.

'She is a very excitable person,' said Thom. 'There is a certain amount of formality in her general behaviour, but she now and then utters romantic and flighty observations.' The description fitted the defence case, suggesting that Isabella had a public self and a diary self, wild inner fancies beneath her shell of decorum.

Thom was asked to read aloud from the diary an entry of 3 June 1854, in which Isabella recorded her impressions of him. 'His great eyes seemed like pale violets,' read out Thom, 'shaded with heavy, drooping lids; his cheeks were hollow, and there was a look of intense dejection about his whole person.' There was laughter in the courtroom at Thom's rendition of this lushly romantic description of himself. He read on, turning to Isabella's report of her own demeanour during the meeting between them: 'My cheeks flushed, tears came every second to my eyes, and my voice was choked. We talked long and earnestly.'

Phillimore asked Thom what he made of this account.

'It is highly coloured and exaggerated,' replied Thom, 'and I was not in a state of dejection or depression.'

Phillimore called Thom's attention to an entry of 4 July 1854, about his meeting with Isabella at Moor Park. This, too, said the young man, was a 'highly coloured' rendition of the facts.

Finally, Phillimore asked Thom about the entry of 15 July 1854, which included the reference to 'that tree, which I never see without thinking of my escapade with Mr Thom'.

'The word "escapade",' said John Thom, 'is inexplicable to me. I remember one day that I was reading under a tree in the garden with Mrs Robinson, when Mr Robinson approached, and Mrs Robinson then ran round a corner, in order apparently to keep out of her husband's way.' He categorically denied that any kind of impropriety had ever passed between Mrs Robinson and himself.

On cross-examination, Thom admitted that he was a friend of Dr Lane: after he had acted as tutor to the Robinson children, he said, Mr Robinson had introduced him to the doctor, with whom he had since remained upon 'terms of intimacy'.

With this, the trial was adjourned.

Over the next three weeks the Robinson case threw the Divorce Court into deeper confusion. When Cockburn, Cresswell and Wightman returned to it on Monday 21 June, Cockburn said that five of the six judges authorised to sit in the court had concluded that they were unable to dismiss Edward Lane from the suit. The one dissenter was the elderly William Wightman, who argued that there was nothing in the wording of the Act to prevent them from doing so. Cockburn, expressing his regret that Wightman was not in accord with the majority, said that the case would proceed as planned. He invited the barristers to sum up.

Since the judges had agreed that there was no case against Edward, Forsyth was not required to speak. Phillimore, on behalf of Isabella, repeated his argument that the diary was a fabrication; he suggested that his client 'supposed she was writing a sort of novel, in which she evidently thought the scenes she described would have formed an appropriate climax'. Chambers, for Henry, summarised his case by pointing out that though the diary was 'undoubtedly written – as women will sometimes write – in a high-flown strain, it appears to be a perfectly accurate account of things that took place. My learned friend has attempted to disparage it by quoting passages relating to Mr Thom, and then placing Mr Thom in the box to deny the correctness of those passages. But Mr Thom does not deny them. He only says they were exaggerated accounts of what really took place.' Chambers added that Mrs Robinson's age in 1854 was not fifty but forty-one.

Cockburn said that the judges would deliver their verdict in just under a fortnight.

Twelve days later, on Saturday 3 July, a crowd of elegantly dressed ladies squeezed in to the courtroom to hear the conclusion of the Robinson case; but they were soon disappointed. Cockburn announced that he had changed his mind. Like Wightman, he and the other judges now believed that Dr Lane should be dismissed from the suit so that he could appear as a witness. What was more, they had learnt of a Bill to amend the Divorce Act, soon to be presented to Parliament, which would include a clause to allow the dismissal of a co-respondent in a case such as this. Cockburn had decided to adjourn the trial again, to await the passing of the Bill.

The judges continued to consider other petitions. On Monday 14 June, the first day of the Robinson trial, the court had heard that a Mrs Ward wanted to divorce her drunken, violent husband on account of his adultery, cruelty and desertion. She was 'a quiet, hardworking woman', testified their landlady, who after years of 'ill-usage' had seemed 'quite agreeable' to her husband's leaving her. The police confirmed that Mr Ward had beaten his wife. But Cresswell pointed out that if Mrs Ward had been glad to see the back of her husband, the court might have to deny the divorce. 'The act of desertion,' he noted, 'must be done against the will of the wife.' Divorce could not be consensual, nor could it be justified by unhappiness alone. When formulating the new law, the legislature had been keen to avoid the example of the French who, in 1792, had sanctioned divorce on the grounds of incompatibility, with the result that over the next decade one in every eight French marriages was dissolved, nearly three-quarters of them on petitions by wives. Yet Cresswell found a way to give Mrs Ward her freedom. On Wednesday 16 June, after John Thom's appearance in the Robinson case, Cresswell ruled that she was 'clearly entitled to a dissolution on the ground of adultery and cruelty, even if there were any doubt about the desertion'. Thanks to the regulations of the new Act, she would be entitled to keep any property that she subsequently acquired.

The Wards' marriage was one of nine undone that day, a speed of despatch that prompted questions in the House of

Lords. If the judges moved too slowly, they let a rotten union linger in the national consciousness; too fast, and they seemed to be dissolving the institution of marriage before the public's eyes.

On 21 June, after the third adjournment of the Robinson trial, Cresswell delivered his verdict in a case originally heard over four days in May: *Curtis v Curtis*, a wife's petition for a judicial separation by reason of cruelty. Since it was a plea for separation rather than divorce, Cresswell could judge it alone. As in the Robinson case, the court's decision turned on the interpretation of a document written by a woman.

Frances and John Curtis, like Henry and Isabella Robinson, had made an unequal marriage, and Cresswell identified the disparity in the couple's social status as key to their discord. Fanny's father was a barrister of Lincoln's Inn, the same Inn to which Isabella's father and grandfather had belonged, while her husband, like Henry, was a civil engineer. Fanny's parents did not take to John Curtis. On the night before the wedding, John spent four hours quarrelling with his prospective father-in-law about Fanny's marriage settlement. At parties at Fanny's parents' house, John felt he was treated as 'inferior'. Fanny admitted that her mother and father often referred to her husband's work as 'engineering rubbish', though she claimed it was not said offensively.

John became increasingly unstable, suffering an attack of 'brain fever' in 1850 and developing extreme religious views. In her petition for a separation, Fanny alleged that he also became brutal towards her and the children – for instance, she said, he frequently beat his son 'with great violence and with heavy and deliberate blows on his face, head and ears'.

When the case was heard in May, John Curtis's witnesses included Forbes Winslow, who testified that John had fully recovered from his attack of brain fever. To counter the accusations of violence, John produced a letter from Fanny to her mother, written while the family was resident in New York in 1852 – the children, May and John, were aged three and two.

The letter described an afternoon on which John reached home to find his children playing with two girls aged four and six, the daughters of a neighbour, while being supervised by a maid. John railed against Fanny for exposing his son and daughter to strangers – 'all the misery of his life', he told her, 'had arisen from immoral habits learnt from other children'. Though she apologised, he became more and more excited about what could befall his children, talking – as she thought – in a 'disgusting' and 'corrupting' way. She made a sharp remark about his mental state – 'Really, if things go on in this manner I shall be obliged to put my children under the protection of the Government' – and instantly regretted it. The furious John banned her from seeing the children, scolded her in front of them and the servant girl, to whom he made a point of serving breakfast before he served his wife. He also tore up and burnt Fanny's magazines, forbidding her from bringing books and journals into the house without showing them to him first.

'I would to God I could tell what to do,' wrote Fanny to her mother, 'but he seems so wrapped up in the children that I do not like to take them away, in spite of anything I may suffer, and I do not see that they are at present threatened . . . I would to God he would do something that would set me at liberty. I often wish he would strike me, but that he never attempts – indeed, he seemed much kinder for a while; but the plain fact is, that he carries the idea of his authority to a mania . . . I feel my own irresolution and weakness are to be blamed as much as you can blame them, but it is very hard to know what to do.' She feared that John's mind was going. 'The extraordinary mixture of arrogance, self-love, love of power, with religious feeling and enthusiasm, is too much for me to understand,' she wrote, 'and especially when, added to all this, there is the occasional breakdown into tears and misery.' Soon after Fanny's parents received this letter, her father sailed over to New York and arranged for his son-in-law to be detained in a lunatic asylum.

When John was released from the asylum some months later, he went to Spain to work as a railroad engineer and then, in 1857, came looking for Fanny and the children at her father's estate in Ireland. John posted placards in which he offered a £10 reward for information about them. The bills read like lost-property notices, or wanted posters: 'Mrs Frances Henrietta Curtis, native of England, age 35, height 5 feet 3 inches, figure inclining to stout, hair very dark brown, eyes blue, not very prominent, complexion fair and fresh, eyebrows not strongly marked, nose slightly turned up, front teeth rather large, great expression of countenance, manner self-possessed and quiet.' Fanny fled to London, where she and the children adopted assumed names. When John tracked them down, she resorted to the law.

Like Isabella's diary entries, Fanny's letter gave the Divorce Court a vivid, subjective glimpse of daily life inside an unhappy marriage. Fanny Curtis was lonely and confused, devoted to her children, and struggling to conform to the role of subservient wife. Though John had submitted the letter as proof that he was not violent, the palpable anguish of Fanny's words commanded the court's sympathy. Her wish that John would hit her was the strongest proof of her unhappiness. Her moments of pity for her agitated husband were testament to her capacity for tenderness.

In the afternoon of 21 June, Cresswell found against John Curtis, granting Fanny the legal separation that she sought. He conceded in his judgment that her 'excited feelings' had 'caused her to give a somewhat highly coloured account' of her husband's behaviour – a passionate partiality that was a feature of the petitions before the new court – and he expressed sympathy for John, scorned and bullied by his wife's family, prey to desperate insecurities and to spiritual obsessions. But he considered that there was 'an air of truth, sincerity and candour' about Fanny's letter, and that it gave 'a melancholy picture' of her life. Cresswell granted her petition, ruling that John Curtis had shown 'a violent and unreasoning exercise of authority . . . sufficient to excite a well-founded apprehension of further acts of violence'. He declined to adjudicate on whether the children should live with their mother or their father. The Custody of Infants Act had given women (adulteresses excepted) the right to petition for custody, and the new Divorce Court theoretically had the power to grant it. However, Cresswell said, 'the Legislature has not prescribed any rules or principles by which the Court is to be governed in dealing with this peculiarly delicate subject'. He left the matter to the Court of Chancery, decreeing that for the next three months at least the Curtis children should remain with Fanny.

But when Fanny Curtis and her father petitioned Chancery for custody, the judge who heard the case took a radically different view. Vice-Chancellor Kindersley found fault in Fanny's conduct towards John: 'I believe it is the common case that very few wives do consider sufficiently their solemn obligation of obedience and submission to their husbands' wishes, even though they be capricious. However harsh, however cruel the husband may be, it does not justify the wife's want of that due submission to the husband, which is her duty both by the law of God and by the law of man.' He accepted that John had beaten the children when they grew restless during prayers or at grace, but he ruled that this fell within the bounds of reasonable behaviour. Crucially, he did not trust Fanny's letter to her mother: she 'is relating facts in a manner not only exaggerated, but falsely'.

In allocating custody, Kindersley said, the court could not consider what was in the best interests of the children, or chaos would ensue. Rather, the authority of the father must be paramount. Even John Curtis's excesses, after all, were his fixations on two tenets of Victorian society: a man's power over his family and God's power over man. To preserve the institution of marriage entailed preserving the pre-eminence of the father. Kindersley dismissed Fanny's petition and granted custody of the children to John.

Cresswell's judgment in the Curtis case was guided by compassionate common sense; Kindersley made his ruling with an eye to precedent and principle.

Just before the Robinson case began, George Combe had discovered that he was even more closely bound up in it than he had thought. In May 1858, Edward Lane wrote to warn him that his name figured prominently in Isabella's journal. The diary alluded to him often, said Edward, in relation to phrenology and the immortality of the soul. Combe was appalled. To be implicated in Isabella's moral anarchy could destroy the rectitude that he had carefully preserved over the past decades. For years he had rejected accusations of atheism. Now he was at risk of having them brought home to him in the person of a highly sexed woman to whom he had shown kindness. To be associated with Isabella's journals, he told Edward, could 'damage my reputation & ruin the influence of my books'. He insisted that any letters of his that Isabella had quoted were his copyright, and, less plausibly, that any conversations with him might infringe on his rights over his own ideas. He pleaded with Edward to explain more about the references: did he seem to speak blasphemously? Did he come across as irreligious or immoral?

Combe and his friends had the keenest interest in suppressing Isabella's unrepentant account of adultery. Her story was a gift to their enemies. She took their ideas to a logical and lurid conclusion: man was an animal, governed only by appetites; there was no immortal soul, so people could behave as they liked without fear of punishment. The diary contained a vision of what society might become if the new, evolutionary view of the world were to take hold.

Lane, Combe and Robert Chambers lobbied newspapermen for their support. Chambers wrote to Marmaduke Sampson and Eneas Sweetland Dallas at *The Times*, entreating them to publish a leader in Edward Lane's defence. In response, Edward received a letter from Mrs Dallas – the former Isabella Glyn, who in 1851 had dined at the Chambers' house with Isabella Robinson. She assured the doctor that the *Times* editors 'were quite alive, from the first' to the 'monstrous hardship' of his position and that a strong editorial to this effect would appear in the paper.

Eneas Sweetland Dallas's editorial was published on 6 July, three days after Cockburn had suspended the trial. It argued that Isabella, unable to distinguish her compulsive fantasies from reality, had become haunted by a 'dreaming world'. She had not deliberately made things up, Dallas suggested, but had submitted to the forces of her unconscious mind. For her, 'the solid barriers which separate realities from shadows – truth from fiction – the waking from the dreaming world – had no existence. Every wild desire which thrilled through her frame, every vagrant thought which flitted across her disordered brain, was invested with the attributes of personality. She lived in an inner world of her own.' The diary, Dallas claimed, resembled a chapter from Catherine Crowe's study of the supernatural, *The Night Side of Nature*. It dissolved the distinction between memory and imagination.

'Every act of Mrs Robinson's leaves us nothing but the choice between two conclusions,' wrote Dallas – 'either she is as foul and abandoned a creature as ever wore woman's shape, or she is mad. In either case her testimony is worthless.' It was a circular argument: by writing about adultery, Isabella had cast herself out of the realm of reason. The words of a self-confessed adulteress – even her confession – could not be trusted.

The *Examiner*, a weekly paper run by Marmion Savage, another friend of Edward Lane and a regular at Moor Park, immediately reprinted Dallas's *Times* editorial, and also ran an article entitled 'Defects of the Law – the Case of *Robinson v Robinson & Lane*', which expressed outrage that the court had denied a voice to the doctor, 'a gentleman of unimpeached respectability and worth'.

Combe wrote to his friend Charles Mackay, the editor of the *Illustrated London News*, to ask for his help. Mackay assured him that he had already made up his mind that 'Mrs Robinson was crazy – & that Dr Lane was entirely innocent'. In the London clubs that he frequented, he added, 'there is a disposition to exonerate Dr Lane from all blame'. He promised that he would prevent the slightest allusion to the case in his newspaper.

Charles Darwin told a friend on 24 June: 'All those, whom I have asked think that Dr L is probably innocent – Mr Thom's (a very sensible nice young man) evidence; the admitted coldness of Dr Lane's letters – the absence of all corroborative evidence – & more than all the unparalleled fact of a woman detailing her own adultery, which seems to me more improbable than inventing a story prompted by extreme sensuality or hallucination – altogether make me think Dr Lane innocent & that it is a most cruel case. – I fear it will ruin him. I never heard a sensual expression from him.' Three days later he wrote to the same friend: 'I am profoundly sorry for Dr L and all his family, to whom I am much attached.'

Edward asked Combe to secure him a friendly article in the *Scotsman*, and he wrote individually to associates in Edinburgh. His name had been 'dragged through the mire', he told a lawyer friend on 25 June, in 'one of the most abominable, the most cruel, & unjust cases that ever came before a Court of Law . . . My hands have thus been completely tied, & I bid fair to be stabbed in the dark.' He protested his innocence '*on the word and honour of a gentleman*'. The diary, he explained, was 'the frantic raving of a monomaniac, who had long been the prey of a severe uterine disease'. He enclosed with his letter copies of the newspaper reports that defended him.

The press rushed to discredit the diary. The *Daily News* demanded a change in the law to allow Edward to testify, as did the *Observer*: otherwise, this paper warned, 'no man is safe who happens to fall in company with a lady of somewhat mature age, with an excitable imagination and a *cacoethes scribendi*. He may be made to appear to have committed all sorts of enormities, while he is, in fact, perfectly innocent, and so be completely ruined.' *Cacoethes scribendi*, a term coined by the Roman poet Juvenal, was an insatiable urge, or persistent itch, to write. Unless the law was changed, said *The Times*, any gentleman who conducted private interviews with women – such as a clergyman or a physician – would be at risk of being ruined by a false accusation. *The Morning Post* proclaimed: 'Dr Lane is an innocent and an injured man.'

As a hydropath, Edward was especially vulnerable to allegations of impropriety. The previous month, during the debates about the Medical Act of 1858, a commentator in *The Lancet* had classed hydropaths, along with mesmerists and homeopaths, as 'men who have sacrificed science and debased morality'. The medical press none the less lined up behind Dr Lane. His treatments might be unorthodox, argued the *British Medical Journal*, but his plight should concern all physicians: if the diary was accepted as evidence, 'any of our associates with "curls and smooth face", and less-favoured ones, for that matter, may some day find themselves plunged from domestic happiness and pecuniary prosperity into utter ruin'. The journal demanded that Dr Lane be put in the witness box, 'in order himself to break through the extraordinary web which the fancy of Mrs Robinson has woven around him'.

Several papers praised the artistry of the diary, with varying degrees of irony. 'The whole work is not without marks of considerable literary power,' commented *The Morning Post*. The *Saturday Review* likened Isabella to the erotic Greek poetess Sappho. The *Daily News* compared the journal's strain of 'passionate sentimentalism' to Rousseau's *Julie, or La Nouvelle Hélöise*; and its 'more sensuous pruriencies' to Alexander Pope's *Eloisa and Abelard*. Both Rousseau's epistolary novel of 1761 and Pope's poem of 1717 were based on the story of Abelard and Heloise, twelfth-century scholars and lovers who exchanged a series of ardent, erudite letters. Less romantically, Isabella saw herself compared to a witch (by *The Morning Post*) and to Messalina, the violent and promiscuous wife of the Roman Emperor Claudius (in a book by Dr Phillimore's brother John). Much of the reporting about the diary struck a feverish note that not only matched but extended Isabella's own. Some of the men who commented on the case may have insisted on the freakishness of the journal because they feared that readers, especially female readers, might sympathise with its story.

'The diary stands self-convicted of insanity,' said the *Saturday Review* on 26 June. 'But its consequences are terrible.' This weekly journal compared Isabella to Lady Dinorden, a widowed peeress who was that week convicted of libel – she had bombarded her nephew with anonymous letters that accused him of being bankrupt, illegitimate and insane. 'The moral of the matter, we are much afraid, is against literary ladies. Lady Dinorden's epistolary style, and Mrs Robinson's command of descriptive and idyllic writing, have ruined them. They are victims – and others too are victims – to literary skill and felicity in the art of composition.' Female writers, who had become increasingly prevalent by the mid-nineteenth century, were all implicated in the excesses of Isabella's journal.

A further editorial in the same issue of the *Saturday Review* decried Isabella's 'luscious sentimentality', arguing that her diary was indebted to 'the exquisitely pathetic deathbeds of beautiful little girls' in contemporary novels; to the piteous letters from prostitutes that appeared in the pages of the press; and to the dirty pamphlets and pictures sold in Holywell Street, off the Strand, the centre of the British pornography trade. The author of this piece traced a direct line from maudlin emotion to sexual decadence. Isabella, taking her cue from the 'fondling love-scenes' of popular fiction, 'in linked sweetness long drawn out', had dwelt lovingly on her downfall, lingered over her ruin, sentimentalised her sinning. In doing so, she had exposed the connection between romance and pornography.

Though far less explicit than most of the texts hawked in Holywell Street, Isabella's diary conformed to a popular pornographic formula: its narrator was a woman who happily abandoned herself to sex. Its rapturous recollections read like an expurgated version of the exclamations in *The Lustful Turk* (1828): 'Never, oh never shall I forget the delicious transports that followed the stiff insertion; and then, ah me!' Isabella's half-conscious reveries in bed in the morning recalled those of Fanny Hill in John Cleland's *Memoirs of a Woman of Pleasure*, a publication of 1749 that had gone through twenty editions by the middle of the nineteenth century: 'I felt about the bed, as if I sought for something that I grasped in my waking dream, and not finding it, could have cried for vexation, every part of me glowing with stimulating fires.'

Isabella had transgressed by writing down her lascivious thoughts, but the newspapers, as her publishers, were collaborating in her crime. During the Robinson case, said the *Saturday Review*, 'as filthy compositions as ever proceeded from any human pen' had been reprinted at full length in the press. For weeks now the newspapers had been spewing out a 'stream of filth', 'matter which rendered them altogether unfit for the reading of any decent woman, and most dangerous stimulants to the prurience of the young'. It seemed that mid-Victorian society had a compulsion to publish and to read sexual scenes quite as strong as Isabella's compulsion to write them.

John George Phillimore, Regius Professor of Civil Law at Oxford, and the brother of Isabella's counsel, argued that Isabella had 'unsexed' herself in the diary – she had surrendered her femininity with her modesty. He warned that the divorce reports, having 'brought home corruption to our hearths and altars', might end by 'dissolving the foundations of national morality'. The integrity of England, wrote Professor Phillimore, rested on the integrity of marriage: 'In no country was the relation of husband and wife of greater dignity and more hallowed than our own. To maintain this part of our national character, which is a compensation for so many deficiencies – to keep this pearl of great price unbartered, is the concern of every man in whose veins there beats a drop of English blood.'

In the summer session of Parliament in 1857, Lord Palmerston's government had pushed through the Matrimonial Causes Act, which established the Divorce Court, and the Obscene Publications Act, which made the sale of obscene material a statutory offence. Both Acts identified sexual behaviour as a cause of social disorder. A year on, though, they seemed to have come into conflict: police officers were seizing and destroying dirty stories under the Obscenity Act, while barristers and reporters were disseminating them under the Divorce Act. 'The great law which regulates supply and demand seems to prevail in matters of public decency as well as in other things of commerce,' noted the *Saturday Review* in 1859. 'Block up one channel, and the stream will force another outlet; and so it is that the current dammed up in Holywell Street flings itself out in the Divorce Court.'

Parts of the House of Commons were evacuated during the heatwave, and Members of Parliament hung lime-soaked sheets from the windows to keep out the bad air. The river 'reeks and steams', reported the *Saturday Review*, in 'the more than Indian heat' of the city. 'The deathpot boils,' observed the *Illustrated London News*. 'We can colonise the remotest ends of the Earth . . . we can spread our name, and our fame, and our fructifying wealth to every part of the world; but we cannot clean the River Thames.'

George and Cecy Combe were in London at the start of the Robinson trial, in lodgings near the Edgware Road. During their stay they attended the Royal Academy summer exhibition, where Augustus Egg's triptych was on show. Upon the adjournment of the legal proceedings in July, they visited a friend called Mr Bastard, who ran a secular school in Dorset, and then joined the Lanes and the Drysdales at Moor Park. Among their fellow guests was Marmion Savage, who as editor of the *Examiner* was supporting Edward Lane's cause. Combe found his hosts 'all low in spirits', he told his journal, 'altho' relieved, from the load of anxiety and toil' that the case had placed upon them. On 12 July he wrote to Sir James Clark, including in his letter an account of his recent re-examination of the head of the Prince of Wales. Bertie was 'much improved', he said, 'but cerebellic difficulty remains'. 'The difficulty in question,' he noted – that is, sexual desire – 'is one of the great unsolved problems of our civilisation.'

Combe had succeeded in keeping his name and many others out of the court: there had been no mention made during the trial of such figures in their circle as Charles Darwin, the Drysdale brothers, Robert Chambers, Sir James Clark, Alexander Bain, Dinah Mulock or Catherine Crowe. The fall-out from the diary had been contained. It remained to be seen whether Edward and his family, too, could be spared its worst consequences. If the amendment to the Divorce Act were passed, they were told, the doctor might be summoned to testify in November.

'This is my dear Cecy's birthday,' Combe wrote in his diary on 25 July 1858. 'She is happy, and her affection towards me is overflowing. The evening was sunny after a blustering day, and Cecy and I walked into the glade. I found shelter from the wind under high ferns, and sat on the ground, she on her camp stool, and she sung to me several favourite songs, with the sweet tones and expression which no other voice has to me. God bless her and long preserve her.'

The next day George Combe felt unwell, and in the fortnight that followed he developed a violent cough, nausea, 'heat and fuss in the head'. Edward tended to him: he 'is very kind,' Combe told his diary, 'but says nature must best be left to work her own cure'. Sir James Clark came to see his old friend at Moor Park on 4 August, a visit that indicated his acceptance of Edward's innocence. On 11 August, Combe was unable to write, and dictated his diary entry to Cecy. By 13 August he could dictate no longer, so Cecy continued the journal in her own words. 'At 2 a.m. I went to him, fed him, tried to wash his face and hands, and heard the word "darling"; but he grows indistinct, and the voice is low.' At 10 a.m. on 14 August, Combe's breathing slowed and ceased. Cecy recorded the moment in her husband's journal: 'Dr Lane said, "it is over". A profound stillness was in the room.' The cause of death was given as pleuro-pneumonia. 'No son could be kinder than Dr Lane has been,' wrote Cecy, 'no friends more so than the whole family.'

On 15 August the undertakers – Messrs Sloman and Workman – removed Combe's head from his body so that the skull could be subjected to phrenological analysis. Cecy took her husband's remains back to Edinburgh, where Combe's body was buried on 20 August.

CHAPTER TWELVE

THE VERDICT

Westminster Hall, November 1858–March 1859

In the month that George Combe died, Parliament passed a series of amendments to the Divorce Act, among them a clause that authorised the court to dismiss a co-respondent in order to call him as a witness. The judges in *Robinson v Robinson & Lane* duly dismissed and then summoned Edward Lane, for whose benefit the law had been altered. On Friday 26 November the doctor came to Westminster to defend his name. Though the court had already technically cleared him of adultery, his reputation would be in tatters unless Isabella was cleared too.

The morning was clear, dry and unusually warm, the temperature in London having risen over the previous three days from thirteen to fifty-seven degrees Fahrenheit. In Westminster Hall, Cockburn, Cresswell and Wightman had reassembled on the bench.

The doctor took his place at the witness box. William Bovill QC, Isabella's counsel, stood to examine him. Bovill resembled a benign, bespectacled professor, earnest in manner, with a reedy body and a big shiny head that bulged at the temples. Though he had not spoken in the court in June, he was the barrister who, with Phillimore, had formulated Edward and Isabella's defence.

'I am a physician,' said Edward Lane in reply to Bovill's queries, 'and a graduate of the Edinburgh University. I married the daughter of Sir William Drysdale in 1847. My wife is about thirty-one or thirty-two years of age. I have four children.'

Bovill asked the doctor about his friendship with Isabella.

'I became acquainted first with Mrs Robinson in the autumn of 1850 when I was residing at Edinburgh,' said Edward. 'The two families became on intimate terms. She was a lady of considerable literary attainments, and corresponded with literary men. Our acquaintance was renewed at Moor Park, when they were living at Reading. In 1853, when my wife and I went to the Continent, we left our children with the Robinsons for four or five weeks. They also stayed with them on other occasions. Mrs Robinson showed them a great deal of kindness.'

Edward confirmed the dates on which Isabella had visited Moor Park, which included one visit made after Henry's discovery of her journal. She stayed for a day and a night in 1856, he said. 'As well as I can recollect that was about the end of September, or early in October.'

Bovill asked whether Mrs Robinson came to the spa as a friend or a patient.

The doctor replied that though Isabella was 'always an invalid', she usually visited Moor Park as a friend of the family. She first consulted him professionally, he said, in June 1855. 'She told me that she had been suffering from a complaint of the womb for several years. She also told me that she was suffering from continual headaches and a great depression of spirits, and as well from irregularities. She seemed between forty and fifty, a period at which a change in females generally takes place.'

Bovill asked further about the nature of her illness.

'The disease from which she was suffering was one that affects the nerves,' said Edward. 'She was a mixture of calmness and excitement.

'She was exceedingly staid in her demeanour, but was sometimes flighty in her conversation,' he added. 'I did not prescribe for her, but merely gave her advice, and told her she ought to follow a course of tonic treatment.' This method of treatment, designed to stimulate the system, typically involved taking drinks such as chalybeate (iron-rich spring water) or bitters (alcohol infused with bark or quinine), in combination with a regime of exercise, good diet and cold baths.

Bovill asked about the walks that Edward and Isabella took together.

'I was in the habit of walking about daily with the different ladies and gentlemen in my establishment,' said Edward. He emphasised that such walks were far from private. 'The grounds are beautiful and spacious. All the walks are open to the patients, and to the servants, and to visitors. The neighbours who are friends also have access to them.'

Bovill asked him about the time that he was seen emerging from Isabella's quarters.

'When any of the ladies did not appear at breakfast I was in the habit of visiting them in their bedrooms,' Edward informed the court. 'I may have gone into Mrs Robinson's room.'

Cockburn interrupted: 'But I understood she was there not as a patient but as a friend.'

'If I had known that Mrs Robinson was unwell I might have gone into her room,' explained Edward, 'but I don't remember that I ever did go. I cannot swear that I never did, but I have no recollection of having done it. She generally had two rooms while remaining at Moor Park: a sitting room and a bedroom, one leading out of the other.'

Bovill asked about the study in which they were alleged to have had sex.

'The study was free of access to all the patients when they wanted to see me, and friends came in there continually and sat with me during the day or in the evening. It was my private room, and anyone who wanted to communicate with me came to it.' On further questioning, he added, 'There are three doors to my study. One is from the public dining room and another is opposite the pantry door. The servants occasionally use it as a passage room.'

'In the whole of your acquaintance with Mrs Robinson from first to last,' asked Bovill, 'had you ever any criminal connection with her?'

'Never,' said Edward.

'Did you ever take any liberties with her person?'

'I never did.'

'Did you ever conduct yourself towards her in any indelicate or improper manner?'

'Never, in the smallest degree.'

'Did you ever address to her any conversation or observation of an amorous description?'

'I never did,' said Edward. He added that he had once, chastely, kissed her. 'In October 1855 she arrived with one of her children, and she was received in the hall by my mother-in-law and myself, in the presence of a number of other persons. The hall is also a billiard room. On that occasion I gave her a kiss. I will tell you why. In the September previous my wife and I were anxious that our children should go to the seaside for change of air, but we were too busy to absent ourselves, and Mrs Robinson kindly volunteered to accompany them. She did so, and on her return to Moor Park I saluted her as I have stated.' This, he said, was the only loving gesture he made towards her. 'I never put my arm round her waist, or embraced her, or tempted her or caressed her. I never did anything to excite her passions in any way.' He denied having a conversation with her about 'obviating consequences'.

He had seen the diary, he said, and its statements were 'utterly and absolutely false – a tissue of romances from beginning to end, as far as they implicate me in anything improper'.

Did she ever take a lock of his hair?

'She never cut off a lock of my hair.'

And did he walk with her in the evenings?

'I may have walked after dusk with her on a summer's evening, but in the month of October I never walked with her after tea-time.'

Bovill sat down, and John Karslake, Montagu Chambers's junior, took the floor to cross-examine the doctor. Karslake was a striking man – six feet six inches tall, 'magnificently handsome', according to his friend and sparring partner John Coleridge, who was Bovill's junior in the Robinson case, 'manly and straightforward and powerful in all he says'.

In a quick monotone, Karslake asked Edward about the supposedly free access to his study.

The doctor conceded: 'It was understood that the servants were not to pass through the study when I was there. The servants would generally knock before entering.'

Karslake asked him to elaborate on the nature of his friendship with Mrs Robinson.

Edward said that in Edinburgh, 'the intimacy between my family and the Robinsons sprang up rapidly. We saw them nearly every day. We could hardly be more intimate as friends than we were at this time. Mrs Robinson and I frequently talked together on scientific subjects, on books, on phrenology, and other topics. I wrote her letters when she was absent from Edinburgh; sometimes long letters.'

Under further cross-examination, Edward agreed that he had given Isabella a locket.

'I once presented Mrs Robinson with a locket, as a gift from my wife, which contained my children's hair. She and my wife had exchanged lockets. That was at Edinburgh. My wife made her presents of that sort on one or two occasions.'

He was asked again about his visit to Isabella's room.

'Mrs Robinson slept in whatever room was vacant when she came to Moor Park. I repeat, that I never remember having been in Mrs Robinson's room in the morning. I have been in her room in an evening. It was early one evening in 1855. I might have dropped into her room in the evening on more than one occasion but I can't recollect having done so. On that occasion I met Mr Thom there.'

Karslake asked whether this was her bedroom.

'It was her sitting room, not her bedroom,' Edward replied. 'I was never in her bedroom at any time in the evening.'

When in 1856 did Mrs Robinson visit, asked Karslake, and had they corresponded since then? He was trying to establish the extent of their conversation after Henry's discovery of the diaries in May.

'The date of Mrs Robinson's visit in 1856 was August or September,' said Edward, slightly changing his previous estimate of late September or October. 'I may have corresponded with her after that visit. I saw Mrs Robinson last in December 1856.'

He was asked when he had learnt of Henry Robinson's decision to take the case to court.

'I did not know for certain, until July 1857, that Mr Robinson had instituted a suit against Mrs Robinson in the ecclesiastical court. I heard of it from my gardener. I saw a report of some proceedings in the November of that year. It was about two lines, I believe, in *The Times*, stating that a divorce had been obtained. My gardener, John Burmingham, told me his sister had been up as a witness.' This was Sarah Burmingham, who had also testified on Henry's behalf in the current case.

And did he correspond with Mrs Robinson after that?

'I had no communication with Mrs Robinson in 1857,' said Edward, 'or with any person in reference to that lady.'

Bovill rose to re-examine his witness, and asked him to describe more fully what he knew about the divorce suit.

'The report I saw was in *The Times* of the fourth of December 1857,' said Edward. 'It merely stated that the suit was promoted by Mr Robinson against Mrs Robinson by reason of adultery; that Dr Addams was about to open the case for the husband, when the Admiralty Advocate, for the wife, said he would offer no opposition; and that the Court pronounced sentence of divorce.' By 'divorce', here, he meant a divorce *a mensa et thoro*, a separation; the Admiralty Advocate to whom he referred was Dr Phillimore.

Cockburn asked Edward whether Isabella had made contact with him when that case was heard in the church court.

'I was not communicated with on behalf of Mrs Robinson when that suit was commenced. I understood I was implicated in the proceedings instituted by Mr Robinson.'

Bovill reminded Cockburn that the doctor could not have been examined in the suit in the ecclesiastical court.

Cockburn corrected him: it was true that he could not have been examined *ex proprio motu* (of his own accord), he said, but if Mrs Robinson had chosen to resist the suit she could have made him a witness.

Edward was permitted to leave the witness box. He had conducted himself with restraint, refraining from making any attacks on Isabella, calmly denying the charges of adultery. He was courteous, poised, detached, free from rancour, passion or intensity. In his letters to George Combe he had been far more outspoken. Then, he had been keen to persuade Combe of his innocence; now, he had a debt to pay Isabella, who was fighting the divorce petition for his sake.

Bovill summed up for Isabella. Henry's case, he said, rested entirely on the diary. 'I would first observe that it contains no explicit statement of Mrs Robinson's guilt.

Some of the most eminent men in the kingdom have proved that the disease under which she was labouring was likely to excite her imagination, and cause her to imagine what had never taken place. The fact that she had suffered under that disease for several years has also been proved, and the means taken by her and her husband to effect a certain purpose tended to aggravate that disease.' This was a euphemistic reference to the form of contraception used by Henry and Isabella. Bovill did not specify their method: they might have used a device such as a syringe or a cervical cap, which could cause physical irritation and therefore, it was believed, provoke mental derangement; or it might have been that Henry withdrew before ejaculation, with the same consequences.

Bovill drew the court's attention to the diary's frequent references to the writings of Shelley: it was fair to infer, he said, that Isabella had also been struck with events in Shelley's life, and with the fact that he had imagined things that had never existed'. He contended that the diary entries were 'not records of fact but expressions of feeling', pointing out that the apparently incriminating entry of 7 October 1854, in which Isabella and Edward first kissed, was not composed that day but the next, 'after a night of sleeplessness and dreaming'.

Bovill read again several of the diary extracts that tended to show Isabella's instability, drawing attention to one – dated 25 May, in an unspecified year – in which she claimed to have betrayed Henry a month before their marriage. He argued that Henry's counsel had failed to incriminate Edward Lane: 'Several months' notice has been given of the examination of Dr Lane, yet not a single question could be asked him by Mr Karslake tending to impeach his credit.' He returned to the central contention of Isabella's defence, the argument that for a woman to record such disgraceful episodes was itself evidence of madness. 'If what she described occurred,' he asked, 'is it credible that she should day by day have written with her own hand a record of her infamy?'

Rather, Bovill argued, the erotic passages were experiments in fiction. The extracts relied upon by Henry's lawyers, after all, were skilfully constructed. When Isabella recounted her first tryst in the Moor Park glade, she did not blurt out her extraordinary news; she began the entry by recreating the innocence of the morning, withholding from the diary her knowledge that Edward desired her. Such entries, Bovill said, suggested that Mrs Robinson was contemplating a novel.

'I hope that "contemplating a novel",' said Cockburn, 'is no sign of a diseased mind.' There was laughter in the court.

'By no means,' said Bovill, 'but the novel she contemplated was connected with events in which she imagined she had taken part. Never before has it been sought to have a lady found guilty of adultery upon such evidence as this.'

Montagu Chambers then addressed the court on Henry's behalf: 'The very journal shows that Mrs Robinson is a sane woman, capable of discussing even the most abstruse and difficult questions. It is the journal of a very romantic but, nevertheless, of a very clever woman, competent to discuss science and subtle subjects.'

Cockburn interjected: 'There is not a lunatic asylum where you will not find persons able to do the same.' The spectators laughed. The judge had dryly pointed out to Bovill that literary aspirations were not in themselves proof of madness; now he reminded Chambers that intellectual sophistication was not evidence of sanity.

'The foundation of the defence,' continued Chambers, 'is that Mrs Robinson was labouring under a uterine disease, but that foundation is one of sand. No evidence has been given as to her present state of health, or as to the time when her disease was supposed to have terminated. We do not even know precisely what was the disease with which she was afflicted.'

He reminded the court of the early entries about Edward Lane. 'It appears that he was in the habit of reading passages of poetry to Mrs Robinson, and she very clearly records her first love for that gentleman. She called him a handsome man the first time she saw him.' When Edward 'made himself free with another woman', he added, she found him 'not so agreeable'. To Dr Lane's credit, said Chambers, he had for several years rejected the advances of Mrs Robinson, responding to her overtures with coldness and reserve. Eventually, though, 'he unfortunately was not able to resist the temptation that was thrown in his way by the allurements of an agreeable and loving woman'. The fact that no one had seen him act with great familiarity to Mrs Robinson, said Chambers, was only 'proof that he was a cautious man, and not that he was free from guilt'.

Cockburn adjourned the trial. The judges, he said, would take time to consider their decision.

Over the next few days, most of the newspapers that in the summer had been so inclined to exonerate Edward Lane were silent on the subject. The *Daily Telegraph*, which earlier in the year had described the diary as 'nonsense in a notebook', even ran a piece that suggested that the doctor might be guilty: 'No one reading her journal, with the events of each day minutely recorded, could possibly doubt the truthfulness of what is set down.' Edward Lane's evidence, the newspaper argued, had not dispelled the mystery surrounding the case. He had confirmed everything in the diary bar the sex, and his cross-examination had resurrected the prickly question of why Isabella had not denied adultery – and called him as a witness – when the case was heard in the church court. 'Dr Lane has been lucky enough to be able to avail himself of an Act passed, it would seem, specially for his benefit, by which he is empowered to figure in the witness box, and give testimony to his own innocence. But no one who knows much of human nature will be disposed to give implicit credence to the testimony of a gentleman so peculiarly circumstanced.' His lawyers' argument that Isabella was insane, said the *Telegraph*, was 'a very convenient theory'.

Since the summer in which the Robinson trial began, claims of insanity had become highly contentious. In June 1858, the novelist (and hydropathy enthusiast) Edward Bulwer-Lytton had his wife Rosina abducted and forcibly detained in a private asylum after she denounced him as a liar at a public hustings. Rosina was certified insane by John Conolly, the alienist who had treated Catherine Crowe; but when she was re-examined, after a furore in the press, both he and Forbes Winslow declared her sane. Detailed reports also appeared in the newspapers about the apparently unjustified confinements of a Mrs Turner, a Mr Ruck and a Mr Leech. A diagnosis of madness, especially a convenient diagnosis, was now treated with new scepticism.

A string of troubling cases came before the court in the weeks after Edward Lane gave his evidence. On Saturday 27 November, Sir Cresswell Cresswell returned to the petition of Caroline Marchmont, who wanted a judicial separation from her husband, a former clergyman, on the grounds of his cruelty. She had brought the huge sum of £50,000 to their marriage, her petition explained, and she and her husband had quarrelled about money from the start. Mr Marchmont was in the habit of demanding cash from her, she said, £100 at a time. He would stand over her, 'very white', while 'his eyes flashed fire'. He abused her when she refused him, calling her a 'hell-fire, spit-fire cat', a 'dirty slut', a 'drunken faggot' and worse. Mr Marchmont claimed that he was provoked: his wife was stingy and controlling with her money, suspicious, foul-mouthed and irritating, especially on the (frequent) occasions on which she drank too much sherry.

Several witnesses testified that Mr Marchmont had

repeatedly forced his wife back to the family home (when he found her hiding at her sister's, for instance, or in a coal hole, or fleeing over a garden wall) but they gave different accounts of the measure of violence with which he did so. Mrs Marchmont said that her husband once broke into their bedroom to find her writing in an account book in which she kept a record of the treatment that she suffered at his hands. He snatched the book and threw it in the fireplace, at which she reached in to the flames to pull it out. According to Mrs Marchmont, he grabbed the book as she rescued it from the hearth and struck her with it, blackening her face. Mr Marchmont claimed that it was she who smacked him in the face with the burning book, so hard that its clasp cut him under the eye. The jury had to decide whether Mr Marchmont had exercised his rights as a husband or acted with cruelty. On 30 November the court found for Mrs Marchmont and she was granted a judicial separation.

The *Saturday Review* disapproved, arguing that Mrs Marchmont's provocations were quite as bad as her husband's greed and occasional violence. In the interests of the greatest happiness of the many, it insisted, a judicial separation should be granted only in the 'gravest emergency': 'a married couple should endure a very considerable amount of discomfort, incompatibility, personal suffering, and distress, and yet should continue to live together as man and wife'.

In *Evans v Evans & Robinson*, a long-running case that came back before the court on 5 December, the husband's evidence of his wife's adultery had been gathered by Charley Field, the same private investigator employed by Henry Robinson. Field kept a diary of his surveillance. He hired rooms in Mrs Evans's apartment block in Marylebone, and arranged for a gimlet-hole to be bored in her sitting-room door; through this, several servants saw her having sex with another man. Their evidence was admissible, the judge said, but he disapproved of Field's methods of securing it. 'The people of England,' declared Baron Martin, who delivered the verdict, found it abhorrent 'to have men running after them wherever they went and making notes of all their actions.'

In the Divorce Court on 13 December, Esther Keats, the young wife of the owner of the Piccadilly grocery emporium Fortnum & Mason, confessed to having committed adultery with Don Pedro de Montesuma, a Spanish musician, in hotels in London, Dover and Dublin. Mrs Keats's counsel argued that Frederick Keats had neglected his wife by leaving her alone in Brighton for long periods while he attended to business in London, and had later condoned her infidelity by allowing her back in to the family home. Mr Keats's counsel urged the court to dismiss the charge of neglect; otherwise, he said, 'what would become of the wives of members of Parliament, who for six months in the year went to the House of Commons at four or five in the afternoon and remained till twelve or one in the morning? – what would become of the wives of members of the legal profession, who were absent on circuit for six weeks together?' If a husband's absence were justification for a woman's adultery, many of the middle-class wives of England would be licensed to fornicate. Mr Keats's petition for divorce was granted, and Don Pedro was ordered to pay him £1,000 in damages.

On 19 December, *Reynolds's Weekly* observed that the cases in the Divorce Court 'seem to indicate that amongst the high, the moral, the respectable, and the Christian classes . . . adultery is in a highly flourishing, if not exceedingly rampant, condition'. A week later Queen Victoria wrote to Lord Campbell, the chief designer of the Divorce Act, to ask if he could suppress some of the stories coming out of the court. 'These cases . . . fill almost daily a large portion of the newspapers, and are of so scandalous a character that it makes it almost impossible for a paper to be trusted in the hands of a young lady or boy. None of the worst French novels from which careful parents try to protect their children can be as bad as what is daily brought and laid upon the breakfast table of every educated family in England, and its effect must be most pernicious to the public morals of the country.' Campbell replied, regretfully, that he had no power to limit the newspaper stories. On 10 January he confided to his diary his anxieties about the new court: 'like Frankenstein, I am afraid of the monster I have called into existence'.

The stories emerging from the Divorce Court were turning out to be disturbing in two ways: bestial in their violence and lust; and uncertain in their meaning. The court was trying to reform the institution of marriage by subjecting it to scrutiny, but seemed to be succeeding only in exposing its contradictions. A broken marriage always generated incompatible narratives, just as a diary always created a partial story. It might not become clear, either by reading private words or by testing a private relationship in a public forum, what had really happened, let alone where justice lay. The cracked-open marriages brought before the court seemed signs of a society in which men and women had become entrenched in separate worlds.

It took the Divorce Court judges three months to reach a verdict in *Robinson v Robinson & Lane*. On Wednesday 2 March 1859, a fine, mild, dry day in London, Cockburn, Cresswell and Wightman again gathered on the bench. The light leaked in to the courtroom through the glazed panes in the roof and the fans over the doorways.

Cockburn addressed the court. In a judgment that the newspapers characterised as 'elaborate and eloquent', he proceeded to undo all the arguments that had been brought before him, and to set out a new way of deciding the suit.

Henry Robinson's case, he said, rested entirely on the entries in the diary, all the corroborative evidence having been dismissed. The judges had found the journal uncommonly revealing, Cockburn said: Mrs Robinson's 'inmost thoughts and feelings, even where one would most have expected secrecy, are set forth without hesitation or reserve'. She emerged from its pages as a 'woman of more than ordinary intelligence and of no inconsiderable attainments' who appeared to have had 'great and sincere affection' for her children. What she lacked was sound sense and judgment: her imagination was too vivid and her passions too strong.

Cockburn's portrayal of Isabella was far milder and more sympathetic than those that had appeared in the press. His private life may have influenced his view of her – as the lover of an unmarried woman who had borne him two children, he knew that a 'fallen' woman was not necessarily a wicked one. He was also aware of the wretchedness of Isabella's marriage: having read the whole diary, he and his fellow judges knew of Henry Robinson's infidelity and rapacity, neither of which had been alluded to in court.

The judges had found no evidence, said Cockburn, that Mrs Robinson was insane. If the scenes that Isabella narrated had been 'the delusions of a disordered mind,' as the defence lawyers claimed, 'we should, no doubt, have found, what is usual in such cases, the statement or confession of them to others, not a mere recording of them among the other events of her life in a secret journal, to be seen by no eye but her own'. Isabella's capacity for secrecy, he implied, was evidence of sanity.

Not all of the judges had been of this mind the previous summer: Wightman had argued on 21 June 1858 that it was 'evident' that Isabella was 'labouring under delusions of a peculiar character, arising from chronic disease'. Either he had been persuaded to change his views by March 1859, or he was over-ruled by Cockburn and Cresswell.

If Isabella had been mad, Cockburn continued, 'probably, too, we should have found more distinct and unequivocal statements of the full consummation of her desires than are to be met with in the diary. Certainly, we should not have found, in so many instances, complaints of imperfect pleasure or of painful disappointment.' As Cockburn noticed, the realism of the diary rested not only on its naturalistic detail and its precision about dates and times and weather conditions but also on its accounts of sexual frustration (the 'half-realised bliss' of her first encounters with Edward) and of humiliating rejection (at the hands of Thom and Le Petit as well as the doctor). In several passages, Isabella showed herself painfully alive to the discrepancy between her fantasies and her experience. Such entries could hardly be construed as the products of delusion.

Cockburn then turned to the arguments of Henry's lawyers, only to dismiss those too. The diary, he said, was not a confession of adultery. It contained 'no clear and unequivocal admission of adultery having taken place'. The passage that most strongly suggested a consummation, said Cockburn, was that in which Edward, after a passionate encounter with Isabella, 'desired her to take care to "obviate consequences", but even here the "consequences" referred to may have been those of detection in a criminal intimacy, not those resulting from actual adultery'.

In Isabella's descriptions of her amorous moments with the doctor, Cockburn said, 'the language is ambiguous. It may be taken to import actual consummation or to refer only to indecent familiarities and caresses.' He conceded that the court would usually be inclined to 'give the fullest effect' to accounts of this kind, to infer adultery from scenes of illicit intimacy, but he believed that the language of Isabella's diary should 'be construed by a different rule'. When writing about men to whom she was attracted, her imagination and passion led her 'beyond the bounds of reason and truth', and she was 'prone to exaggerate and overcolour every circumstance which tended to her gratification'. Since Isabella had taken erotic pleasure in writing down her experiences, he suggested, she was likely to have heightened and embroidered the truth: the diary's prime purpose was not to document her past but to delight her present. 'It is plain that she dwells with impure gratification on the portraiture of these scenes, and on the details of the guilty endearments and caresses which she narrates,' Cockburn said. 'To statements so made it is not open to us to add anything by way of inference.'

The Divorce Court rarely heard direct evidence of sexual intercourse. It depended on inference, on deducing a consummation from evidence of desire and opportunity. There was little doubt of either in this case. But Cockburn claimed that although something illicit had obviously gone on between Edward and Isabella, he could not be sure of what. By refusing to infer, even from a written confession, he effectively surrendered the court's power to interpret.

Cockburn concluded by dismissing Henry Robinson's petition for divorce. 'We regret the position of the petitioner,' he said, 'who remains burdened with a wife who has thus placed on record the confession of her misconduct; or, at all events, even if the most favourable view be taken of the case, of unfaithful thoughts and unchaste desires; but we can only afford redress on legal proof of adultery, and that proof we cannot find in the incoherent statements of a narrative so irrational and untrustworthy as that of Mrs Robinson.'

Of the 302 petitions for dissolution brought before the court in its first fifteen months, Henry's was one of only six to be refused. Isabella had won.

After Cockburn had delivered his judgment, Bovill asked the court to grant Isabella's costs – that is, to rule that Henry, as the loser, should pay her legal expenses. These amounted to £636, including the court's fees, the solicitors' and barristers' charges, the cost of copying the diary and the allowances paid to the witnesses. Cockburn briskly dismissed the application. Given the peculiar circumstances of the case, he said, and the fact that Isabella had an independent income, she must foot her own bill. Bovill asked whether the court would order Mr Robinson to pay Dr Lane's costs. Cockburn said that he had not expected this request, and was not prepared to decide upon it. Edward's lawyers could raise the issue at a later date, he said, adding, sharply, 'if in the exercise of their discretion his counsel think fit to do so'. Having so narrowly secured a victory, he implied, they would be ill-advised to press their point.

Cockburn and Wightman withdrew, leaving Cresswell to deal with the rest of the day's business.

The few editorials about Cockburn's judgment simply reported that Dr Lane had been exonerated. The *Examiner* – under the editorship of the Moor Park patient Marmion Savage – airily asserted: 'it is enough to state that the divorce has been refused, with the result of substantially as well as formally establishing the innocence of the male defendant. The judgment will be highly satisfactory to the public, on account of Doctor Lane. It now appears that opinion was not more general in his favour than it was just, when the subject was so much in discussion last summer.' The *Medical Times & Gazette* claimed that 'Dr Lane has been the victim of the erotic maniacal ravings of the unfortunate woman who was proved to have committed adultery in her heart'.

The story that endured was that Isabella's journal was a fiction and Dr Lane was entirely innocent. The barrister John Paget in 1860 cited the case as an example of the power of delusion: 'nothing could be clearer, more explicit, or more astounding' than the diary's account of Isabella's affair with Edward Lane, Paget wrote; but 'it was established beyond a doubt that the lady, though apparently conducting herself like other people, and giving no external sign of disordered intellect, was upon this particular subject altogether insane'.

But Cockburn in his judgment had said nothing of the

kind. Rather, he had deemed Isabella sane and her diary essentially truthful. Though the journal contained elements of melodrama and sentimental fiction, the judges considered that as a whole it told a nuanced story, rendered credible by its self-recrimination, disappointment and doubt. Its exaggerations and excesses were those familiar to any diarist, to any desperately unhappy person or to anyone in love. It was ultimately not a work of madness but of realism, an account of the limits of romantic dreams. In effect, the court had decided to let Edward off on a technicality: since Isabella had not explicitly detailed a sexual consummation, the judges ruled, the degree of her intimacy with Edward was impossible to gauge.

Cockburn and his fellow judges afterwards supplied the editors of a legal digest of the early Divorce Court cases with the sections of Isabella's diary upon which they had relied. Since the verdict had turned entirely on the diary, the editors wrote, it was 'thought advisable to print the following extracts from that journal, and some pains have been taken to choose such portions as should give a fair idea of the whole'. The extracts amounted to about 9,000 words, almost double the number that appeared in the newspapers during the trial. They included half of the entries Isabella wrote in Edinburgh in 1850 and 1852; nearly all of those she wrote at Ripon Lodge between 1852 and 1854; and most of those she composed at Moor Park and Boulogne in 1855. This last batch, in which Isabella recorded Edward's passion dissolving into indifference, most powerfully established the journal's veracity. The extra material appeared in a book directed at legal specialists – Swabey and Tristram's *Reports of Cases Decided in the Court of Probate and in the Court for Divorce and Matrimonial Causes*: *Volume I* (1860) – and went unreported in the press.

After the trial, Edward was able to return to his family and his work. Isabella was left impoverished, disgraced and friendless, with the same confused desires that had propelled her into this mess: her impulse to write, her hunger for sex, her yearning for companionship, her intellectual curiosity, her wish to be with her sons.

Yet she had achieved some of her desires: she had defeated Henry, sacrificed herself for Edward, and made some amends to the women whose trust she had abused. As George Combe had recommended, she had harnessed the energies of her oversized faculties: she resisted the divorce suit because, with her Amativeness, she loved Edward Lane; because, with her Adhesiveness, she treasured her attachment to him and his family; because, with her Love of Approbation, she longed for them to respect her; and because, with her small organ of Veneration, she set no store by the social and judicial systems that required her to obey her husband or the law. By her moral code, Henry deserved to be punished and Edward, Mary and Lady Drysdale to be spared.

As she had written in her last letter to Combe, her one wish after the loss of her diary and her sons was to 'atone to this friend & his family in some degree for the serious mischief & sorrow I have so wantonly but unintentionally occasioned them'. For them, she wrote, 'I have entertained nothing but the deepest regard & gratitude, *wholly so*'. Her 'confession' that the diary was a delusion was 'the only poor reparation I have now at command'. The harm that she had inflicted on herself, and on her three boys, was, in any case, beyond fixing.

Isabella had proved herself capable of restraint and self-sacrifice: she had allowed herself in the course of the trial to be made the focus of the most fervid contemporary anxieties about suppressed female sexuality and madness. Yet her pride was not extinguished. She was still defiant as well as sorry, angry with the world as well as with herself. She was furious with Henry, whose crime in reading her journal she believed far surpassed her own in writing it, and also with a society that had sanctioned his sexual conduct while it condemned hers: 'Is the infamy of his own private life,' she asked, 'not to be taken into account?'

In August 1859, Parliament passed a further series of amendments to the Divorce Act, including a provision to protect public morality: 'The Court, when for the sake of Public Decency it shall so think fit, may hold its Sittings with closed Doors.' The doors of a court, like the covers of a diary, were sometimes best kept shut.

CHAPTER THIRTEEN

IN DREAMS THAT CANNOT BE LAID

1859 & after

After the fierce blaze of the trial, the Robinsons, the Lanes and most of their associates returned to lives of relative anonymity.

Edward Lane's reputation survived the scandal. 'I am glad to say that not one of Dr Lane's patients has given him up,' reported Charles Darwin in 1859, '& he gets a few fresh ones pretty regularly.' Darwin was finally publishing his book about evolution. The attendant anxiety brought on attacks of ill health, and with them repeated trips to Moor Park.

In 1860, Edward and Mary Lane and Lady Drysdale moved to a spa at Sudbrook Park in Richmond, Surrey, equipped with one of the first Turkish baths in Britain. By the time that Darwin took the water cure at the new premises in June that year, he had become famous: 'The controversy excited by the appearance of Darwin's remarkable work on the *Origin of Species*,' said the *Saturday Review* in May, 'has passed beyond the bounds of the study and lecture room into the drawing room and the public street.'

Edward continued to promote the benefits of good diet, clean air, plentiful exercise and hot and cold water. He had published a book on the subject – *Hydropathy; or, the Natural*

System of Medical Treatment: an Explanatory Essay – in 1857, and he followed this with *Medicine Old and New* in 1873 and a pamphlet, *Hygienic Medicine*, in 1885. It is likely that the Drysdale family forgave him his entanglement with Isabella Robinson, just as they had forgiven George when his sexual urges prompted him to fake his own death in the 1840s. Mary and Edward's relationship had been forged in the pain and sadness of George's breakdown, and Lady Drysdale knew how to welcome home a prodigal son.

The novelist Catherine Crowe, who had withdrawn from the public eye after her naked escapade in Edinburgh, visited Sudbrook Park in December 1860. She found Lady Drysdale 'as young and jolly as ever'. Though Mrs Crowe was apparently restored to sanity, she still communed with spirits: 'the Love of my youth, and indeed the love of all my life . . . protects me and takes care of me', she confided in a letter to a friend that winter. 'I am perfectly willing to take the eternal vows and he says the same of himself. I wd at any time have forsaken all the world for him and would now if her were "*in the human*", that's what he calls being in the body.' She was in love with a ghost.

John Thom secured a job at the monthly newspaper *Home News*, run by Edward's patient Robert Bell and distributed in India and Australia. But after a couple of years in a damp City office he decided to migrate to Australia himself. Charles Darwin contributed £20 towards his travel costs, and Thom sailed for Queensland in 1863.

Edward and Mary's eldest son, Atty, died at Sudbrook Park in 1878 aged twenty-nine, after a lifetime of ill health. The family moved the next year to Harley Street, a Georgian terrace in Marylebone renowned for its specialist physicians. They remained there for the next decade. Lady Drysdale died in 1887, aged one hundred, bequeathing a substantial fortune of £47,000 to her children. When Edward and then Mary followed her – in 1889 and 1891, aged sixty-six and sixty-eight – they left their money to their sons William and Sydney, both stockbrokers. Their youngest, Walter, had been removed from his father's will in 1888, for 'certain family considerations'.

George and Charles Drysdale practised together as doctors in London into the twentieth century, lobbying all the while for women's suffrage, contraception and freer sexual relations. George repeatedly revised and reprinted the radical book about sex that he had written as a medical student, known after 1861 as *The Elements of Social Science*. Charles became the spokesman for the brothers' beliefs. He edited *The Malthusian* magazine and wrote dozens of books and pamphlets on venereal disease, poverty, prostitution and overpopulation.

Neither George nor Charles married but both lived with women. Charles had two sons with Alice Vickery, one of the first women in England to obtain a medical degree. George shared a house in Bournemouth, Dorset, with Susannah Spring, a widow listed in the 1901 census as his housekeeper, to whom he bequeathed two properties in the town. After George's death in 1904, Charles revealed that his older brother was the author of *The Elements of Social Science*, which was now in its thirty-fifth edition and had sold 90,000 copies. It had been published anonymously, Charles said, to protect their mother from scandal. Charles died three years later.

After the Robinson trial, Sir Cresswell Cresswell remained in charge of the Divorce Court for a further four years, acquiring a reputation as a friend to married women. 'Sir Cresswell Cresswell represents 5,000,000 of English wives,' ran a piece in *Once a Week* in 1860. 'Brother husbands! We are betrayed!' By the time that he died in July 1863, after a fall from his horse, he had ruled on more than a thousand matrimonial cases, only one of which had been reversed on appeal. Lord Palmerston, who in 1857 had steered the Divorce Act through Parliament, was himself cited as a co-respondent in a divorce suit four months after Cresswell's death; the case was dismissed only because it was not clear that the petitioner and respondent were married. In 1867, on the tenth anniversary of the Divorce Act, *The Times* claimed that this piece of legislation had set in motion 'one of the greatest social revolutions of our time'. The revolution in sexual attitudes precipitated by the publication of George Drysdale's book – and even of Isabella Robinson's diary extracts – was to prove no less significant.

Sir Alexander Cockburn continued to preside over celebrated cases in the law courts. On occasion he was criticised for vanity and for flaws in his logic; but he was admired for his worldly common sense as a judge. In 1864, Queen Victoria refused to give him a peerage on the grounds that he had a 'notoriously bad moral character'. He was appointed Lord Chief Justice in 1875, and died five years later, leaving most of his fortune to his illegitimate son.

It turned out that George Combe had been right to predict the sexual delinquency of the Prince of Wales. Queen Victoria believed that her husband's death in 1861 was due in part to the shock of learning that the nineteen-year-old Bertie had lost his virginity to an actress in Ireland. Over the remaining forty years of his mother's reign, the future Edward VII gained a reputation as a tireless philanderer.

Like Isabella, Combe had not had the chance to sift and sort his private papers before they fell into the hands of others. After his death in 1858, Cecy preserved his correspondence, and his trustees donated it to the National Library of Scotland in 1950. They may not have noticed – as Isabella did not notice on a first reading – that in his letters of February 1858 he had coached Mrs Robinson into pleading insanity.

Eneas Sweetland Dallas, the journalist who wrote the *Times* editorial defending Edward Lane, in 1866 published *The Gay Science*, a book that expanded on his theory of 'the human soul as double; or at least leading a double life', possessed of 'a secret flow of thought which is not less energetic than the conscious flow, an absent mind which haunts us like a ghost or a dream'. In terms that anticipated Sigmund Freud's theory of the unconscious, Dallas described an intense and wayward inner world: 'In the dark recesses of memory, in unbidden suggestions, in trains of thought unwittingly pursued, in multiplied waves and currents all at once flashing and rushing, in dreams that cannot be laid . . . we have glimpses of a great tide of life ebbing and flowing, rippling and rolling and beating about where we cannot see it'. Fifty or a hundred years later, Isabella might have located the source of her turbulence and desire in this wild and ungovernable secret realm, rather than in her organ of Amativeness or in uterine disease. Later still, in a return to the principles that had guided George Combe, neurologists would argue that the origins of mania and depression might be physiological after all.

Eneas Sweetland Dallas's marriage fell apart in 1867 when his wife, Isabella Glyn Dallas, accused him of adultery after reading a letter that he had written to another woman. He denied the charge and demanded that Mrs Dallas sign a document saying that her accusations were based on insane delusions. When she refused, he left her. Seven years later she petitioned for a divorce on the grounds of her husband's desertion and adultery and was briefly interned in Holloway prison because she refused to give up documents pertaining to the case. Unlike Isabella Robinson, Isabella Dallas managed to hold on to her private papers, but she surrendered her liberty in their place. The divorce was none the less granted.

Two of the female authors who had frequented Moor Park went on to write novels about diaries. Georgiana Craik, with whom Darwin had sparred, published *My First Journal* in 1860. The novel opens with the eleven-year-old narrator's uncle giving her a diary bound in scarlet, an initiation into the adult world. Having encouraged her to record her thoughts and feelings, he attempts to read what she has written. 'Uncle

Robert . . . tried to peep over my shoulder, and see what I was saying, but I wouldn't let him, and shut up the book, and then he tried to steal it away from me, and I held it so tight he couldn't get it, and we had such laughing about it.' Dinah Mulock (who later married Miss Craik's cousin George Lillie Craik, a man fifteen years her junior) wrote *A Life for a Life* (1859), a 'double diary' that alternated the narratives of a woman and the doctor with whom she falls in love. At the end of the novel, the female diarist's new husband urges her to throw her journal into the sea, but she is reluctant: 'It would feel something like dropping a little child into this "wild and wandering grave".'

Wilkie Collins had already used secret diaries as vehicles for his stories, and in *The Woman in White* (1860) he included a scene of a diary's discovery: when Marian Halcombe succumbs to a delirious fever, Count Fosco opens her journal and reads of her hatred of him. In *Armadale* (1866), Collins took up the question of why a woman would preserve a record of her dark deeds. 'Why do I keep a diary at all?' asks his villainous heroine Lydia Gwilt. 'Why did the clever thief the other day (in the English newspaper) keep the very thing to convict him in the shape of a record of everything he stole? Why are we not perfectly reasonable in all that we do? Why am I not always on my guard and never inconsistent with myself, like a wicked character in a novel? Why? Why? Why? I don't care why! . . . There's a reason that nobody can answer – myself included.'

The brooding, dreaming, dissatisfied wife became a mainstay of the 'sensation novels' of the 1860s. 'It is curious,' observed Eneas Sweetland Dallas in 1866, 'that one of the earliest results of an increased feminine influence in our literature should be a display of what in women is most unfeminine.' Dinah Mulock defended books about 'lost women': it was better to read such stories, she contended, than 'be swaddled up for ever in the folds of silken falsehood'.

Many of the unhappy heroines of these novels merely dreamt of escape, but Mrs Henry Wood's bestseller *East Lynne*, serialised between 1860 and 1861, gave an unsettlingly sympathetic portrait of a wife who acted upon her adulterous wishes. Lady Isabel Carlyle, having married a country solicitor, becomes increasingly infatuated with a 'fascinating' young man, for whom she can no more suppress her desire 'than she could suppress her own sense of being'. When separated from the object of her obsession, 'a miserable feeling of apathy stole over her: a feeling as if all whom she loved in the world had died, leaving her living and alone. It was a painful depression, this vacuum in her heart which was making itself felt in its keen intensity.' Lady Isabel is tormented by her dreams: 'Oh, those dreams! They were painful to awake from; painful from the contrast they presented to reality; and equally painful to her conscience, in its striving after what was right.' She betrays her husband in Boulogne-sur-mer. When he learns of her infidelity, he divorces her. She is haunted for the rest of her life by her longing for her children.

Henry Robinson was enraged by the Divorce Court's verdict: the trial had left him out of pocket, humiliated, and saddled with a wife who, as the world now knew, despised him. The impression that the diaries had made upon him, he said, could never be eradicated: he would always believe that Isabella was an adulteress or at the very least 'an adulteress in her heart'. Still pursuing his claims to the point of obsession, he appealed to the House of Lords in 1859 to overturn the verdict, but after two years was forced to back down because he was unable to afford the expense – a projected £400–£500 – of copying the legal proceedings and the journal afresh. When ordered to pay Isabella's costs in the aborted case, he resisted. His position, he told the appeals committee, was one of 'great hardship', his business with the West Indies having incurred heavy losses during the civil war in North America.

The scandal had left Isabella estranged from her mother as well as her friends. Shortly after the discovery of the diary in 1856, Bridget Walker made a will in which she left her small personal estate (of less than £2,000) to her sons Frederick and Christian and her younger daughter Julia, the wife of Albert Robinson. The will made no mention of Isabella. Early in 1859, Bridget wrote a letter to Christian's infant son in which she emphasised the importance of shoring up intellectual endeavour with faith: 'little Children & their kind Teachers must take all the pains they can *to teach* & *to learn*; but they must not forget to pray to their Father in Heaven, to bless their labours'. When Bridget died in May that year, the Ashford Court estate passed to Frederick. It afterwards fell to him, as Isabella's trustee and legal representative, to fight Henry on her behalf. Frederick filed a Bill in the Court of Chancery for the return of the railway stock that Henry had bought with Isabella's money. Henry responded by insisting that Isabella had agreed that he purchase the stock and hold it in trust for their sons.

In her small rented cottage in Reigate, Isabella took two lodgers: Joseph Humphrey, a local carpenter in his thirties; and Emily Lucretia Wright, a four-year-old girl whose parents and brothers lived next door. Through this arrangement, Isabella gained a little extra income, as well as the company of a younger man and a child. In reply to the queries of the census-taker in 1861, she gave her marital status as 'widow' and knocked five years off her age. She continued to support Alfred, though he was often away from home – in the early 1860s he was apprenticed to marine engineers, first in Liverpool and then in Bolton, Lancashire. Her income rose by £30 in 1860, when she agreed to let Henry keep the railway stock that he had bought with her money on condition that he pay her the dividends; but by 1861 she had managed to pay only £100 of the £636 that she owed for the divorce trial.

Henry sold Balmore House in 1861, and rented two properties in London: a house in Talbot Square, Marylebone, where Otway and Stanley stayed with him in the holidays; and an office in Park Street, near Hyde Park, in which he employed a nephew, Tom Waters.

Otway left Tonbridge School in 1861, aged sixteen, and promptly fled his father's house to move in to his mother's cottage in Reigate. Henry was furious: 'contrary and in defiance' of his wishes, he said, Isabella had 'secretly exercised an influence' on Otway, and 'induced' the boy to run away. Alfred, said Henry, had connived in Otway's escape. When Otway turned seventeen in March 1862, he was entitled by law to choose where he lived. He remained with his mother.

In 1863, seven years after he began hiring agents to gather evidence against his wife, Henry at last obtained the proof of adultery that he required. A lawyer's clerk called Louis Philip Vincent and a man called William Lines witnessed her sharing a room with a man at the Victoria Hotel in London on 19 and 20 June 1863; and another room, with the same man, at the Grosvenor Hotel on 27 June. The splendid Victoria Hotel, built in 1839, flanked the great Doric arch in front of Euston Square railway station; the Grosvenor, which dated from 1861, was a more modern and equally opulent establishment near Victoria station, equipped with a hydraulic elevator, or 'rising room'. Isabella denied adultery, but Justice James Wilde, who, after Cresswell's death, had become Judge Ordinary of the Divorce Court, decreed in June 1864 that the case was sufficiently proved. With no press coverage at all, the Robinsons' marriage was dissolved on 3 November 1864.

The events of the past few years had not stopped Isabella from pursuing her desires, but they may have encouraged her to choose her partners more carefully. Her paramour in the hotel rooms in 1863 was Eugene Le Petit, the tutor with whom she had been besotted in Boulogne. Le Petit had no reputation to lose in England, and after the assignations in

London was able to return to France and resume his life as a teacher. He played no part in the divorce proceedings. In Boulogne in the 1860s, he tutored the son of an Irish nobleman and in the 1870s conducted a survey of local primary schools.

At fifty-eight, Henry Robinson was at last free to take another wife. In Dublin in May 1865 he married Maria Arabella Long, the twenty-four-year-old daughter of a former registrar of the Irish Court of Chancery. He was one of forty-eight divorced men to remarry that year. Having set up and sold on a company to run steam packets in Singapore and Batavia in the early 1860s, he continued to negotiate the sale of sugar mills from his office in London. His nieces, the daughters of a sister who lived in Brighton, recalled that their brother Tom had a 'horror' of working at Uncle Henry's office, 'and no wonder'. Henry reneged on a promise to help fund Tom's passage to the Far East, where Albert Robinson was establishing an iron works (in Shanghai) and a dockyard (in Yokohama, Japan). He showed little loyalty even to his ailing and forgetful father. Unlike the kindly Albert, one of the nieces noted, 'HOR will not trouble to do anything for the poor old man'. Henry's sister Helena and her daughters referred to him privately as 'the Turk'.

Stanley, the youngest of Henry and Isabella's children, was permitted little contact with his mother. He had a difficult adolescence. He often stayed with his widowed aunt, Helena Waters, in Brighton in the early 1860s, but she and her daughters found him a burden. On a visit to their house during the school holidays, he was said to have propositioned one of the female lodgers. In November 1863, when Henry had just filed his second divorce petition, Helena wrote to one of her daughters that Stanley 'seems very anxious to come back to us, poor child, and I shall not like to refuse to take him – but would much rather he was safe with someone else as he is a great care and trouble to me'. A month later she reported: 'Stanley has gone to his

Pater to London, and I hope will not return to me – latterly I have found him *very* unmanageable.' Henry transferred Stanley from Tonbridge School to the Edinburgh Academy the next year. He disappears from the record after his graduation in 1866 – he may have left England to join one of the several Robinson enterprises overseas.

In the late 1860s, Henry moved back to Edinburgh with his new wife, and took over a yard in Glasgow on the River Clyde, which was replacing the Thames as the centre of iron shipbuilding. In 1869 he patented a design to improve the operation of dredgers, boats that used a revolving ladder of buckets to heave mud and silt off the riverbed.

Isabella left Reigate in the late 1860s and moved into a rented house on the village green in Frant, Kent. Henry's sister Helena was living a few miles away, having moved with her family from Brighton to Tunbridge Wells. Despite all the disclosures of the diary and the court, Helena and her children seemed to think more highly of Isabella than of Henry. In April, one of Helena's daughters wrote in the family journal that she had received a letter from Isabella: 'a splendid letter writer!' she reported, 'and whatever her faults may be [she] is a good mother to her sons. I cannot but feel much interested for her.' Helena invited Isabella to call on them. On 4 April, Helena's son Ernest wrote in the family journal: 'Mrs Robinson (Stanley's Mother) came at Mother's invitation to see us on Saturday and stayed to tea, having walked in from Frant a distance of about three and a half miles. I went down to the Station with her in the evening.' On a return visit to her house in Frant, Ernest met Alfred, who had now qualified as a marine engineer.

In 1874, Alfred, at thirty-three, married the eighteen-year-old Rosine Cooper, the daughter of a silversmith. Two years after that he went into partnership with his younger half-brother Otway who, after dabbling in the cotton business in the 1860s, had joined the Merchant Navy. Otway and Alfred bought and sailed iron cargo ships: they purchased the *Trocadero*, the *Frascati*, the *Alcazar* and the *Valentino* in South Shields in the 1870s, and the *Harley* in Glasgow in the 1880s. Otway sometimes acted as master of the vessels, and Alfred as first engineer.

Henry moved back down to England, and by 1876 was living in Norwood, Surrey. 'He has become quite an old broken down man,' reported a niece. 'He has almost lost his memory.' Henry's business, too, was faltering – 'the firm is not making a penny just now' – and in 1877, Tom Waters broke with his uncle: 'He could not stand his idiotic interferences any longer.' The second Mrs Robinson, to whom Henry's sister Helena referred as 'poor little "Marie",' bore her husband three sons.

Isabella, restless as ever and perhaps pursued by her reputation, moved from Frant to St Leonards-on-Sea, Sussex, and then to a house called Fairlight in Bromley, Kent.

Each of the famous fictional adulteresses of the nineteenth century – Flaubert's Emma Bovary, Tolstoy's Anna Karenina and Zola's Thérèse Raquin – died at her own hand, her sins having engulfed her in grief and shame. Isabella too was killed by her own hand, though in less sensational circumstances. At her house in Bromley on 20 September 1887 she discovered an infected abscess on one of her thumbs. Three days later she died of septicemia, with Otway at her side. On the death certificate, he gave her age as seventy, and her marital status as widow. That December, Henry died in Dublin aged eighty.

Isabella left everything to Otway – she had made her will in 1864, soon after he alienated himself from his father by running away to join her. Otway did not marry. When he died in the seaside town of Whitstable, Kent, in 1930, aged eighty-five, he bequeathed his land and cottages and furniture (worth about £6,000) to a friend and neighbour called Alfred Harvey. He stated in his will that he wished to leave the remainder of his estate – about £7,000 – to the German conscripts wounded in the First World War; and, if that proved impossible, to those soldiers injured by British forces in the Boer War. He told Harvey that he was 'fed up with England', a phrase that *Time* magazine used as a headline when it ran a short article about Captain Robinson's unusual bequest. Otway's sympathies lay with the soldiers of countries defeated by the British Empire: men who, like him, had been dragged into wars of others' making and left hurt and humiliated by fights that they had not started.

The original diaries and the copies made of them were, as far as we know, destroyed.

CODA

DO YOU ALSO PAUSE TO PITY?

In a court of law, the value of Isabella's diary was dubious. Like any book of its kind, it was a work of anticipation as much as memory – it was provisional and unsteady, existing at the edge of thought and act, wish and deed. But as a piece of raw emotional testimony, it was a startling work, an awakening or an alarm. The diary gave its Victorian readers a flash of the future, as it gives us a flicker of our own world taking shape in the past. It may not tell us, for certain, what happened in Isabella's life, but it tells us what she wanted.

Isabella's journal offered a glimpse of the freedoms to which women might aspire if they gave up their belief in God and in marriage – rights to possessions and money, to the custody of children, to sexual and intellectual adventure. It also hinted at the pain and confusion that such freedoms would entail. In the decade in which the Church relinquished its control over marriage and Darwin threw into deeper doubt the spiritual origins of mankind, her journal was a sign of the tumult to come.

In an undated diary entry, Isabella explicitly addressed a future reader. 'One week of a new year already gone,' she began. 'Ah! If *I* had the hope of another life of which my mother speaks (she and my brother wrote kindly this day), and which Mr B urged us to secure, all would be bright and well with me. But, alas! I have it not, nor can possibly obtain *that*; and as to this life, anger, sensuality, helplessness, hopelessness, overpower and rend my soul, and fill me with remorse and foreboding.'

'Reader,' she wrote, 'you see my inmost soul. You must despise and hate me. Do you also pause to pity? No; for when you read these pages all will be over with one who was "too flexible for virtue; too virtuous to make a proud, successful villain".' Isabella was quoting loosely from Hannah More's play *The Fatal Falsehood* (1779), in which a young Italian count – a 'compound of strange, contradicting parts' – falls desperately in love with a woman promised to his best friend.

When Edward Lane first read the diary, this entry in particular drew his anger and scorn: 'The address to the Reader!' he wrote to Combe. '*Who is* the Reader? Was this precious journal, then, intended for publication, or if not quite so bad as that, was it meant for an heirloom for her family? On either supposition, I say there is clear madness here – and if there were not another passage in the whole farrago to warrant that view, to my mind this one alone wd be sufficient.'

Yet Isabella's address to an imagined reader might, on the contrary, point to the clearest explanation of all for why she kept her diary. Part of her, at least, wanted to be heard. She harboured a hope that somebody considering her words after her death would hesitate before damning her; that her story might one day be met with compassion, even love. In the absence of a spiritual afterlife, we were the only future she had.

'Good night,' she ended, with a desolate blessing: 'May you be more happy!'

NOTES

Abbreviations used in the Notes and Bibliography

CD – Charles Darwin
EWL – Edward Wickstead Lane
GC – George Combe
HOR – Henry Oliver Robinson
IHR – Isabella Hamilton Robinson
Lady D – Lady Drysdale
MD – Mary Drysdale
RC – Robert Chambers

HLA – House of Lords Archives, London
NA – The National Archives, London
NLS – National Library of Scotland, Edinburgh
NPG – National Portrait Gallery, London
ODNB – The Oxford Dictionary of National Biography (2004)
WG – Williams/Gray Papers, Tairawhiti Museum and Art Gallery, Gisborne, New Zealand

BOOK I: THIS SECRET FRIEND

CHAPTER 1: HERE I MAY GAZE AND DREAM

3 *they moved to Edinburgh that autumn.* The Robinsons arrived in the city with letters of introduction from the wife of Henry's former colleague John Scott Russell. See letter GC to Sir James Clark, 19 Dec 1857. This and all subsequent letters to and from George Combe are held in the Combe Collection, an archive at the NLS.

4 *A servant let Isabella in to the building . . . and shining shoes.* Account of Lady Drysdale's party based on brief references in

IHR's journal, quoted in court on 14 Jun 1858, along with information from Cecil Cunnington's *English Women's Clothing in the Nineteenth Century* (1952), Penelope Byrde's *Nineteenth-Century Fashion* (1992); pictures of the exteriors of the houses at Royal Circus in the early-nineteenth century and plans and personal observation of the interiors; weather reports in the *Scotsman* of 4 Dec 1850; and description of the New Town, including its lighting, in John Stark's *Picture of Edinburgh* (1823). Robert Chambers also refers to the party in his diary, RC papers, NLS.

4 *an 'uncongenial partner . . . selfish, proud'*. IHR's journal, 14 Mar 1852. This and all subsequent diary entries are taken from the extracts printed in M. C. Merttins Swabey DCL and Thomas Hutchinson Tristram DCL, *Reports of Cases Decided in the Court of Probate and in the Court for Divorce and Matrimonial Causes: Vol. I* (1860).

4 *'a man who had only a commercial life'*. Letter IHR to GC, 26 Feb 1858.

5 *'my errors of youth . . . as a friend, as a mistress'*. IHR's journal, Nov 1850.

5 *'Thou know'st that thou has made me . . .'*. Burns's 'A Prayer in the Prospect of Death', circa 1781–82. Isabella slightly misquoted the original, adding a hint of compulsion to the line 'Thou knowst that thou has formed me' by replacing 'formed' with 'made'.

5 *She was born in Bloomsbury, London . . .* According to the St Pancras parish records, she was christened on 8 May 1813.

6 *'a large pretty Garden . . . Dogs & Cats & Kittens'*. Letter from Bridget Christian Walker to her grandson Thomas Walker, 3 Jan 1859. Private collection (Ruth Butler, née Walker).

6 *The house was set in 230 acres . . . rented out the rest.* Information on the Walkers' estate at Ashford Carbonel from Phyllis M. Ray's *Ashford Carbonel: a Peculiar Parish; A Brief History* (1998).

6 *Isabella and her seven siblings . . .* These were: John Curwen, born 1811; Harriet Elizabeth, born 1815; Caroline, born 1817; Julia, born 1818; Charles Henry, born 1822; Charles Frederick, born 1823; Christian Henry James, born 1831.

Another brother, James Burrough, was born in 1825 but died in the same year. See parish records of St Mary's Church, Ashford Carbonel. A sister, also Isabella, had died as a baby in 1810 – her death was reported in *Jackson's Oxford Journal*, 27 Oct 1810.

6 *'an independent & constant thinker'*. Letter IHR to GC, 24 Oct 1852.

6 *The ceremony . . . up the hill from her house.* Parish records of St Mary's Church, Ashford Carbonel.

6 *a widowed Royal Navy lieutenant of forty-three.* He was born in 1794 and joined the Navy in 1815, according to the *Navy List* (1835).

6 *'headstrong passion'*. IHR's journal, 29 Jan 1855.

6 *He brought . . . £6,000 to the marriage.* According to the will made by his father, Richard Dansey.

7 *This capital . . . about £900 a year.* Isabella's funds yielded more than £400 a year, and the income from Edward Dansey's larger settlement would have exceeded this.

7 *Alfred Hamilton Dansey, in February 1841.* Alfred was born on 21 Mar 1841, according to his birth certificate, and christened in St Lawrence's Church, Ludlow, two days later.

7 *Ludlow 'had balls . . . love affairs there'*. See Henry James's *Castles and Abbeys* (1877).

7 *The Danseys' house . . . down to the River Teme.* David Lloyd's *Broad Street: Its Houses and Residents through Eight Centuries* (2001).

7 *Isabella . . . installed at the heart of Shropshire society.* In the census of May 1841, three servants were listed as resident in their house.

7 *'Poor Mr Dansey . . . this most painful of all trials'*. Letter from Bridget Walker to her brother Henry Curwen, 18 Dec 1841, Curwen archive, Cumbria Record Office and Library, Whitehaven, Cumbria.

7 *Dansey died of 'a diseased brain'*. According to his death certificate, he died on 11 May 1842.

7 *a young lieutenant with the Royal Bombay Fusiliers.* Celestin Edward Dansey was born to Edward Dansey's first wife, a Frenchwoman, in France in 1824. He married in 1851 and died in 1859.

7 *Isabella inherited nothing.* Edward Dansey's will, made at the Queen's Hotel, Cheltenham, on 27 Jan 1840, and proved in London in Jun 1842.

8 *produced 8,000 gallons of spirits a year.* See *Accounts and Papers relating to Customs and Excise, Imports and Exports, Shipping and Trade, 1831–32, House of Commons Papers,* Vol. 34.

8 *fast-growing profession . . . about 900 engineers in Britain.* See R. A. Buchanan's 'Gentlemen Engineers: the Making of a Profession', in *Victorian Studies*, Vol. 26 (1983). According to the *Daily News* of 3 Aug 1854, Henry and Albert went into business with their father in 1838. When Henry was elected an associate of the Institution of Civil Engineers in 1841, he was sharing a terrace house near Waterloo station with his father, James, and his mother, Jane (census returns of 1841). In the *Post Office Directory* of 1843 Henry was listed as a civil engineer for the colonies with an office at 10 Old Jewry, Cheapside. For details of his parents' early life, see Arthur William Patrick Buchanan's book about the family of Henry's mother, who was born Jane Buchanan: *The Buchanan Book: the Life of Alexander Buchanan, QC, of Montreal, Followed by an Account of the Family of Buchanan* (1911).

8 *'I suffered my scruples . . . wedlock like one fated.'* Letter IHR to GC, 26 Feb 1858.

8 *After a wedding . . .* They were married by the Dean of Hereford at St Peter's Church in St Owen's, Hereford. Isabella and Henry's fathers were witnesses to the marriage. Isabella gave as her address Henry's sister's house in the parish of St Owen's. Henry gave his parish as St Pancras in London.

8 *was born . . . just under a year later.* Charles Otway Robinson was born at 78 Camden Road Villas on 20 Feb 1845, according to his birth certificate.

8 *Henry and his brother Albert . . . boats and mills on site.* By 1845, Henry was established at Millwall – in September he took on an apprentice, a Hereford boy called Henry James. See Lord Askwith's *Lord James of Hereford* (1930). According to the census of 1851, Albert Robinson employed 700 men at Millwall. See also *Survey of London,* Vol. 33/34. Scott Russell helped to organise the Great Exhibition of international

industry in Hyde Park in 1851, at which the company displayed sugar mills and models of their steamships.

8 *In one project . . . under his supervision.* The Ganges project is described in Albert Robinson's *Account of Some Recent Improvements in the System of Navigating the Ganges by Iron Steam Vessels* (1848).

9 *In 1848 the Robinson brothers . . . a decade earlier).* See A. J. Arnold's *Iron Shipbuilding on the Thames* (2000).

9 *On the day of the* Taman's *launch . . . the river.* See *Illustrated London News*, 18 Nov 1848.

9 *Henry's marriage . . . his wife's property.* Henry's property at the time of his marriage, by contrast, consisted of a quantity of furniture, plate and china. Discussion of the settlement system in Mary Lyndon Shanley's 'One Must Ride Behind: Married Women's Rights and the Divorce Act of 1857', in *Victorian Studies*, Vol. 25 (1982); Mary Poovey's *Uneven Developments: the Ideological Work of Gender in Mid-Victorian England* (1988); and Lawrence Stone's *Road to Divorce: England 1530–1987* (1990). The system was designed less to protect women than to ensure that a man's grandsons would be provided for even if their father proved profligate.

9 *'a person of very imperious temper' . . . to keep accounts.* Bill of Complaint filed in the Court of Chancery by Frederick Walker, acting on IHR's behalf, on 26 Feb 1858, and HOR's answer of 17 Apr 1858, NA, C15/550/R24.

10 *higher echelons of the upper middle classes.* According to an analysis of the population of the United Kingdom in 1867 in R. D. Baxter's *National Income* (1868), 1.2 per cent of the population earned £300 or more. Of these, a ninth (about 50,000 people) earned £1,000 or more; the remaining eight-ninths (150,000 people) earned between £300 and £1,000, the sum required to run a home with servants. The remainder of the country – about 10 million people, or 98 per cent of the population, earned less than £300.

10 *When her father died . . . additional £1,000.* Charles Walker died on 23 Dec 1847, aged seventy-six, according to his memorial at St Mary's Church, Ashford Carbonel. In his will (proved in London on 28 Jan 1848) he confirmed settling

funds of £5,000 on Isabella, £4,500 on her younger sister Julia, and £5,400 on his youngest surviving child, Christian. The older boys had been separately provided for.

10 *London & North Western Railway stock.* This company, formed in 1846 from a merger of three existing railway companies, ran trains from Euston station to the Midlands, the North-West and Scotland.

10 *Isabella claimed that Henry . . . settled property.* Letter IHR to GC, 21 Feb 1858.

10 *'irresolute': 'chafing; yet still passive'.* Letter IHR to GC, 26 Feb 1858.

10 *'With every knowledge . . . one thing after another.'* Letter IHR to GC, 21 Feb 1858.

10 *At the time of his birth she was . . .* According to his birth certificate, he was born at 19 Cannon Place on 6 Feb 1849. 'Stanley', the name by which he was known, was the maiden name of the wife of Isabella's uncle Henry Curwen.

10 *identified her ailments as signs of 'uterine disease'.* Testimony of Joseph Kidd in *Robinson v Robinson & Lane*, 16 Jun 1858.

10 *Henry was away on business . . .* The dissolution of his partnership with Scott Russell was reported in *The Law Times*, 17 Apr 1849.

10 *Isabella began to keep a diary . . .* According to HOR's counsel in *Robinson v Robinson & Lane*, 14 Jun 1858.

10 *'I know not where . . . ray of comfort I possess.'* IHR's journal, 27 Mar 1852.

11 *a bond 'of* no common *strength'.* Letter IHR to GC, 21 Feb 1858.

11 *renowned for its liberal and moderately priced schools.* According to Adam and Charles Black's *Black's Guide Through Edinburgh* (1851), the educational establishments 'attract many strangers who desire to secure for their families a liberal education at a moderate expense'.

11 *Here, their boys could be . . .* Letter GC to Sir James Clark, 19 Dec 1857.

11 *at a cost of about £150 a year.* To rent a house in Moray Place cost between £140 and £160 a year in 1844, according to *Black's Guide* (1851). K. Theodore Hoppen's *The*

Mid-Victorian Generation, 1846–1886 (1998) estimates that the middle classes spent an average of 10 per cent of their income on rent.

11 *The Robinsons kept four servants* . . . In the Scottish census returns of 1851, in which the family is listed as 'Robertson', the servants at 11 Moray Place were Andrew McIntosh, Agnes Thomson, Eliza Power and Mary Graham. This number of servants more or less accorded with the family's income. According to Mrs Beeton's *Book of Household Management* (1861), a household with £1,000 a year would usually employ five: a cook, two housemaids, a nursemaid, and a manservant.

12 *a 'strawberry feast'*. Robert Chambers's diary, RC papers, NLS.

12 *successful lady novelists such as Susan Stirling.* A professor's daughter, she was the author of the bestselling *Fanny Hervey, or, The Mother's Choice* (1849). IHR refers to 'our mutual friend Mrs Stirling' in a letter to GC on 16 Aug 1852.

12 *according to Charles Piazzi Smyth, the Astronomer Royal for Scotland.* In a letter to a friend in 1851, quoted in Miriam Benn's *Predicaments of Love* (1992).

12 *'so warm-hearted and unselfish a woman.'* Letters from Elizabeth Rigby to John Murray, 29 Dec 1842 and to Hester Murray, 10 Feb 1843, in *The Letters of Elizabeth Rigby, Lady Eastlake* (2009), ed. Julie Sheldon.

12 *Lady Drysdale was a keen philanthropist . . . marriage.* Among the Italian exiles in Lady Drysdale's circle was G. B. Nicolini, an ardent Republican who was preparing a coruscating history of the Jesuits. IHR refers to him in a diary entry of 31 Aug 1852. Lady Drysdale's enthusiasm for Polish refugees is noted in Lady Priestley's *The Story of a Lifetime* (1908).

12 *A photograph of Henry . . . nose in a long face.* Photograph in collection of Robinson family.

13 *Isabella said . . . illegitimate daughters.* Letter IHR to GC, 21 Feb 1858.

13 *Within months . . . the Drysdales almost every day.* EWL's testimony to Divorce Court, 26 Nov 1858.

13 *'to parse & interpret any line of poetry . . . or other people's!'* Letter IHR to GC, 26 Feb 1858.

13 *Edward, in turn, often invited Isabella . . . play on the rocks and sand.* Letters GC to Jane Tennant and Sir James Clark, 28 Dec 1857 and 4 Jan 1858.

14 *'the port of Leith, the Frith . . .'.* The Firth of Forth, where the River Forth flows into the North Sea, was more usually known as the Frith of Forth until the 1860s.

14 *'Oh, thought I . . . more weary of life.'* Her description was echoed in a passage in Charles Dickens's *A Tale of Two Cities*, published in 1859, which suggested 'that every one of those darkly clustered houses encloses its own secret; that every room in every one of them encloses its own secret; that every beating heart in the hundreds of thousands of breasts there, is, in some of its imaginings, a secret to the heart nearest it!'

14 *If she and Henry were to part . . . she was of good character.* See Kelly Hager's *Dickens and the Rise of Divorce* (2010).

15 *to smoke a cigar . . . a distinctly rebellious, unfeminine act.* As *Blackwood's Edinburgh Magazine* put it in an article earlier that year, 'a man, when he sees his wife after dinner cross her legs, put her feet on the fender and smoke a cigar, will have, to say the least, sensations of doubt'. See article on 'bloomerism', the phenomenon of women wearing bloomers instead of skirts, cited in Karen Chase and Michael Levenson's *The Spectacle of Intimacy: a Public Life for the Victorian Family* (2000).

15 *They discussed an essay by Edward . . .* 'Pronouncers', an unsigned article collected in *Chambers's Edinburgh Journal*, Vol. 17 (1852).

16 *She and Edward talked . . . Samuel Taylor Coleridge's 'Dejection: An Ode'.* This poem included a reference to the dramatist Thomas Otway, after whom Isabella may have named her second son.

17 *'My mind is a chaos . . . I weary of my very self, yet cannot die.'* Isabella's words echoed a line in Alfred Tennyson's 'Mariana' (1830), in which the lonely maiden pines for her lover: 'I am aweary, aweary,/ I would that I were dead!'.

18 *This was one of a series of talks . . .* See Anna M. Stoddart's *John Stuart Blackie* (1895).

18 *an 'elastic and buoyant' public speaker . . .* Quoted in Stuart Wallace's *John Stuart Blackie: Scottish Scholar and Patriot* (2006), p. 142.

19 *At the party at Royal Circus . . . swathes of wavy hair.* Engraving of Robert Chambers in the 1840s by D. J. Pound, after John Jabez Edwin Mayallin, in the NPG.

19 *The next May . . . young actress Isabella Glyn.* For IHR's social engagements with RC, see RC's diary, RC papers, NLS.

19 *'Lines Addressed to a Miniature, By a Lady,' appeared under the initials 'IHR'.* Collected in *Chambers's Edinburgh Journal,* Vol. 16 (1852).

CHAPTER 2: POOR DEAR DODDY

21 *Edward Wickstead Lane . . . Terrebonne, Quebec.* His parents, Elisha Lane and Harriet Wickstead, married at Christ Church Cathedral in Montreal on 27 Mar 1819.

21 *When Edward was nine . . .* Arthur Benjamin Lane was born on 28 Jan 1828, and christened at the Holy Trinity Church in Quebec. Harriet Lane died on 19 Apr 1832, aged thirty. See *The Lower Canada Jurist,* Vol. 8 (1864).

21 *Elisha Lane . . . built up a business . . .* In 1851 he clubbed together with three other Presbyterian wholesalers to build a Free Church in Montreal, an offshoot of the reformed Church established in Edinburgh by the Rev. Thomas Guthrie. See www.eglisesdequebec.org.

21 *Within a decade his company had assets . . .* The company was Gibb & Lane; see entry on James Gibb in Frances G. Halpenny and Jean Hamelin's *Dictionary of Canadian Biography,* Vol. 8 (1985).

21 *The Lane boys lodged . . .* They and nine other boys were lodging with a Mr and Mrs Morrison at 24 Northumberland Street in 1841, according to the census returns.

21 *Edward won prizes for his achievements . . .* Prizes listed in the *Caledonian Mercury,* 1 Aug 1840.

22 *Afterwards . . . he won six prizes in his first year.* See *Caledonian Mercury,* 7 May 1842.

22 *Edward read Law at Edinburgh University . . .* EWL was elected to the Speculative Society on 15 Nov 1842, and granted extraordinary membership in 1845. See *The History of the Speculative Society 1764–1904* (1905).

22 *George's parents, Sir William* . . . William Drysdale was knighted in 1842.

22 *These concerned George* . . . George Drysdale's biography is drawn from Tomoko Sato's 'George and Charles Drysdale in Edinburgh' in *Journal of Tsuda College Tokyo*, Vol. 12 (1980) and Benn's *Predicaments of Love.* Sato first wrote about George's crisis of the 1840s in 'George Drysdale's Supposed Death and *The Elements of Social Science*' published in Japanese of the *Hitotsubashi Ronsu*, Vol. 78, (1977). His story is also discussed in Gowan Dawson's *Darwin, Literature and Victorian Respectability* (2007) and Michael Mason's *The Making of Victorian Sexuality* (1994). First-hand accounts of George's life are in his *The Elements of Social Science* and Charles Drysdale's 'Memoir of the Author' in the edition of 1904.

22 *George was at university in Glasgow* . . . Letter from William Copland (Lady Drysdale's son from a previous marriage) to John Murray, 5 Dec 1843. Murray archive, NLS.

22 *George suffered a breakdown* . . . George and Charles were the subject of a photograph taken at this period by the pioneering Edinburgh photographers Octavius Hill and Robert Adamson. George, aged about eighteen, is plumply handsome, curly-haired, brooding, leaning on a chair with a hand on his hip; he looks down and away from the camera. Charles, aged about sixteen, is sitting in front of him, thin-faced, with a high white forehead, a long lick of hair across his scalp, legs tight in checked trousers, gazing into the middle distance (calotype in the NPG).

22 *'The deceased's mother and friends . . . I almost ever knew.'* Letter from Cockburn to Francis Jeffrey, 26 Mar 1846, in *Lord Cockburn: Selected Letters* (2005), ed. Alan Bell. He was Henry Thomas Cockburn, 1779–1854, a Lord of Session and of Justiciary; not to be confused with Sir Alexander James Edmund Cockburn, 1802–80, Chief Justice of the Common Pleas in 1856 and later Lord Chief Justice of England, before whom the Robinsons' divorce case was heard in 1858.

23 *But Mary . . . strengthened by the trials he has undergone'.* Letter MD to Jane Williams, 19 Mar 1846, in the 'Journals of

Jane Williams (née Reid)' at the State Library of Tasmania, NS213/1/1/2.

24 *The theory of his chosen branch of medicine* . . . Simpson described homeopathy as 'a creed which ninety-nine out of a hundred medical men deem to be utterly false'. J. Y. Simpson's *Homeopathy, its Tenets and Tendencies, Theoretical, Theological and Therapeutical* (1853).

24 *Mary reported to her friend . . . till he shd see us all once more'*. Letter MD to Jane Williams, undated but probably May 1846, State Library of Tasmania, NS213/1.

26 *In his study of involuntary ejaculation* . . . In French, *Des pertes seminales involontaires*; in English, *A Practical Treatise on the Causes, Symptoms and Treatment of Spermatorrhea.*

26 *The work of Lallemand* . . . For the spermatorrhea panic, see Ellen Bayuk Rosenman's *Unauthorised Pleasures: Accounts of Victorian Erotic Experience* (2003).

26 *Masturbation was the dark corollary* . . . See analysis of Victorian attitudes to masturbation in Thomas Laqueur's *Solitary Sex: a Cultural History of Masturbation* (2003).

26 *'been obliged to hurry home . . . he should himself forget it poor fellow'*. Letter MD to John Murray, Murray archive, NLS.

27 *'A bystander saw . . . flames hid him from sight'*. See Sir James MacPherson Le Moine's *Quebec Past and Present: a History of Quebec, 1608–1876* (1876).

27 *The ceremony took place* . . . Mary Drysdale was born at 8 Royal Circus on 24 Mar 1823, according to *Blackwood's Magazine*.

27 *Mary said that she had never seen her brother look better* . . . Undated letter from Jane Drysdale to John Murray, Murray archive, NLS.

27 *He was later remembered . . . like a vast mountain or a granite wall'*. Typescript by Florence Fenwick Miller, quoted in Benn's *Predicaments of Love*, p. 30.

28 *Mary became pregnant in Dublin* . . . Letter from Lady D to James Young Simpson, 30 Mar 1848, Royal College of Surgeons of Edinburgh Library and Archive. It did not become common to administer chloroform at childbirth until after Queen Victoria gave birth to Prince Leopold with the help of chloroform in 1853.

28 *In Dublin in 1848* . . . Scottish census return of 1851.

28 *The Royal Infirmary . . . as a result of this practice.* EWL's thesis, 'Notes on Medical Subjects, Comprising Remarks on the Constitution and Management of British Hospitals, etc.', (1853).

29 *One patient . . . an overdose of aconite.* For account of the practices in the Royal Infirmary, see Bill Yule's *Matrons, Medics and Maladies: Edinburgh Royal Infirmary in the 1840s* (1999).

29 *To combat this evil . . . Both agreed.* Letter of 23 Oct 1852 in *The Letters of Charles Dickens,* Vol. 6 (1988), ed. Madeline House, Graham Storey and Kathleen Tillotson.

29 *During his time on the wards . . . best human skill can furnish'.* In his belief in 'self-cure', Edward drew on the ideas of his friend Andrew Combe, the brother of George Combe and a celebrated physician who had died of tuberculosis in Edinburgh in 1847. Dr Combe, wrote Edward in his thesis, 'probably did more by his writings and his practice than any man of his time, to inculcate a trust in nature and natural agents in the treatment of disease as well as the preservation of health'. James Young Simpson, who secured the Chair of Obstetrics at Edinburgh with the help of Sir William Drysdale, was also a fierce advocate of hygiene in hospitals (*ODNB*).

30 *John, the homeopath . . . he claimed, great success.* See John Henry Clarke's *The Life and Times of James Compton Burnett* (1904).

30 *He was not the only object of her affections* . . . Letter GC to Sir James Clark, 19 Dec 1857.

30 *He lived in the New Town with his wife* . . . Combe was forty-five when he married the thirty-nine-year-old Cecilia Siddons in 1837; the £15,000 that she brought to the marriage allowed him to retire from the law, and instead devote himself to phrenology.

30 *'quite filial in its character'*. Letter IHR to GC, 21 Feb 1858.

30 *'the exponent of a clearer . . .'*. Letter IHR to GC, 17 Nov 1854.

30 *'a man of singular integrity . . . human beings I have ever known'*. In Fanny Kemble's *Record of a Girlhood,* Vol. 1 (1879).

31 *'I often think of you . . . with my own nature.'* Letter from Marian Evans to GC, Mar 1852, in *The George Eliot Letters, Vol. VIII, 1840–70* (1978), ed. Gordon S. Haight.

31 *Combe's book . . . published by Robert Chambers.* A volume of sales exceeded only by *Robinson Crusoe*, *Pilgrim's Progress* and the Bible, according to Harriet Martineau's obituary of Combe in the *Daily News* in Aug 1858.

31 *The cerebellum . . . fatter necks than other creatures.* See Combe's *A System of Phrenology* (1843).

31 *Another of Combe's subjects . . . will soon give trouble.'* They consulted him during the royal visit to Edinburgh in 1850, and again in 1852, when Combe made his observation about Amativeness. See David Stack's *Queen Victoria's Skull: George Combe and the Mid-Victorian Mind* (2007).

32 *'wild freshness of morning'* . . . GC's journal, 25 Jul 1857. This and all subsequent quotations from GC's journal are taken from manuscripts in the Combe Collection, NLS.

32 *Combe declined to go into further detail . . . a veritable ecstasy.'* See Combe's translation from the French of Josef Franz Gall's *On the Functions of the Cerebellum* (1838). See also Michael Shortland's 'Courting the Cerebellum: Early Organological and Phrenological Views of Sexuality', in *British Journal for the History of Science*, Vol. 20 (1987).

34 *The novelists . . . agitated me to pain sometimes.'* See Sally Shuttleworth's *Charlotte Brontë and Victorian Psychology* (1996).

35 *They took walks in the city or to the sea* . . . RC's diary, NLS.

35 *All three sailed from Hull to Sweden . . . a candle to read the time.* Ibid., and William Swan's 'On the Total Eclipse of the Sun on Jul 28, 1851, observed at Goteborg; with a description of a new Position Micrometer' in *Proceedings of the Royal Society of Edinburgh*, Vol. 3 (1857).

35 Vestiges *was condemned by many . . . and all sprung from apes.'* See James A. Secord's *Victorian Sensation: the Extraordinary Publication, Reception, and Secret Authorship of Vestiges of the Natural History of Creation* (2000).

35 *The authorship of* Vestiges *had been the subject of speculation* . . . Ibid.

36 *In his journal of 1839 . . . motions of a confined leech'*. GC's

Notes on the United States of North America, During a Phrenological Visit in 1838–40, Vol. 2 (1841).

36 *'a natural history of myself'*. Herbert Spencer's *An Autobiography* (1904).

CHAPTER 3: THE SILENT SPIDER

37 *Albert and Richard Robinson were pulling out* . . . Letter IHR to GC, 24 Oct 1852.

37 *'His advertising material . . . and then too much'*. See the advertising pamphlet 'A Description of Robinson's Steam Cane Mill' (1845) and 'Robinson's Patent Sugar Cane Mills' in *The Mechanics' Magazine*, 2 October 1841.

37 *in Tirhoot, India* . . . The Robinsons persuaded the indigo growers of Tirhoot to succumb to the sugar craze in 1845, but the planters sustained heavy losses when they discovered that their soil was not conducive to the cultivation of cane. By 1850 they had reverted to indigo. 'The Lion King stretched out his hand,' ran a local poem, 'Speaking of the cheapness of labour and the richness of land . . ./ Then things went on right jolly/ Till the district was dotted o'er with monuments of folly.' See Minden Wilson's *History of Behar Indigo Factories* (1887).

38 *For three months in 1852 . . . Welsh landscapes.'* Letter IHR to GC, 16 Aug 1852.

38 *A railway station had opened in April* . . . The line from Shrewsbury to Ludlow was completed in Apr 1852. According to Phyllis M. Ray's *A Peculiar Parish*, a station was opened at Ashford Bowdler but remained in operation for just a few years – in the census of 1861 only a crossing keeper was listed in the village. The Shrewsbury & Hereford Railway Company promised the Walker family £2,500 for five acres of land on which they built a section of railroad. See *Report of Cases Decided in the High Court of Chancery* (1853).

38 *Two of Isabella's younger siblings* . . . Julia Walker was five years younger than Isabella. According to the records of St Mary's Church, Ashford Carbonel, she was born on 22 Dec 1818, and married Albert in Jan 1849. Charles Henry died aged twelve, in 1834, according to a memorial stone in St

Mary's. Caroline was buried at St Mary's in 1838, aged twenty-one. One other sister – Harriet, born in 1815 – had probably also died. She was not mentioned in either of her parents' wills nor does her name seem to appear in census or marriage records.

39 *'There is so much bias from self-love . . .'* From 'Pronouncers', *Chambers's Edinburgh Journal,* Vol. 17 (1852).

40 *Many upper-middle-class families . . .* Andrea Broomfield's *Food and Cooking in Victorian England* (2007), pp. 65–66.

43 *Reading lay in a . . .* See *Post Office Directory of Berkshire* (1854) and *Murray's Guide to Berkshire* (1860).

43 *'like a river of blood'.* See Grace Greenwood's *Haps and Mishaps of a Tour of Europe* (1853).

43 *Isabella and the children . . . three times a week.* Letters IHR to GC, 24 Oct and 11 Dec 1852.

43 *Although her eldest . . . some amount of obstinacy'.* Letters IHR to GC, 16 Aug and 24 Oct 1852.

43 *Henry planned to establish . . . theology.* Letter HOR to GC, 25 Dec 1853.

44 *'cold as a garret . . . every corner of her heart'.* Quotes from *Madame Bovary* are taken from the first English translation, published in 1886. The translator – Karl Marx's daughter Eleanor – retained the original French word *ennui*, for which there was no direct equivalent in English. Colloquially, though, a sufferer from ennui could be described as plagued by visits from 'the blue devils', or 'the blues'. The narrator of Anna Brownell Jameson's popular novel *The Diary of an Ennuyée* (1826) gives her journal the alternative title 'the Diary of a Blue Devil'. This usage is the origin of the expressions 'to have the blues' and 'to feel blue'. See 'The Blues', in *Eliza Cook's Journal* of 1 Nov 1851 and Eric Partridge's *A Dictionary of Slang and Unconventional English,* ed Paul Beale (eighth edition, 1984).

44 *Her father, Charles . . .* Charles Walker, who was born in 1775, had been called to the Bar at Lincoln's Inn in 1801, according to James Whishaw's *A Synopsis of the Members of the English Bar* (1835). Bridget was born at Workington Hall in 1788.

45 *Charles had inherited some land . . .* Charles's father, Thomas,

had died in London in 1802, leaving most of his land in west Yorkshire and Shropshire to his eldest son, Thomas, along with two houses in Lincoln's Inn Fields (probate granted 16 Feb 1802). But in 1828 the younger Thomas died a bachelor, and left his property to Charles, substantially increasing his holdings (probate granted 28 Feb 1828).

45 *The Curwens were an ancient* . . . For Curwen and Christian family history, see John F. Curwen's *A History of the Ancient House of Curwen* (1928); Edward Hughes's *North Country Life in the Eighteenth Century* (1952); A. W. Moore's *Manx Worthies* (1901). Information about Bridget's birth and Charles and Bridget's first meeting from letter of 1911 by their youngest son, Christian Henry James Walker (private collection, Ruth Walker). In the *Cumberland News* of 4 Aug 2000, Denis Periam argues that Wilkie Collins used Ewanrigg as the model for Limmeridge Hall, the home of the heroines of *The Woman in White* (1860). Collins and Dickens toured Cumberland in 1857.

45 *Bridget's mother, Isabella* . . . Romney's portrait of Isabella Curwen, NPG.

45 *To show his fellow feeling* . . . John Christian Curwen introduced the Suffolk Horse and the Lothian plough to his district, established a herd of Shorthorn cattle and imported Merino sheep to cross with a native breed. See J. V. Beckett's entry in *ODNB*.

45 *Even her mother . . . was closed to her.* In 1841, when Isabella and most of her siblings had moved out, Ashford Court still housed three male and six female staff, according to the census returns.

45 *'many leisure hours . . . most women'*. Letter IHR to GC, 24 Oct 1852.

46 *'is a pleasant place . . . to make many agreeable ones.'* Ibid.

46 *'You do not know . . . if I dared to hint at them.'* Letter IHR to GC, 28 Feb 1854.

47 *'all is dark . . . once I quit this world'*. Ibid. In Matthew Arnold's 'Dover Beach', composed in about 1851 though not published until 1867, the doubting poet finds himself 'alone as on a darkling plain'.

47 *Isabella's loss of faith . . . the rest of her life'*. Letter EWL to GC, 17 May 1858.

47 *She said she knew . . . for avoiding blame'.* Letter IHR to GC, 16 Aug and 24 Oct 1852.

47 *Combe firmly discouraged . . . need not lead to atheism.* The Edinburgh philosopher Sir William Hamilton warned in the 1820s: 'Phrenology is implicit atheism . . . Phrenology – Physical Necessity – Materialism – Atheism – are . . . the precipitous steps of a logical transition.' 'Correspondence between Sir William Hamilton and Mr Combe' in *The Phrenological Journal and Miscellany*, Vol. 5 (1829).

47 *'does away with the usually received . . . from animal existence?'* Letter IHR to GC, 11 Dec 1852.

48 *At the very least . . . & a degree of charity.'* Letter IHR to GC, 10 Feb 1853.

48 *'There are those living . . . as they may think fit.'* Letter IHR to GC, 24 Oct 1852.

48 *'I arrive at the conclusion . . . to leave Edinburgh.'* Letter GC to Robert Tait, 16 Apr 1853.

49 *'I can safely promise . . . inclination for abstract meditations.'* Letters IHR to GC, 10 Feb and 27 May 1853. Having read the draft treatise, Isabella wrote a letter of congratulation to Combe, but she admitted that she was disappointed to find that he had stopped short of atheism. 'I,' she explained to him, 'am obliged to . . . live without the cheering belief that a great and Beneficent Ruler exists whose mind is in relation with ours. I could not reply with the perfect candor that is natural to me, unless I made this remark in speaking of your book, – & yet, I fear, it is my own fault that I do not see with you on this point.' Letter IHR to GC, 28 Feb 1854. Another of his trusted early readers, by contrast, was so horrified by the manuscript's apparent attack on immortality that he begged Combe to suppress it; Combe none the less incorporated the essay in his *The Relation between Science and Religion* (1857).

49 *'some lines of mine about . . .'.* Letter IHR to GC, 26 Feb 1858.

49 *'A Woman and Her Master' . . .* See *Chambers's Edinburgh Journal*, Vol. 19 (1853).

49 *a work of 'deep & thoughtful philosophy'.* Letter IHR to GC, 11 Dec 1852, referring to Herbert Spencer's *Social Statics; or,*

The Conditions Essential to Happiness Specified, and the First of Them Developed (1851).

49 *'the degradation . . . atmosphere of command'*. See first edition of *Social Statics*, published in 1851. That year Marian Evans met and fell in love with Herbert Spencer. He rejected her, and by the summer of 1852, Evans felt herself doomed to spinsterhood: 'You know how sad one feels when a great procession has swept by one,' she wrote to a friend, 'and the last notes of its music have died away, leaving one alone with the fields and the sky.' Spencer subsequently repudiated his proto-feminist ideas, and erased them almost completely from the edition of *Social Statics* published in 1856. See Nancy Paxton's *George Eliot and Herbert Spencer: Feminism, Evolutionism, and the Reconstruction of Gender* (1991).

50 *He had recently been granted a patent . . .* Patent sealed on 8 Apr 1853, and described in *Newton's London Journal of Arts & Sciences* in 1854.

51 *was dark where his brothers were fair . . .* GC's journal, 30 Aug 1856. Combe examined the heads of the Lane boys, noting that Arthur had large organs of Benevolence, Adhesiveness, Conscientiousness and Wonder; William, who his parents thought 'soft and dull', had large Philoprogenitiveness and Adhesiveness; while Sydney had 'large, enormous Wonder' and a small faculty of Conscientiousness: 'He will have a difficulty in keeping to truth', Combe concluded.

51 *from which Edward sent several letters to Isabella*. EWL's testimony to Divorce Court, 23 Nov 1858.

51 *its 'shady lanes' and 'murmuring river'*. *Chambers's Edinburgh Journal*, 3 Apr 1851 (EWL identified as author in authors' ledger, RC papers, NLS).

51 *On their return . . . Robinsons for a day and a night*. EWL's testimony to Divorce Court, 23 Nov 1858.

51 *'cheating November of its gloom . . . likes very much.'* Letter HOR to GC, 25 Dec 1853.

52 *her first husband's brother.* George Dansey and his wife had lived a couple of houses down the hill from Edward and Isabella in Ludlow in 1841, according to the census returns.

52 *who lived with his family in Tasmania*. John Walker was accountant to a bank in Derwent, where he was trying to establish himself as a teacher.

53 *It was, Mrs Ellis wrote . . . own houses'*. Sarah Ellis's husband was the educational reformer William Ellis, a friend of Combe. The Combes and the Ellises toured south Wales together in the summer of 1852, despite the fact that disquieting rumours about Ellis had reached Combe in Edinburgh: he was said to be 'viciously licentious in his conduct in respect to women', Combe wrote to a friend in 1850; 'he had even communicated disease to his wife'. Letter GC to M. B. Sampson, Jul 1850.

CHAPTER 4: MY IMAGINATION HEATED AS THOUGH WITH REALITIES

55 *In 1854 a new man . . .* John Thom had been previously employed as a teacher in Germany and Edinburgh. Letter IHR to GC, 28 Feb 1854.

56 *His letters . . . Isabella exchanged*. In a conversation reported in a letter from GC to Sir James Clark, 4 Jan 1858.

57 *They 'proceed from . . . impressions of the other.'* Catherine Crowe, *The Night Side of Nature* (1848), p. 42. 'One faculty, or more than one, bursts asunder the bonds which enthralled it,' wrote Robert Macnish in *The Philosophy of Sleep* (1830), 'while its fellows continue chained in sleep . . . and thereby indulges in the maddest and most extravagant thoughts.'

58 *'Dreaming all night . . . and Mr Lane.'* The entries refer to Edward as 'Mr Lane' rather than 'Dr Lane', which should suggest that they were written before he qualified in the summer of 1853; but Isabella seems not to have started to call him 'Dr' until seeing him *in situ* at his water-cure spa in the summer of 1854.

58 *'the accumulation . . . going mad'*. From 'Cassandra', written in 1852 but not published during its author's lifetime; quoted in Mark Bostridge's *Florence Nightingale* (2008), p. 372.

58 *'passional nature . . . evil of dreaming'*. In a note made on 24 Dec 1850, quoted in Bostridge's *Florence Nightingale*, p. 127.

59 *The story of Mrs Crowe's . . . to the world.* Catherine Crowe Collection, Kent University, F191882; *The Letters of Charles Dickens* and RC papers, NLS. The episode is investigated in 'Naked as nature intended? Catherine Crowe in Edinburgh, Feb 1854', a blog posted by Mike Dash on www.aforteanint-hearchives.wordpress.com on 29 Sep 2010. The Catherine Crowe Collection also contains a letter about the episode from Marian Evans to GC, which expresses sympathy for Mrs Crowe and her great friends, the Combes.

59 *At the end of May, Henry abandoned* . . . Isabella said that the school failed to win support because of local opposition to social and religious liberalism; and also because Henry was too busy in London. Letter IHR to GC, 25 Sep 1854.

61 *When Thom left the Robinsons'* . . . By the mid-nineteenth century, the neighbourhood's cachet had declined a little, chiefly because of the ugly new military camp at Aldershot, and it had become affordable to entrepreneurs such as Smethurst and Lane. Smethurst set up his establishment at Moor Park in 1851, when he took out advertisements in *The Lancet* and *The Critic*. He was later to be tried for bigamy and murder.

61 *Thom accepted Isabella's suggestion* . . . Letter from Mary Butler to CD, Dec 1862. For this and subsequent letters to and from Charles Darwin, see Darwin's correspondence database online at www.darwinproject.ac.uk.

61 *The consultation fee* . . . Information from 'Moor Park Hydropathic Establishment [a Prospectus]' (1856) Combe Collection, NLS; and letter CD to William Fox, 10 Apr 1859.

62 *and Atty continued to be prone* . . . The six-year-old boy was 'in a precarious state', in the autumn of 1854, Isabella told GC in a letter of 25 Sep 1854.

62 *The theory was that immersion* . . . See, for example, E. S. Turner's *Taking the Cure* (1967); J. Bradley's *Taking the Watercure* (1997); and Alastair Durie's essay in *Repositioning Victorian Sciences* (2006).

62 *Edward Lane said that many* . . . Edward Bulwer-Lytton's *Confessions of a Water Patient* (1846) noted that hydropathy spas were frequented by those who lived 'hard and high, wine-drinkers, spirit-bibbers'.

62 *his 'everlasting species-Book'* . . . Letter CD to Charles Lyell, 13 Apr 1857.

62 *'I have seen many cases . . . distressingly great.'* Letter of 1882 from EWL to Dr B. W. Richardson, read out at a lecture in St George's Hall, Langham Place, 22 Oct 1882. Information on Darwin at Moor Park from Ralph Colp's *Darwin's Illness* (2008) and from Darwin's correspondence.

62 *Edward said that . . . he had to 'struggle* . . . 'To the minds of a large number of persons,' wrote Lane, 'a water-cure establishment is a country retreat for patients, where a kind of merry inquisition goes on from morning to night, a jocular torture in sport. The patients are pictured as everlastingly gibbering in cold and wet sheets, in a state, it must be presumed, of the highest discomfort, to say the least, and only tolerable to poor deluded mortals who have well-nigh parted with their senses.' Lane's *Hydropathy* (1857).

63 *She caught a train from Reading . . . his own pace'.* Description of the house and the grounds at Moor Park in this and the following chapter from Marianne Young's *Aldershot, and All About It* (1857); 'Moor Park, As It Was and Is', an anonymous piece in the *New Monthly Magazine*, May 1855; *Black's Guide to Surrey* (1861); Charles T. Tallent-Bateman's *A Home Historical: Moor Park, Surrey* (1885); *Sketches of the Camp at Aldershot* (anon, 1858); Thomas Babington Macaulay's *The History of England from the Accession of James II* (1848); Richard John King's *A Handbook for Travellers in Surrey, Hampshire, and the Isle of Wight* (1865); Egerton Brydges' *The Autobiography, Times, Opinions, and Contemporaries of Sir Egerton Brydges* (1834); Dinah Mulock's 'The Water-Cure' (1855) and *A Life for a Life* (1860); and personal observation.

64 *To the right of the terrace* . . . Jane Austen's *Mansfield Park* includes a reference to 'a Moor Park', a strain of apricot cultivated by Sir William Temple.

66 *'She who is faithfully . . . romance.'* Cited in Nancy Armstrong's *Desire and Domestic Fiction: a Political History of the Novel* (1987), p. 274.

67 *The plot on which Henry was building* . . . Particulars and plan in Balmore House estate sale catalogues (1861 and 1865), Local Studies Dept, Reading Central Library.

68 *The next month, Thom took a post* . . . Letter IHR to GC, 25 Sep 1854. Thom 'finds the office an interesting and satisfactory one,' Isabella told Combe. Information on Duleep Singh (1838–93) from Amandeep Singh Madra's entry in *ODNB*.

68 *he 'clings to my heartstrings . . . his image.'* Quoted in Cockburn's judgment on the case, 2 Mar 1859.

69 *In the summer of 1854 Henry checked* . . . HOR's answer to IHR's Bill of Complaint in the Court of Chancery, 17 Apr 1858, NA, C15/550/R24.

69 *They argued –* . . . HOR's response of 1 Feb 1862, Divorce Court file, NA, J77/44/R4; IHR's reply of 4 Mar 1862; and letter IHR to GC, 26 Feb 1858.

69 *Though he had refused the £15* . . . HOR's answer to IHR's Bill of Complaint in the Court of Chancery, 17 Apr 1858, NA, C15/550/R24.

69 *Albert now lived in Westminster* . . . Census returns of 1851, *The Daily News* of 2 Dec 1852 (on the flotation of shares in the Eastern Steam Navigation Company) and *The Morning Chronicle* of 27 Jun 1853 (on the schooner *Dolphin*'s trip to Greenland).

69 *Albert refused to pay Henry* . . . See *The Daily News*, 3 Aug 1854.

CHAPTER 5: AND I KNEW THAT I WAS WATCHED

70 *Isabella twice visited* . . . Divorce Court file, NA, J77/44/R4.

70 *Elizabeth Drysdale . . . of the great establishment'*. In Henrietta Litchfield's *Emma Darwin, Wife of Charles Darwin: Vol. II* (1904).

70 *'Dr Lane & wife* . . . Letter CD to J. D. Hooker, 25 Jun 1857.

71 *He did not subscribe . . . can explain'*. Letter CD to W. D. Fox, 30 Apr 1857.

71 *George Combe agreed . . . good nature & frankness'*. Letter GC to M. B. Sampson, 11 Jan 1858.

71 *Combe remarked . . . depended on women'*. Letter GC to Sir James Clark, 19 Dec 1857.

71 *'Benevolence and Love . . . their kindness.'* Letter GC to M. B. Sampson, 11 Jan 1858.

71 *Good company . . . his own ailments'*. Lane's *Hydropathy* (1857).

71 *'There are few pleasures . . . fellow creatures.'* Letter EWL to GC, 23 Aug 1857.

72 *'very . . . agreeable, Society'*. GC's journal, 28 Aug 1856.

72 *'kindness and attention' of his hosts . . .* Alexander Bain, *Autobiography* (1904); it was he who recommended the establishment to Darwin.

72 *All the residents ate together . . . at seven) . . .* EWL's evidence, 23 Nov 1858.

72 *'I have been playing . . . splendid strokes!'* Letter CD to W. E. Darwin, 3 May 1858.

73 *'The physician has his patients . . .'* Lane's *Hydropathy* (1857).

73 *'I strolled a little . . . had been formed.'* Letter CD to Emma Darwin, 28 Apr 1858.

73 *'what a play of forces . . . becomes extinct.'* Letter CD to J. D. Hooker, 3 Jun 1857.

73 *'I had such a piece . . . Master's nests.'* Letter CD to J. D. Hooker, 6 May 1858. The slave-makers were *Formica sanguinea* and their slaves *Formica nigra*.

74 *'thare whare a grate many eggs . . .'* Letter from J. Burmingham to CD, 10 Sep 1858.

74 *Darwin took . . . part of the body).* Letter CD to W. D. Fox, 30 Apr 1857.

74 *For dyspeptics . . . directed at the pelvis*. See Rachel P. Maines's *The Technology of Orgasm* (1999).

74 *To take Edward's hot air bath . . .* GC's journal, 29 Aug 1856.

74 *Another enthusiast . . . as an ostrich'*. See Captain J. K. Lukis's *The Common Sense of the Water Cure* (1862). The sitz-bath – which resembled a sixteen-foot-wide washing tub – was recommended by Lane's predecessor, Smethurst, as a treatment for diseases of the womb, as well as constipation: the patient should sit in the tub and rub his or her stomach for ten or fifteen minutes a day, he suggested. William Temple's *Of Health and Long Life* (1701, edited by Jonathan Swift) also recommended hot bathing: it 'opens the pores, provokes Sweat, and thereby allays Heat; supples the joints and sinews'. Friction, wrote Temple, 'is the best way of all forced

Perspiration . . . I have heard of Persons, who were said to cure several Diseases by stroaking'.

74 *When taking the water . . . the actual hour'*. See Edward Bulwer-Lytton's *Confessions of a Water-Patient* (1845).

75 *The illnesses . . . hypochondriasis and hysteria*. According to Lane's predecessor at Moor Park, Thomas Smethurst, in his *Hydrotherapia* (1843).

75 *conditions thought . . . body and the mind*. See Jane Wood's *Passion and Pathology in Victorian Fiction* (2001).

75 *The novelist Dinah Mulock . . . and an easy mind'*. See her novel *A Life for a Life* (1860). For hypochondria, including an account of Darwin's illness, see Brian Dillon's *Tormented Hope: Nine Hypochondriac Lives* (2009).

75 *In an influential work . . . to conceal them'*. See Robert Brudenell Carter's *On the Pathology and Treatment of Hysteria* (1853).

75 *'I am afraid it cannot . . . the monomania'*. Dinah Mulock in *Chambers's Edinburgh Journal*, Vol. 7 (1857), reprinted in *A Woman's Thoughts About Women* (1858).

76 *'My object here . . . read much novels.'* Letter CD to Charles Lyell, 26 Apr 1858.

76 *'Mrs Lane agrees . . . written by a man!'* Letter CD to Emma Darwin, 25 Apr 1858. *'Beneath' the Surface* is Darwin's error – *Below the Surface* is the correct title.

76 *the novelist and poet Marguerite Agnes Power* . . . See Adrian Room's *Dictionary of Pseudonyms: 13,000 Assumed Names and their Origins* (fifth edition, 2010).

76 *'I like Miss Craik . . . – on every subject?* Letter CD to Emma Darwin, 28 Apr 1858, and footnote.

76 *'never was anyone more genial . . . and animated.'* Letter of 1882, EWL to Dr B. W. Richardson, read out at a lecture in St George's Hall, Langham Place, 22 Oct 1882.

77 *A water-cure spa* . . . A census return that records the guests at Lane's hydropathic spa (from 1861, by which time it had relocated to Richmond) lists eight unmarried men and four unmarried women aged between twenty and forty-one, as well as three adolescent girls (two of them unaccompanied) and a married couple with two daughters. About twelve servants, including bath attendants, catered to them and the Lane family.

77 *Occasionally . . . 'disgusted' her.* Cited in letter from GC to EWL, 23 Feb 1858.

77 *In 1855, Miss Mulock published . . .* Dinah Mulock's 'The Water-Cure' appeared in the *Dublin University Magazine*, Apr 1855, and was collected in *Nothing New: Tales* (1857).

78 *A lawyer from Lincoln's . . . I call it divine.'* See 'Moor Park, As It Was and Is', *New Monthly Magazine*, May 1855.

79 *In this cave . . . Temple's housekeeper.* Victorian commentators were disapproving of Swift's libertinism and his ruthless treatment of Esther and the other women he wooed: see, for instance, William Howitt's *Homes and Haunts of the Most Eminent British Poets* (1857), which accused him of a tendency to 'pluck and torture' the hearts of women.

79 *'The meadows interlaced . . . taller woods.'* Swift's 'A Description of Mother Ludwell's Cave' (1692–93), reproduced in *Collected Poems by Jonathan Swift* (1958), ed. Joseph Horrell.

80 *Goethe's most famous novel . . .* The urgent intimacy with which Isabella spoke to her diary – the exclamations and apostrophes – was similar in style to that of the introspective, despairing, love-struck Werther: 'My only consolation is: She may have turned to look back at me! Perhaps! Good night! Oh, what a child am I!', *The Sorrows of Young Werther* (1787).

85 *'we spoke of his early age, thirty-one . . .* Isabella did not mention that it was Edward's birthday, although the reference to his age may have been prompted by that fact. If he was thirty-one, he was born in 1823; but he was later to argue that his date of birth was 10 Oct 1822, which would have made him twenty-one in Feb 1844, old enough to be assigned part of his father's estate. This became crucial in 1864, when the estate was divided upon Elisha Lane's death, and the children of his second wife (whom he had married in Montreal in 1848) tried to claim it all as their own – see *The Lower Canada Jurist*, Vol. VIII (1864).

86 *The late-eighteenth-century guide . . . coach cushions altogether. Harris's List* was published in 1788; quoted in Stone's *Road to Divorce* (1990), p. 110.

CHAPTER 6: THE FUTURE HORRIBLE

88 *At Boulogne harbour* . . . For Boulogne, see Charles Dickens, 'Our French Watering-place', *Household Words*, 4 Nov 1854; A. C. G. Jobert's *The French-Pronouncing Hand-Book for Tourists and Travellers* (1853); and John Murray's *Hand-Book for Travellers in France* (1854).

88 *'We have established ourselves . . . town.'* Letter IHR to GC, 17 Nov 1854.

88 *Now they joined* . . . The school was unusual in refraining from the use of corporal punishment, according to Henry Melville Merridew's *Visitor's Guide to Boulogne* (1864).

89 *More than 7,000 British* . . . Murray's *Handbook for Travellers in France* (1854).

89 *'It is a bright, airy, pleasant . . . bonnes in snow-white caps.'* Dickens's 'Our French Watering-place'.

90 *That November* . . . See *The Life and Correspondence of Thomas Slingsby Duncombe: late MP for Finsbury*, Vol. 2 (1868).

90 *When Henry visited Boulogne* . . . Letter IHR to GC, 28 Feb 1855.

90 *'unhappy turn of mind . . . delusions'*. Quoted in Cockburn's judgment, 2 Mar 1859.

90 *she had 'nothing bright . . . information, or reproof.'* Letter IHR to GC, 17 Nov 1854.

91 *Combe wrote back . . . act out our love in good deeds.'* Letter GC to IHR, 7 Dec 1854.

91 *'Nature alone cures . . . act upon him.'* Florence Nightingale, *Notes on Nursing* (1860).

92 *On 10 October . . . in early November.* In spite of her new vocation, Nightingale continued to be plagued by ill health and nervous conditions, for which she sought help at the hydropathic clinic at Malvern in 1857 and 1858. She was mildly scornful about hydropathy – 'a highly popular amusement . . . amongst athletic invalids who have felt the tedium vitae and those indefinite diseases which a large income and unbounded leisure are so well calculated to produce' – but she admitted that her spell at Malvern did her good. See Bostridge's *Florence Nightingale*, p. 125.

92 *Combe was 'deeply mortified' . . . cause of religious freedom'*. Letter GC to Charles Bray, 15 Nov 1854.

93 *'Bible of the Brothel'*. Cited in William H. Johnson's *Life of Charles Bradlaugh, MP* (1888).

94 *Among the neo-Malthusians . . .* See Tomoko Sato's 'E. W. Lane's Hydropathic Establishment at Moor Park' in the *Hitotsubashi Journal of Social Studies*, Vol. 10, (1978).

95 *She was 'a treasure . . . remarkably modest'*. *The Letters of William and Dorothy Wordsworth*, Vol. IV (1967), ed. Ernest de Selincourt, p. 495.

96 *She asked her husband . . . and their future children.* Account of John Wordsworth's behaviour in letter from Henry Curwen to his son Edward, dated 30 Jan 1846, Curwen archive, Whitehaven, DCu/3/31. 'The old Poet I know has altered his will,' Curwen wrote, '& left all to Isabella's children, out of his JW powers, and I have done the same.'

96 *He wrote to his son-in-law . . .* In *William Wordsworth: a Biography* (1965) Mary Trevelyan Moorman makes a cryptic reference to this letter: 'A letter from old Mr Curwen exists,' she writes, 'in which John is unmercifully abused,' p. 598. She had evidently read the letter, but she gave no clue to its whereabouts nor any detail of its contents. Even a century later, it seems, a biographer of Wordsworth felt bound to protect his family's honour.

97 *Isabella continued to correspond . . .* Letter IHR to GC, 28 Feb 1855.

97 *'sweet, mournful little note . . . they missed each other.* IHR's journal, 27 Apr 1855.

97 *'I have found more employment . . . to prepare.'* Letter IHR to GC, 28 Feb 1855.

98 *Unknown to Henry . . .* HOR's answer to IHR's Bill of Complaint in the Court of Chancery, 17 Apr 1858, NA, C15/550/R24.

98 *Henry's house was Italianate in design . . . kitchen.* Details from Balmore House sale catalogues (1861 and 1865), Reading Central Library.

99 *As soon as Isabella . . . a fortnight's water therapy.* EWL's testimony to Divorce Court, 23 Nov 1858.

99 *The establishment at Moor Park . . .* Letter IHR to GC, 4 Nov 1855.

102 *douche the vagina with a syringe.* The syringe is recommended, for instance, in Charles Knowlton's bestselling *Fruits of Philosophy; or, The Private Companion of Young Married People* (1832). See also Angus Maclaren's *Birth Control in Nineteenth-Century England* (1978).

103 *'It is very far from finished . . .'* Letter IHR to GC, 4 Nov 1855.

103 *Queenwood School . . .* See 'A Mid-Nineteenth-Century Experiment in Science Teaching' by D. Thompson in *Annals of Science*, Vol. 2, (1955).

104 *'long been on the worst of terms . . . be called sane'.* Letter IHR to GC, 21 Feb 1858.

105 *marital bond as a 'superstition' . . .* Letter GC to Sir James Clark, 19 Dec 1857.

105 *Mrs Norton set out the injustices . . . to destroy'.* See *A Letter to the Queen on Lord Chancellor Cranworth's Marriage and Divorce Bill* (1855).

105 *'one of the chief instruments for the degradation of women . . .'* See *Physical, Sexual, and Natural Religion* (1854).

106 *the longest and gravest diphtheria epidemic . . .* See Ernest Abraham Hart, 'On Diphtheria' (1859), a pamphlet reprinted from *The Lancet*.

106 *'Boulogne sore throat'.* A French physician had dubbed it 'diphtheria' in 1855; the term derived from the Greek word *diphthera*, meaning leather, a reference to the thick, dry throat membrane that characterised the condition. See Charles Creighton's *A History of Epidemics in Britain* (1891).

106 *As she lay in her bed . . .* HOR's response of 1 Feb 1862 in NA, J77/44/R4.

BOOK II: OUT FLEW THE WEB

CHAPTER 7: IMPURE PROCEEDINGS

111 *'The Robinsons married in 1844 . . .* Details of the trial of *Robinson v Robinson & Lane* are taken from reports in *The Times, Morning Chronicle, Liverpool Mercury, Manchester Times, Reynolds Newspaper, The Era, Daily News, Daily Telegraph, Observer, Caledonian Mercury* and *The Morning*

Post published 15–22 Jun 1858; 5–6 Jul 1858; 27–30 Nov 1858; and 3 Mar 1859; and from Swabey and Tristram's *Reports*. Most of the quotations from counsel are attempts to translate back into direct speech the continuous prose of the legal and press accounts. For instance, the line given in *Reports* as: 'He proposed to put in evidence certain diaries written by Mrs Robinson' is here given as 'I propose to put in evidence certain diaries written by Mrs Robinson.'

111 *The three judges* . . . See entries in *ODNB*; (Michael Lobban on Cockburn, Joshua S. Getzler on Cresswell); Edward Foss's *Biographia Juridica: A Biographical Dictionary of the Judges of England from the Conquest to the Present Time* (1870); Mr Serjeant Robinson's *Bench and Bar, Reminiscences of One of the Last of an Ancient Race* (1894); Justin McCarthy's *Reminiscences: Vol. II* (1899); and John Duke Coleridge's memoirs.

112 *The judges had decided* . . . This was one of twenty-two cases – for divorce or for judicial separation – to be heard before the full court without a jury in 1858.

112 *The sun funnelled* . . . Description of the architecture, the judges' bench and the spectators from an engraving of the new divorce court at Westminster Hall published in the *Illustrated London News*, 22 May 1858, and from the series 'Divorce a Vinculo', *Once a Week; Vols I & II* (1860).

112 *The temperature climbed* . . . See *The Annual Register 1858* (1859) and reports in *The Times*.

112 *Mr Chambers* . . . For Montagu Chambers, see his obituary in *The Law Times*, 1885, and lithograph after Robert Samuel Ennis Gallon, 1852 or after, printed by M. and N. Hanhart, NPG.

115 *In moments of impatience* . . . 'Divorce a Vinculo', *Once a Week*.

117 *The Divorce Court investigated adultery* . . . Barbara Leckie argues in *Culture and Adultery: the Novel, the Newspaper and the Law, 1857–1914* (1999) that the partial perspectives of the Divorce Court narratives influenced the emergence of the unreliable narrator in English fiction; her book includes a chapter on the Robinson case.

118 *The law required . . . to this effect*. See Richard Thomas

Tidswell and Ralph Daniel Makinson Littler's *The Practice and Evidence in Cases of Divorce and other Matrimonial Causes* (1860).

120 *Proximate acts might include* . . . Ibid.

121 *'The testimony of discarded . . . and alarm.'* John J. J. S. Wharton, 'An Exposition of the Laws Relating to the Women of England, showing their Rights, Remedies and Responsibilities' (1853), quoted in Stone's *Road to Divorce* (1990).

122 *Most of the petitioners* . . . The *Parliamentary Papers: Accounts & Papers 1859*, Vol. 19, paper 131, reports that the earliest of the 356 instances of adultery alleged in the court (by men and by women) in its first eighteen months took place in 1833; most, though, were from the 1850s – 30 in 1853, 27 in 1854 (including Isabella and Edward's), 32 in 1855, 41 in 1856, 53 in 1857, and 53 in 1858.

122 *The new law stipulated . . . bourgeois society.* See David M. Turner's *Fashioning Adultery: Gender, Sex and Civility in England 1660–1740* (2002); Ann Sumner Holmes's 'The Double Standard in the English Divorce Laws, 1857–1923' in *Law and Social Inquiry*, Vol. 20 (1995); and Lynda Nead's *Myths of Sexuality: Representations of Women in Victorian England* (1998). The issue of whether men and women should be equal under the divorce law had been debated in the Houses of Lords and Commons. In a vote in the Lords on 25 May 1857, the motion to approve a distinction in the divorce laws between men and women was carried by 71 to 20; in the Commons on 7 Aug it was carried by 126 to 65. George Drysdale objected to the double standard by which 'For a man to indulge his sexual appetites illegitimately, either before or after the marriage vow, is thought venial; but for a woman to do so, is the most heinous crime.' Women were granted equal rights in divorce in 1923, soon after they won the vote.

123 *'a light literature entirely based . . . Saturday Review*, Jul 1857.

124 *a notorious haunt of prostitutes and suicides.* Thomas Hood's poem 'The Bridge of Sighs' (1844) had forged the association of this spot with sexual transgression and self-destruction. The poem commemorated the suicide of a prostitute washed

up on this bank of the river: 'Still for all slips of hers,/ One of Eve's family – / Wipe those poor lips of her/ Oozing so clammily.' The fallen woman was redeemed and purified by her remorse and death, but also preserved as an object of gruesome erotic fascination. John Everett Millais made an etching inspired by the poem in 1858.

CHAPTER 8: I HAVE LOST EVERY THING

126 *Henry refused to allow her back* . . . HOR's answer to IHR's Bill of Complaint, Court of Chancery, 17 Apr 1858, NA, C15/550/R24.

126 *moved twenty miles south* . . . Letter IHR to GC, 26 Feb 1858.

126 *'gloom & solitude'* . . . *shattered by illness.* Letter IHR to GC, 21 Feb 1858.

127 *'I have lost every thing* . . . Ibid.

127 *His first plan was to sue* . . . Ibid. 'He tried, in the autumn of '56 a direct legal attack; *that, of course, failed'*.

128 *a lawyer called Gregg* . . . This may have been the William Gregg who read Law at Edinburgh University with Edward, graduating with an MA in 1844.

128 *Neither Edward nor Isabella* . . . See letters IHR to GC, 21 and 26 Feb 1858.

128 *The cost could run to* . . . This cost was estimated at anything between £200 and £5,000, according to Gail L. Savage's 'The Operation of the 1857 Divorce Act, 1860–1910: A Research Note' in *Journal of Social History* (1983). The cost of a separation was far lower: Stephen Lushington, a judge in the Consistory Court, estimated in 1844 that the minimum cost of an uncontested suit was £50, rising to a maximum of £800 for a contested suit. See Stone's *Road to Divorce* (1990), p. 188.

128 *'cosey, dosey, old-fashioned* . . . Charles Dickens, *David Copperfield* (1850).

129 *'Lady Drysdale is taken ill* . . . This and subsequent quotations from GC's journal, 3 Jul–3 Aug 1857.

129 *George suffered from digestive* . . . *anxiety.* See Stack's *Queen Victoria's Skull*, p. 156.

129 *In these letters Miss Smith* . . . From F. Tennyson Jesse's *The*

Trial of Madeline Smith (1927), quoted in Leckie's *Culture and Adultery* (1999).

130 *Within a few days . . . unabated interest.* RC's journal, RC papers, NLS.

131 *Though Henry . . . acquaintances in Edinburgh.* Divorce Court file, NA, J77/44/R4.

131 *In the meantime . . . case came to court.* See *Register of Tonbridge School* (1893).

131 *Otway was selected . . . Rule 13.* See *The Tonbridgian* of October 1861 and D. C. Somervell's *A History of Tonbridge School* (1947).

131 *Henry's petition . . . under the old system.* For workings of the ecclesiastical courts, see Stone's *Road to Divorce* (1990).

131 *The Times* reported the case in a few lines . . . *The Times*, 4 Dec 1857.

132 *'scarcely enough to live as a gentlewoman'.* IHR's petition to the House of Lords Select Committee on Appeals, 6 Jun 1861, HLA. Her brother Frederick invested her settlement in Three Per Cent Consols (government bonds). Though she asked him to invest instead in stocks that might achieve a higher rate of return, he refused. After an international commercial crisis in 1857, he may have felt it incumbent upon him to be cautious on her behalf. See IHR's response of 4 Mar 1862 in NA, J77/44/R4.

132 *£300 a year was considered the minimum . . .* According to R. D. Baxter's *National Income* (1868).

132 *Henry was staying . . . society in Reading.* Letter IHR to GC, 21 Feb 1858.

132 *'impassioned and disgusting' . . .* Letter GC to Mrs Tennant, the half-sister of Mary Lane, 28 Dec 1857.

132 *'reverenced the conjugal vow' himself.* Letter GC to Sir James Clark, 19 Dec 1857.

133 *'half out of her mind . . . such a scandal.'* Letter EWL to GC, 29 Dec 1857.

133 *'You will believe my solemn words . . .* Letter Lady D to GC, 1 Jan 1858.

133 *Edward went to Edinburgh . . .* Letter EWL to GC, 31 Dec 1857.

133 *He claimed that he had not flirted . . .* Letter GC to Sir James Clark, 4 Jan 1858.

133 *I never wrote a line to Mrs R* . . . Letter EWL to GC, 11 Jan 1858.

134 *She was 'a rhapsodical & vaporing fool* . . . Letters EWL to GC, 5 Feb and 17 May 1858.

134 *'the consummation of human meanness* . . . Letter EWL to GC, 17 May 1858.

134 *'anxious to escape* . . . Letter EWL to GC, 29 Dec 1857.

134 *Combe . . . the doctor's honour.* Letter GC to HOR, 12 Jan 1858.

134 *She 'professed a great . . . all interest for us'.* Letters GC to Sir James Clark, 19 Dec 1857 and 4 Jan 1858.

135 *'an extraordinary . . . her own infamy'.* Letter Sir James Clark to GC, 22 Jan 1858.

135 *'by devoting himself . . . a victim.'* Letter from M. B. Sampson to GC, 9 Jan 1858.

135 *Disingenuously . . . private and confidential'.* Letter HOR to GC, 4 Jan 1858.

136 *'Now, your offer . . . his defence.'* Letter GC to HOR, 18 Jan 1858.

136 *'you have acted towards me . . . malignant' manner.* Letter EWL to GC, 5 Feb 1858.

136 'I speak to you . . . much moment'. Ibid.

136 *'May I . . . our only safety.'* Letter from Lady D to GC, 2 Mar 1858.

137 *When the Court of Divorce* . . . See *Parliamentary Papers: Accounts and Papers 1859*, Vol. 22, paper 106.

137 *The new court conducted . . . before 1858.* Tidswell and Littler's *Practice and Evidence* (1860).

138 *In February 1858, Henry served papers* . . . HOR's response of 1 Feb 1862 in NA, J77/44/R4.

138 *On 22 April, Isabella . . . Edward did the same.* Isabella's solicitor was Francis Hart Dyke, Queen's Proctor, a former practitioner in Doctors' Commons; Edward's was John Young of Desborough, Young & Desborough, in the City of London.

138 *Edward organised for the diary* . . . Letter EWL to GC, 26 May 1858.

138 *In the first five months* . . . The *Birmingham Daily Post* reporting on recently published Parliamentary Return, 25 Jun 1858. According to *Parliamentary Papers: Accounts and Papers*

1859, Vol. 22, 302 petitions for a full dissolution of marriage were presented to the court in its first fifteen months. Of these, 244 were filed in 1858, according to *Vol. XXVI: Return of Proceedings (Session 1)*.

139 *On 12 May, a solicitor . . .* See *Daily News*, 13 and 14 May 1858, and Swabey and Tristram's *Reports*.

139 *'Everybody with whom . . .'* See *Daily News*, 28 May 1858.

139 *Even Queen Victoria . . .* See Roger Fulford's *Dereast Child: Letters Between Queen Victoria and the Princess Royal Previously Unpublished*(1964), p. 99.

CHAPTER 9: BURN THAT BOOK, AND BE HAPPY!

140 *Lord Brougham may have been aware . . .* Brougham also had first-hand knowledge of mental illness – he was afflicted by spells of hypochondriacal depression and mania; his sister was insane and his wife had suffered from nervous illness ever since the birth of their second daughter in 1822. Henry Brougham had several affairs and in 1826 paid the courtesan Harriette Wilson to keep his name out of her memoirs (see Michael Lobban's entry in *ODNB*).

140 *He enjoyed the limelight . . . court.* The *Daily Telegraph* of 17 Jun 1858 noted that this was the first case heard before the new court to be reported in detail in the press.

143 *Caroline Suckling . . . a distant relative of Lord Nelson.* See William R. O'Byrne's *A Naval Biographical Dictionary* (1849).

143 *Combe described . . . her mother advice'.* GC's journal, 28 Aug 1856.

147 *Phillimore was probably . . . repentant self-flagellation.* See H. C. G. Matthew's *Gladstone* (1997), pp. 90–95.

148 *I might, for instance . . . that he masturbated.* William Acton alluded to this in his *Functions and Disorder of the Reproductive Organs, in Childhood, Youth, Adult Age, and Advanced Life, Considered in the Physiological, Social, and Moral Relations* (1857) when he wrote that Rousseau 'pries into his mental and moral character with a despicably morbid minuteness', a 'hideous frankness' that perpetuated the condition it described. Quoted in Stephen Marcus's *The Other*

Victorians: a Study of Sexuality and Pornography in Mid-Nineteenth-Century England (1966), p. 24.

148 *The edition of 1848 omitted . . . regret their loss'.* From a review of the third edition of the diary in *Blackwood's Magazine*, which observed that 'the great charm of the book is its utter freedom from disguise'. 'Diary of Samuel Pepys', *Blackwood's*, Vol. 66 (1849).

148 *Pepys had been edited . . . honesty.* Also edited out of the historical record – by Pepys himself – were the private confessions of Mrs Pepys, as he explained to his diary on 9 Jan 1663. On that day Elizabeth Pepys pulled from a locked trunk a copy of a piece of writing that she had tried to show her husband before. She started to read it aloud. She had written, said Pepys, about 'the retirednesse of her life and how unpleasant it was'. He was horrified to find that it was written in English (his own diary was encrypted) and therefore 'in danger of being met with and read by others'. 'I was vexed at it and desired her and then commanded her to teare it – which she desired to be excused it; I forced it from her and tore it, and withal took her other bundle of papers from her and leapt out of the bed and in my shirt clapped them into the pockets of my breeches that she might not get them from me; and having got on my stockings and breeches and gown, I pulled them out one by one and tore them all before her face, though it went against my heart to do it, she crying and desiring me not to do it.' Pepys's panic and rage was caused by the fact that his wife had written a document that others might read, carrying her private thoughts into a public realm.

150 *The preface quoted . . . 'due to his memory'.* According to Kathryn Carter's analysis of the *English Catalogue of Books* in this period, in 'The Cultural Work of Diaries in Mid-Century Victorian Britain', *Victorian Review*, Vol. 23 (1997).

151 *The Diary of an Ennuyée . . .* Jameson was a good friend of Cecy Combe's cousin Fanny Kemble, and an acquaintance of the Combes.

151 *pastiche inspired a string of imitations . . .* These included Anne Manning's *The Maiden and Married Life of Mary Powell: afterwards Mistress Milton* (1849); *Passages from the Diary of Margaret Arden* (1856) by Holme Lee (Harriet

Parr); *The Diary and Houres of the Ladye Adolie, a Faythfulle Childe, 1552* (1853), 'edited' by Lady Charlotte Pepys; and the anonymous *Ephemeris: or Leaves from ye Journall of Marian Drayton* (1853), *The Diary of Martha Bethune Baliol, from 1753 to 1754* (1853); and the *Diary of Mistress Kate Dalrymple, 1685–1735* (1856).

151 *Dinah Mulock . . . secret journal of a governess.* Mulock, *Bread upon the Waters* (1852).

151 *two tales in the guise of journals by women.* Wilkie Collins's 'Leaves from Leah's Diary', the framing device of his collection *After Dark*; and his proto-detective tale *The Diary of Anne Rodway*.

152 *'Use your diary . . .* Advertisement from the 1820s, quoted in David Amigoni's *Life Writing and Victorian Culture* (2006), p. 27. The essayist Isaac D'Israeli spelt out the purpose of a diary in his *Curiosities of Literature* (1793): 'We converse with the absent by letters, and with ourselves by diaries . . . [they] render to a man an account of himself to himself.'

152 *bound in cloth or in red Russian calf hide . . .* See advertisement for Letts diaries in David Morier Evans's *The Commercial Crisis 1847–48* (1849).

152 *The word 'diarist' . . .* See John Craig's *A New Universal Etymological, Technological, and Pronouncing Dictionary of the English Language* (1859).

153 *in three volumes after her death in 1840.* See Carter's 'The Cultural Work of Diaries in Mid-Century Victorian Britain'.

153 *'Your journal all about feelings . . .'* See *Letters and Memorials of Jane Welsh Carlyle*, Vol. II (1913), ed. James Anthony Froude.

154 *In* Mr Nightingale's *. . . fantasies.* See Charles Dickens and Mark Lemon's *Mr Nightingale's Diary: a Farce in One Act* (1877).

154 *The play parodied . . . self-diagnostic 'diaries of health'.* These had become popular since the publication in 1820 of Henry Matthews's *The Diary of an Invalid; Being the Journal of a Tour in Pursuit of Health; in Portugal, Italy, Switzerland, and France, in the Years 1817, 1818, and 1819.* Darwin kept a diary of his symptoms between 1849 and 1855.

154 *'Burn that book, and be happy!'* Dickens and Lemon,

Mr Nightingale's Diary. In *My Wife's Diary: a Farce in One Act,* a play by Thomas William Robertson that opened at the Royal Olympic Theatre in London in 1854, a husband gloats as he unlocks his wife's desk with a duplicate key: 'diaries are a devilish good invention'. See Carter's 'The Cultural Work of Diaries in Mid-Century Victorian Britain'.

CHAPTER 10: AN INSANE TENDERNESS

155 *At lunchtime* . . . 'Divorce a Vinculo', *Once a Week.*

155 *malfunction in the uterus itself.* The term 'uterine disease' was too much for most newspapers: *The Times* (16 Jun 1858) translated it for its readers as 'a disease peculiar to women'.

155 *He was an Irish Quaker* . . . See Walter Kidd, *Joseph Kidd 1824–1918: Limerick, London, Blackheath: A Memoir* (privately printed, 1920, revised 1983). Kidd went on to become physician to William Gladstone and, from 1877, to Benjamin Disraeli, whose health rallied after he advised him to drink claret instead of port. Disraeli died holding Kidd's hand.

156 *Their task was to confirm* . . . Doctors who gave evidence about insanity in the criminal courts, observed the alienist John Charles Bucknill, 'may usually be divided into two classes: those who know something about the prisoner and nothing about insanity, and those who know something about insanity and nothing of the prisoner'. The physicians before the Divorce Court that day fitted these categories: Kidd knew Isabella, but little about sexual mania; the others were well versed in women's diseases, but had not examined Isabella.

156 *The first of the specialists* . . . See portrait of James Henry Bennet by Ferdinand Jean de la Ferté Joubert, after a mezzotint by Édouard Louis Dubufe, 1852, NPG.

157 *the modern school of gynaecology.* The term gynaecology was first included in a dictionary in 1849.

157 *He was an authority* . . . Obituary of James Henry Bennet, *British Medical Journal*, 12 Sep 1891.

157 *The speculum was controversial* . . . In *On the Pathology of Hysteria* (1853) Robert Brudenell Carter wrote that he had 'more than once seen young unmarried women, of the middle

classes of society, reduced, by the constant use of the speculum, to the mental and moral condition of prostitutes; seeking to give themselves the same indulgence by the practice of solitary vice; and asking every medical practitioner, under whose care they fell, to institute an examination of the sexual organs'. Stephen Smith's *Doctor in Medicine: and Other Papers on Professional Subjects* (1872) discussed the danger of women being afflicted by 'speculum-mania', a condition that could lead to depravity and insanity.

157 *The second was Sir Charles Locock* . . . See G. T. Bettany's entry in *ODNB* and Locock's obituary in *British Medical Journal*, 31 Jul 1875. As a young man, Locock had fallen 'devilishly in love' with a pretty and well-connected young woman, but she aroused his disgust when she 'appeared rather too forward and loving . . . I always look with a cursedly jealous eye upon that very *coming* disposition in young ladies.' From a letter to a friend in 1823, quoted in Russell C. Maulitz's 'Metropolitan Medicine and the Man-Midwife: the Early Life and Letters of Sir Charles Locock', *Medical History* 26 (1982).

157 *He was the author of nearly* . . . His research suggested that young women who indulged in intercourse or masturbation while menstruating could experience convulsive fits, and he experimented in treating sexual mania with potassium bromide (this turned out to be highly effective in the treatment of epilepsy).

157 *Dr Forbes Winslow, shiny-pated* . . . Photograph of Forbes Winslow in 1864 by Ernest Edwards in NPG, and Jonathan Andrews's entry in *ODNB*.

158 *Though the press reported sparingly* . . . The condition of *furor uterinus*, or excessive sexual feeling in women, was identified during the Renaissance. See Carol Groneman's 'Nymphomania: the Historical Construction of Female Sexuality' in *Signs: Journal of Women in Culture and Society*, Vol. 19 (1994).

158 *about ten per cent of sufferers* . . . According to Charles Bucknill and Daniel H. Tuke's *A Manual of Psychological Medicine* (1858), quoted in Shuttleworth's *Charlotte Brontë and Victorian Psychology* (1996).

158 *After giving birth . . . local irritation.'* Bennet's *A Practical Treatise on Inflammation of the Uterus, Its Cervix, and Appendages, and on Its Connection with Uterine Disease* (third edition, 1853). In a later edition, published in 1864, Bennet revised this sentence to make explicit that nymphomania could lead to 'self-abuse'. W. Tyler Smith's *Manual of Obstetrics* (1858) also made a connection between childbirth and sexual mania: 'sexual excitement is sometimes apparent during or after labour in a very high degree; indeed cases of this kind may pass into erotomania after parturition'.

159 *Alternatively, the trigger . . .* See E. J. Tilt's *The Change of Life in Health and Disease* (1857).

159 *Forbes Winslow, too . . .* In his *Journal of Psychological Medicine and Mental Pathology* (1854), Forbes Winslow wrote: 'Sometimes erotism breaks out at the time of the suppression of the catamenia [menstruation], and is evidently connected with a special state of the sexual organs.'

159 *Tilt argued that 'sub-acute ovaritis'.* Tilt, *The Change of Life.*

159 *When Euphemia Ruskin petitioned . . .* Information on the Ruskins' divorce from Phyllis Rose's *Parallel Lives: Five Victorian Marriages* (1983). Euphemia was seeking an annulment because she had fallen in love with the artist John Millais, who was painting her husband's portrait.

159 *These were distinct illnesses . . .* Esquirol's book was published in France in 1838, and translated into English in 1845. His ideas had been introduced to Britain a decade earlier, in James Cowles Prichard's *A Treatise on Insanity and Other Disorders Affecting the Mind* (1835). Monomania could afflict anyone, however seemingly sane, wrote Esquirol, and it could depart as swiftly as it had arrived. The clever and inquisitive were especially susceptible: 'The more the understanding is developed, and the more active the brain becomes, the more is monomania to be feared.'

159 *erotomania was a disorder . . .* 'Erotomania is the result of an excited imagination,' explained James Copland in *A Dictionary of Practical Medicine* (1858), 'unrestrained by the powers of the understanding; satyriasis and nymphomania proceed from the local irritation of the sexual organs, reacting upon the brain, and exciting the passions beyond the restraints of reason.'

According to the Scottish alienist Sir Alexander Morison, erotomania was revealed in 'restlessness, melancholy and silence'; he observed one sufferer 'continually writing the name of the beloved object on paper, on the walls of the room, or on the ground'. See Morison's *Outlines of Lectures on the Nature, Causes, and Treatment of Insanity* (1848).

159 *Nymphomaniacs were less prone . . . she met a man.* Horatio Storer's 'Cases of Nymphomania' in *American Journal of Medical Science,* Vol. 32 (1856), quoted in Groneman's 'Nymphomania: the Historical Construction of Female Sexuality'.

160 *'The two may exist together . . . in the head.'* See Daniel H. Tuke's 'On the Various Forms of Mental Disorder' in *The Asylum Journal of Mental Science*, Vol. 19 (1857).

160 *Older women were especially likely . . .* See Mary Poovey's *Uneven Developments: the Ideological Work of Gender in Mid-Victorian England* (1988). The phrase 'redundant women' is from W. R. Greg's 'Why are Women Redundant?' in the *National Review*, Apr 1862.

160 *The 'redundant women' . . .* See Tilt, *The Change of Life.*

160 *Though Dr William Acton famously . . .* In Acton's *Functions and Disorders of the Reproductive Organs*. In a later edition, published in 1862, Acton seemed to have (slightly) modified his views on the basis of this and other divorce cases. He added: 'It is too true, I admit, as the divorce courts show, that there are some few women who have sexual desires so strong that they surpass those of men, and shock public feeling by their exhibition. I admit, of course, the existence of sexual excitement terminating in nymphomania, a form of insanity that those accustomed to visit lunatic asylums must be fully conversant with; but, with these sad exceptions, there can be no doubt that sexual feeling in the female is in abeyance, and that it requires positive and considerable excitement to be roused at all; and even if roused (which in many instances it never can be) is very moderate compared with that of the male.'

161 *back of her skull with cold water.* See Alexander Morison's *The Physiognomy of Mental Diseases* (1840). George Combe's brother had also insisted that sexual disorders

were based in the brain: 'the affection of the generative organs,' wrote Andrew Combe, 'is generally the effect, and not the cause, of the cerebral disturbance'. Andrew Combe studied Esquirol's work in France in the 1840s. 'Remarks on the Nature and Causes of Insanity', *The Phrenological Journal*, Vol. 15 (1842).

161 *hip baths, deep baths and showers*. In *A Practical Treatise on Inflammation of the Uterus*, Bennet noted that uterine inflammation was particularly prevalent immediately after childbirth – the time that Isabella first consulted Kidd. The symptoms, Bennet wrote, included 'intense headache, great depression and lowness of spirits, and groundless terrors', often 'accompanied by delusions or hallucinations, and by the fear of insanity'.

161 *Locock advised the application* . . . In his entry on amenhorrhea in the *Cyclopaedia of Practical Medicine* (1833).

161 *A London surgeon relieved* . . . *The Lancet*, 5 Jun 1853. In the early 1850s the physician Isaac Baker Brown performed his first successful clitoridectomy, upon his sister, and he was to become notorious for the practice in the 1860s. See Ornella Mosucci's 'Clitoridectomy, Circumcision and the Politics of Sexual Pleasure in Mid-Victorian Britain' in *Sexualities in Victorian Britain* (1996), ed. Andrew H. Miller and James Eli Adams.

161 *'My dear Lady Drysdale* . . . Letter IHR to Lady D, 14 Feb 1858.

163 *The tone was 'too light* . . . *actual occurrences'*. Letter GC to Lady D, 3 Mar 1858.

163 *She begged him: 'assist me* . . . *me to retain'*. Letter IHR to GC, 21 Feb 1858.

163 *In his reply* . . . *vindicate yourself & Dr Lane'*. Letter GC to IHR, 23 Feb 1858.

165 *On the same day* . . . *is insanity'*. Letter GC to EWL, 23 Feb 1858.

165 *'It looks like insanity.'* Letter GC to HOR, 6 Jan 1858.

165 *'The woman was not mad* . . . *down as facts.'* Letter GC to Sir James Clark, 4 Jan 1858.

165 *'I will make my reply* . . . *but the writer's.'* Letter IHR to GC, 26 Feb 1858.

166 *Gustave Freytag's* Debit and Credit . . . Mrs Malcolm's translation of the novel was reviewed in *The Times*, 31 Dec 1857.

166 *'Could I dream* . . . not *how* this can be.' Letter IHR to GC, 26 Feb 1858.

168 *'I have been reconsidering . . . another word to add.'* Letter IHR to GC, 28 Feb 1858.

169 *Isabella's latest letter . . . on the brink of insanity'.* Letter GC to EWL, 2 Mar 1858.

169 *In a letter to Lady Drysdale . . . 'an* insane *account'.* Letter GC to Lady D, 3 Mar 1858.

169 *George Combe believed* . . . Combe was drawing here on the teachings of his younger brother Dr Andrew Combe, who in *Observations of Mental Derangement* (1831) had warned of what might happen to upper- or middle-class women who had no outlet for their energies: 'their own feelings and personal relations necessarily constitute the grand objects of their contemplations: these are brooded over till the mental energies become impaired, false ideas of existence and providence spring up in the mind, the fancy is haunted by strange impressions, and every trifle which relates to self is exaggerated into an object of immense importance'.

169 *to his friend William Ivory, an advocate* . . . Ivory had been a classmate of George Drysdale at the Edinburgh Academy from 1834 to 1841. See *Edinburgh Academy Register 1824–1914* (1914).

169 *To this end, he wrote . . . in Edinburgh.* Letter GC to EWL, 29 Feb 1858. There is room for confusion between the Bennett who Combe hoped would appear in court and the Bennet who did appear as an expert witness. The legal reports on the case spell the witness's name as 'Bennet', and describe him only as an MD, not a professor, which identifies him as James Henry Bennet, the London doctor who specialised in women's diseases, rather than John Hughes Bennett, the Edinburgh doctor and lecturer to whom Combe alluded. The two were likely to have known one another – in his book on uterine inflammation, J. H. Bennet makes admiring reference to J. H. Bennett's work on cancer of the uterus.

169 *'a fantastical, vain . . . corrupt imagination'.* Letter EWL to GC, 13 Apr 1858.

170 *(all three were 'speculumisers')* . . . In *The Elements of Social Science* (1861), George praised 'Bennett's [sic]' work on uterine inflammation and commended his use of the speculum.

170 *patient of the homeopath John Drysdale.* Kidd's obituary in *British Medical Journal.* John Drysdale treated Kidd in Liverpool in the early 1850s, and advised him that he should take holidays from work.

170 *'a history of events . . . innocent person'.* Letter RC to Cecilia Combe, 26 Feb 1858.

170 *'Had you only seen the Journal* . . . Letter RC to GC, 2 Mar 1858. His allusion was to Christ's warning, in the Gospel of St Matthew, that 'anyone who looks at a woman lustfully has already committed adultery with her in his heart'.

170 *'whether peace . . . a sea of uncertainty.'* Letter EWL to GC, 16 Mar 1858.

171 *'perfectly impassable & determined'.* Letter EWL to GC, 25 Mar 1858.

171 *'evidently does not wish . . . a complete fanatic'.* Letter EWL to GC, 28 Mar 1858.

CHAPTER 11: A GREAT DITCH OF POISON

172 *The heat of London* . . . Details of weather from *The Annual Register 1858* (1859).

172 *It was 'pestiferous* . . . See *The Morning Post,* 20 Jun 1858.

172 *'A great ditch of poison* . . . See *Illustrated London News,* 19 Jun 1858.

172 *In the Westminster courts* . . . See *Annual Register 1858.* A barrister in the Court of Exchequer asked the judge if they could dispense with their wigs.

173 *When a wife sued for divorce . . . behind her back'.* See John Fraser Macqueen's *A Practical Treatise on Divorce and Matrimonial Jurisdiction* (1858).

176 *When formulating the new law* . . . See Stone's *Road to Divorce* (1990), p. 322.

177 *On 21 June* . . . Account of *Curtis v Curtis* from divorce papers in NA, J77/8/4; from Swabey and Tristram's *Reports;*

and, for the Court of Chancery proceedings, from the *Law Times*, 24 Sep 1859.

177 *Fanny's father* . . . Later, as Attorney General of Gibraltar, Fanny's father, Frederick Solly Flood, set in motion the conspiracy theories about the *Mary Celeste*, a merchant ship that was found abandoned 600 miles west of Portugal in 1872. In Gibraltar's Vice-Admiralty Court, Solly Flood refused to countenance an innocent explanation for the ship's desertion. Instead, he suggested that the crew had mutinied, murdering the captain and his family; or that the captain had murdered the crew, and then handed the ship to a co-conspirator to claim the reward for finding an abandoned vessel; or that the crew of another ship had murdered all those onboard in order to claim the salvage reward. The Court found no evidence for any of these suggestions, concluding instead that the ship had been abandoned because she was sinking, and that her crew had been subsequently lost at sea. None the less, Solly Flood's theories passed into legend, notably through Arthur Conan Doyle's short story 'J. Habakuk Jephson's Statement' (1884). See Bob Solly's 'Solly-Flood Family Notes' in the Nov 1999 edition of *Soul Search*, the journal of The Sole Society.

177 *John Curtis's witnesses included* . . . According to *The Times*, 21 May 1858.

180 *The Custody of Infants Act* . . . See Ann Sumner Holmes's 'The Double Standard in the English Divorce Laws, 1857–1923', in *Law and Social Inquiry*, Vol. 20 (1995).

181 *Kindersley dismissed Fanny's petition* . . . In spite of this ruling, all three Curtis children were by 1861 living with their mother in Lyme Regis in Dorset, according to the census returns; while their father was alone in a house behind the National Portrait Gallery in London. Twenty years later Mrs Curtis had moved to a house under the cliff in Dover, which she shared with her two daughters, art students aged twenty-seven and thirty-two. Fanny Curtis died in Dover in 1896, aged seventy-one.

181 *In May 1858 . . . immortality of the soul.* Letter EWL to GC, 17 May 1858.

181 *'damage my reputation . . . or immoral?* Letters GC to EWL, 17 and 22 May 1858.

182 *'were quite alive . . . appear in the paper.* Letter EWL to GC, 30 Jun 1858.

183 The Examiner . . . *respectability and worth.'* See *Examiner,* 26 Jun 1858.

183 *'Mrs Robinson was crazy* . . . Letter from Charles Mackay to GC, 21 Jun 1858. Mackay was the author of *Extraordinary Popular Delusions and the Madness of Crowds* (1841), which explored the collective fantasies that could lead to anything from economic bubbles to witchhunts. 'Men, it has been well said, think in herds,' he wrote; 'it will be seen that they go mad in herds, while they only recover their senses slowly, and one by one.'

183 *All those, whom I have asked . . .'* Letter CD to William D. Fox, 24 Jun 1854. Darwin was undergoing personal and professional crises of his own: he had just learnt of the existence of an essay that threatened to pre-empt his own theory of natural selection; and his youngest son was extremely ill. On 1 Jul his friends presented his theory in public for the first time at a meeting of the Linnean Society in London. Darwin was unable to attend as his son, Charles Waring Darwin, had died the previous day.

183 *'I am profoundly sorry . . .'* Letter CD to William D. Fox, 27 Jun 1858.

183 *Edward asked Combe* . . . Letter EWL to GC, 30 Jun 1858.

183 *His name had been 'dragged* . . . Letter EWL to Thomas Jameson Torrie, 25 Jun 1858, quoted in Benn's *Predicaments of Love*, p. 242.

184 The Daily News *demanded* . . . See *Daily News*, 25 Jun 1858.

184 *'no man is safe . . . completely ruined.'* See *Observer*, 20 Jun 1858.

184 *'Dr Lane is an innocent* . . . See *The Morning Post*, 8 Jul 1858.

184 *'any of our associates with "curls . . .'* See *British Medical Journal*, 10 Jul 1858.

185 *Both Rousseau's epistolary novel* . . . Rousseau's modern Heloise, like Isabella in the diary, seduced her lover in a 'bosquet', an arbour or grove. Pope's Eloisa, like the dreaming Isabella, seemed to cleave to a succubus: 'I hear thee, view

thee, gaze o'er all thy charms,/ And round thy phantom glue my clasping arms'.

185 *'The diary stands self-convicted* . . . See *Saturday Review*, 26 Jun 1858.

186 *'Never, oh never shall I forget* . . . Discussed in Marcus's *The Other Victorians*, pp. 197–216.

186 *glowing with stimulating fires.'* See *Fanny Hill: Memoirs of a Woman of Pleasure* (Wordsworth Editions, 2000), p. 31. See Peter Gay's characterisation of Holywell Street pornography in *Education of the Senses: the Bourgeois Experience, Victoria to Freud*, Vol. I (1984).

186 *For weeks now the newspapers had been spewing* . . . See *Saturday Review*, 26 Jun 1858: 'A man has neither morally nor, as we think, legally any better right to corrupt the public morals by increasing than by originating the circulation of such publications.' In *Novels and Novelists of the Eighteenth Century* (1871), William Forsyth – Edward Lane's counsel – compared the 'polluting details' in the newspaper reports of the Divorce Court proceedings to the licentious passages in eighteenth-century novels; he upbraided editors for allowing 'this strain of vulgarity, now driven out of fiction, to find a home in their pages'.

187 *John George Phillimore . . . drop of English blood.'* See Phillimore's *The Divorce Court: Its Evils and the Remedy* (1859), p. 71, in which he observed that Isabella had felt a 'morbid excitement in gloating over the accumulated proofs of her own licentiousness'.

187 *In the summer session* . . . Palmerston had long had a reputation as a ladies' man. He recorded his sexual exploits in a pocket diary. See David Steele's entry, *ODNB*.

187 *'The great law which regulates* . . . The author of both was probably the Victorian essayist and lawyer James Fitzjames Stephen, who often railed against the sentimental excesses of Dickens's fiction. With the rumours now circulating about Dickens's private life, Stephen's attacks on his literary dishonesties had a sharper edge.

187 *'Block up one channel* . . . 'Old Father Thames has got a rival,' observed 'Old Bachelor' in an anonymous pamphlet published in 1859 or 1860: 'the accumulated filth that

floats on his venerable bosom is not so noxious as the poison that is daily distributed under the sanction [of] our Christian legislature. And to what do we owe this scandal? To ourselves – to our accommodating morals – to the manner in which we educate our women – to the fearful license we grant them.' Quoted in Leckie's *Culture and Adultery* (1999), p. 71.

188 *'The deathpot boils . . . the River Thames.'* See *Illustrated London News*, 26 Jun 1858.

188 *George and Cecy Combe . . .* Letter GC to EWL, 2 Jun 1858.

188 *During their stay . . .* Jane Welsh Carlyle to Thomas Carlyle, 27 Jun 1858, Carlyle letters online, carlyleletters.dukejournals.org.

188 *Upon the adjournment . . . had placed upon them.* GC's journal, 12 Jul 1858.

188 *Bertie was 'much improved . . . our civilisation.'* Letter GC to Sir James Clark, 12 Aug 1858.

188 *If the amendment to the Divorce Act . . .* Letter J. B. Stewart to GC, 3 Jul 1858.

189 *'This is my dear Cecy's . . . than the whole family.'* GC's journal, 25 Jul–14 Aug 1858 and Charles Gibbon's *The Life of George Combe, the Author of 'The Constitution of Man'* (1878).

189 *On 15 August the undertakers . . .* See Stack's *Queen Victoria's Skull*, p. 2.

CHAPTER 12: THE VERDICT

190 *Bovill resembled a benign . . .* See print of Bovill in NPG, and *The Reminiscence of Sir Henry Hawkins, Baron Brampton*, Vol. II (1904), ed. Richard Harris.

194 *In a quick monotone . . .* E. H. Coleridge's *The Life and Correspondence of John Duke Coleridge: Lord Chief Justice of England* (1904).

196 *could have made him a witness.* The issue of whether Lane could have appeared at the church court was the source of some confusion. In *The Times*, Cockburn was reported as saying he 'could have been examined' of his own accord, but this was a misprint: Cockburn had actually said that Lane

could *not* volunteer to testify. Lane's solicitors pointed this out in a letter to the paper on 29 Nov.

199 *'nonsense in a notebook'*. See *Daily Telegraph*, 17 June 1858.

199 *'No one reading her journal . . .'* See *Daily Telegraph*, 24 Nov 1858.

200 *Detailed reports also appeared in the newspapers . . .* See Nicholas Hervey's 'Advocacy or Folly: the Alleged Lunatics' Friend Society, 1845–63' in *Medical History*, Vol. 30 (1986). In Aug 1858, in a letter quoted in the British and American papers, Charles Dickens tried to restore his damaged reputation by describing his estranged wife Catherine as suffering from a 'mental disorder'.

200 *A string of troubling cases . . .* Accounts of cases from Swabey and Tristram's *Reports* and from articles in *The Times* and *Daily News*.

201 *The* Saturday Review *disapproved . . . Saturday Review*, 4 Dec 1858. Condonation and connivance remained bars to divorce for another century. In order to get a divorce, an 'innocent' husband or wife had to prove the guilt of his or her spouse; the evidence often consisted of staged assignations in hotel rooms. An Act of 1969 opened the way to consensual divorce.

202 *A week later Queen Victoria wrote . . .* See *Letters of Queen Victoria: a Selection from Her Majesty's Correspondence between the Years 1837 and 1861* (1907), quoted in the *Report of Royal Commission on Divorce and Matrimonial Causes* (1912).

203 *In a judgment that the newspapers . . .* John Thom pointed out to *The Times*, 5 Mar 1859, that it had misquoted Cockburn: 'his Lordship is made to say that Mrs Robinson wrote "to" me in the most impassioned language, saying that "passion clung to her heartstrings" &c. This is a mistake. Mrs Robinson never addressed me in such a manner. She may have written "of" me in such terms in her diary, which is a very different thing.'

204 *The judges had found no evidence . . .* Forbes Winslow, in the *Journal of Psychological Medicine and Mental Pathology*, Vol. 12 (1859), expressed his annoyance that Cockburn had dismissed the medical testimony out of hand, and had made

the unfounded assertion that sex maniacs always confessed their obsessions to others.

205 *Such entries could hardly be construed . . .* After the publication of the anonymous erotic memoir *My Secret Life* in the 1880s, many questioned whether it was a work of fact or fantasy. Those who argued for its authenticity pointed to the frequently mundane detail in the book, and to the scenes in which the author chronicled his sexual failures and disappointments. See Marcus's *The Other Victorians.*

206 *Bovill asked the court . . . allowances granted to the witnesses.* IHR's petition to House of Lords Select Committee on Appeals, 6 Jun 1861, HLA. For expenses see: *A Handy Book on the New Law of Divorce and Matrimonial Causes* (1860).

207 *'it is enough to state . . . discussion last summer.'* See the *Examiner*, 5 Mar 1859.

207 *Medical Times and Gazette . . .* In the edition of 12 Mar 1859.

207 *'nothing could be clearer . . . altogether insane'.* Collected in John Paget's *Paradoxes and Puzzles* (1874). Even in 1910, the barrister H. E. Fenn wrote in his memoir that the Divorce Court always looked upon a wife's confession of adultery 'with very grave suspicion, and does not, in any case, act upon it without full corroboration, and quite right too, otherwise who would be safe from the utterings of a hysterical woman? . . . There is no doubt that some women do "romance", especially if they are of a nervous disposition, imagining things which they would not really object to happen.'

210 *its Sittings with closed Doors.'* By 1860 women were usually excluded from the courtroom in any case, unless they were appearing as witnesses: 'Divorce a Vinculo', *Once a Week.*

CHAPTER 13: IN DREAMS THAT CANNOT BE LAID

211 *'I am glad to say . . . pretty regularly.'* Letter CD to William Fox, 12 Feb 1859.

211 *Hydropathy; or, the Natural System of Medical Treatment:*

an Explanatory Essay. The work was dismissed in the establishment medical journal *The Lancet* as containing 'nothing particularly new or clever', being merely an example of a hydropathist 'puffing his own wares'; but greeted in the *Living Age* as 'luminous and able . . . by far the clearest and most rational exposition [of the water cure] that has yet been given'. Both Combe and Darwin recommended the work to friends: it was 'rational & scientific', said Combe; Darwin declared it 'very good & worth reading'. Lane sent a copy to Dickens, who, less enthusiastically, replied with a letter of thanks for 'your little book'.

212 *'the Love of my youth . . . being in the body.'* Letter from Catherine Crowe to Helen Brown, 25 Jan 1861, Crowe Collection, F191822.

212 *to migrate to Australia himself.* Letter from Mary Butler to CD, Dec 1862.

212 *sailed for Queensland in 1863.* Letter from J. P. Thom to CD, 14 Jan 1863.

213 *for 'certain family considerations'.* Probate of Elizabeth Drysdale (dated 14 May 1887), Edward Wickstead Lane (30 Oct 1889) and Margaret Mary Lane, née Drysdale (15 Aug 1891). Lady Drysdale died in Harley St, Edward in Boulogne, and Mary in Connaught Square, near Hyde Park.

213 *Charles became the spokesman . . .* He was a witness for the defence when Annie Besant and Charles Bradlaugh were prosecuted for obscene libel after publishing a book on birth control in 1877. In spite of his efforts, the pair were convicted of circulating material 'liable to deprave and corrupt', a test of obscenity devised by Sir Alexander Cockburn in 1868 and still in use today.

213 *Charles had two sons with Alice Vickery . . .* Their sons were Charles Vickery Drysdale and George Vickery Drysdale.

213 *George shared a house . . . died three years later.* Wills of George Drysdale (proved 10 Dec 1904) and George Drysdale (proved 21 Dec 1907). Both died in the same house in West Dulwich, Surrey. Susannah Hamilton Spring in census returns of 1891 and 1901.

213 *By the time that he died in July 1863 . . .* See Joshua S. Getzler's entry in *ODNB*.

214 *'one of the greatest social revolutions . . .'* *The Times*, 28 May 1867.

214 *Queen Victoria believed . . . an actress in Ireland.* See Christopher Hibbert's *Queen Victoria: a Personal History* (2000), p. 299.

215 *might be physiological after all.* In 1854, the French alienist Jean-Pierre Falret had described a form of mania that he named '*la folie circulaire*'; it was the first identification of the illness now known as manic depression or bipolar disorder. When manic, the sufferers could experience a heightened sexual drive, wrote Falret, accompanied by the delusion that the objects of their lust reciprocated their feelings; they sometimes sought out sex with reckless abandon. When depressed, they were subject to profoundly melancholic, even suicidal feelings. Falret pointed out that victims of this circular madness often appeared normal: they did not experience thought disorder, and their extreme moods were often interrupted by lucid intervals. These symptoms corresponded to the sensations of being 'crazed' and then 'crushed' that Isabella recorded in her diary. Though the doctors who testified in the Robinson trial probably knew of Falret's findings (they were reported in the British medical press in 1854), his theory did not support the case for Isabella's madness: a victim of *la folie circulaire* might misinterpret sexual intentions, but she was not likely to hallucinate sexual acts.

216 *Dinah Mulock . . .* A Life for a Life. *A Life for a Life* and George Eliot's *Adam Bede* were the most borrowed library books of 1859, according to Sally Mitchell's *Dinah Mulock Craik* (1983). Dinah Mulock married Georgiana Craik's cousin, George Lillie Craik, in 1865, when she was forty and he twenty-five.

216 *'sensation novels' of the 1860s.* The narrator of *The Serpent on the Hearth: a Mystery of the New Divorce Court* (1860), for instance, cannot help 'dwelling on the past . . . though there is an agony in that past, there is still for me an exquisite delight, and a pleasure, which I can, in writing this mystery only, again and again recall'.

216 *'It is curious . . . most unfeminine.'* See E. S. Dallas's *The Gay Science* (1866).

216 *books about 'lost women' . . . silken falsehood'.* Dinah Mulock's 'To Novelists – and a Novelist', a review of George Eliot's *The Mill on the Floss* in *Macmillan's Magazine*, 1861.

217 *'an adulteress in her heart'.* HOR's response of 1 Feb 1862 in NA, J77/44/R4.

217 *he appealed to the House of Lords . . .* Minutes of the Appeal Committee of the House of Lords, 25 Jun 1860, and HOR's petition to withdraw appeal, 3 Jun 1861, HLA.

217 *When ordered to pay . . . North America.* HOR's rejoinder of 14 Apr 1862, in NA, J77/44/R4.

218 *'little Children & their kind . . .'* Letter from Bridget Curwen Walker to her grandson Thomas Walker, 3 Jan 1859, private collection (Ruth Walker).

218 *When Bridget died . . .* Bridget Christian Walker's will, proved 28 May 1859.

218 *estate passed to Frederick.* When Frederick died in 1880, aged fifty-seven, the estate was valued at £41,000. It passed to John Walker, Isabella's eldest brother, and his son, who subsequently barred the entail and sold it. Frederick left a widow, Henrietta, their two children, Isabella and Frederick, having predeceased him.

218 *Henry responded by insisting . . .* HOR's reply of 17 Apr 1858 in the Court of Chancery and his response of 1 Feb 1862 in NA, J77/44/R4.

218 *She continued to support Alfred . . .* Papers in NA, J77/44/R4 and census return of 1861.

218 *on condition that he pay her the dividends . . .* HOR's response of 1 Feb 1862 and IHR's reply of 4 Mar 1862 in NA, J77/44/R4.

218 *but by 1861 she had managed to pay . . .* IHR's petition to the House of Lords Select Committee on Appeals, 6 Jun 1861, HLA.

219 *Henry sold Balmore House . . .* HOR's rejoinder of 14 Apr 1862, in NA, J77/44/R4. Henry described the Talbot Square property – a four-storey terraced building – as a 'small house', which he was about to give up because of his business losses. In the spring of 1861, according to the census returns, he was resident there with Otway, Stanley, three servants, and two of his nieces. The house in Park Street cost £84 a year, according to the rejoinder.

219 *Otway left Tonbridge School* . . . See *Register of Tonbridge School* (1893).

219 *'contrary and in defiance'* . . . HOR's rejoinder of 14 Apr 1862, in NA, J77/44/R4.

219 *In 1863, seven years . . . Hotel on 27 June*. HOR's petition to the Court for Divorce and Matrimonial Causes, 2 Nov 1863, sworn in Paris before the British Consul and resworn in London a week later before being filed on 10 Nov, Court minutes, *Robinson v Robinson & Le Petit*. Both documents in NA, J77/44/R4.

219 *The splendid Victoria Hotel* . . . See John Henry Sherburne's *The Tourist's Guide; or Pencillings in England and on the Continent* (1847).

219 *'rising room'*. T. C. Barker and M. Robbins, *A History of London Transport* (1963).

219 *dissolved on 3 November 1864*. Court minutes, *Robinson v Robinson & Le Petit*, NA, J77/44/R4.

219 *Her paramour in the hotel rooms* . . . HOR's petition to the Court for Divorce and Matrimonial Causes, 2 Nov 1863, in NA, J77/44/R4.

220 *son of an Irish nobleman* . . . Lord Rossmore's *Things I Can Tell* (1912).

220 *a survey of local primary schools*. See *Memoires de la Société academique de l'arrondissement de Boulogne-sur-Mer* (1880).

220 *In Dublin in May 1865 he married* . . . Marriage reported in the *Belfast News-letter*, 4 May 1865. The ceremony took place at St Stephen's Church.

220 *men to remarry that year*. See *Annual Reports of the Register-General of the Births, Deaths and Marriages in England* (HMSO, 1878–1902).

220 *Having set up and sold on* . . . Details of steam-packet venture in J. Forbes Munro's *Maritime Enterprise and Empire* (2003).

220 *Henry reneged on a promise* . . . In a letter from Tom's sister, Amy Waters, to their sister Lucy on 19 Jun 1864, which describes Henry as behaving 'most shamefully', WG 9/6. This and all subsequent correspondence between members of the Waters family from Williams/Gray Papers at the Tairawhiti Museum and Art Gallery, Gisborne, New Zealand.

220 *Unlike the kindly Albert* . . . When the census of 1871 was taken, Albert was staying in Westbourne Park with his eighty-nine-year-old widowed father. In 1881, Albert's wife Julia, with her children Alice and Hubert, was taking the waters at Great Malvern.

220 *'HOR will not trouble . . .'* Letter from Helena Waters (née Robinson) to her daughter Lucy, 19 Jun 1864, WG 9/6.

220 *privately as 'the Turk'*. In letters from Helena to her daughter Lucy Waters, 31 Dec 1868, and from Carry Cowan to her sister Lucy Waters early in 1864. Carry added that Henry had just come back from a trip to the East, 'very oleaginous minded . . . & very grey & mysterious old donkey', WG 9/6. Albert, by contrast, was referred to lovingly by his nieces as 'dear Albert'. He and his sister Helena were members of the Plymouth Brethren, an evangelical Christian sect founded in Dublin in the 1820s, and Albert was the chief negotiator when the Robinson firm agreed to build a flour mill, at cost price, for the paupers of Hereford (see Jean O'Donnell, *John Venn and the Friends of the Hereford Poor*, 2007).

220 *Stanley 'seems very anxious . . .'*. Letter from Helena Waters to Lucy Waters, 23 Nov 1863, WG 9/6.

220 *'Stanley has gone . . . unmanageable.'* Letter from Helena Waters to Lucy Waters, 25 Dec 1863, WG 9/6.

221 *Henry transferred Stanley* . . . See *Register of Tonbridge School* (1893) and the *Edinburgh Academy Register*, which records Stanley's attendance from 1864 to 1866.

221 *In the late 1860s, Henry* . . . The *Scottish Commercial List* shows HOR in Glasgow in 1869.

221 *In 1869 he patented* . . . Patent listed in *Chronological Index of Patents* (1869).

221 *'a splendid . . . interested for her'*. Waters family journal, 13 Apr 1870, WG 10/7.

221 *'Mrs Robinson . . . in the evening.'* Waters family journal, 4 Apr 1870, WG 10/7.

221 *On a return visit* . . . Waters family journal, 7 Apr 1870, WG 10/7.

221 *In 1874, Alfred, at thirty-three* . . . According to the marriage certificate, both bride and groom were living in Rupert Street, Westminster when they were married on 21 Sep 1874.

221 *cotton business in the 1860s* . . . Otway is listed as having dissolved a partnership in a firm of Liverpool cotton dealers in the *London Gazette*, 24 Aug 1867.

221 *joined the Merchant Navy*. Otway received his master's certificate in London on 19 Feb 1873, according to *Lloyd's Captains' Registers 1851–1947*, NA, ref BT 122/86.

222 *Alfred as first engineer.* See, for instance, census of 1871, where Otway is listed as the master of a ship docked at Cardiff, and Hamilton as his first engineer. Otway was the captain of the *Frascati* when it docked at Bute in 1875, according to *The Western Mail* of 15 Jun that year.

222 *'He has become quite . . . his memory.'* Letter from Lucy Gray (née Waters) to her husband Charles, 12 Mar 1876, WG 9/3.

222 *'He could not stand his idiotic . . .'* Letter from Lucy Gray to her sister Adelaide, circa May 1877, WG 10/2.

222 *'poor little "Marie"'* . . . Letter from Helena Waters to Lucy Waters, 31 Dec 1868, WG 9/6.

222 *bore her husband three sons.* Oliver, born in 1867, became a naval surgeon; Arthur, born in 1871, became a shipwright; and Ernest, born in 1877, became a naval engineer. See census returns of 1871, 1881 and 1891.

222 *to a house called Fairlight in Bromley, Kent*. Isabella bought a house and land on the corner of Newman Road and Tweedy Road in Bromley from Dorothea Tweedy of Belvedere in the early 1870s, according to schedules of deeds in the Bromley public library; she sold off parts of the land in the early 1880s.

222 *Flaubert's* Emma Bovary. The quotations from *Madame Bovary* in this book are taken from the first English translation, by Karl Marx's daughter Eleanor, which appeared in 1886, a year before Isabella Robinson's death. In 1898, Eleanor killed herself with prussic acid after discovering that her lover, the atheist Edward Aveling, had married a young actress.

222 *At her house in Bromley* . . . According to her death certificate, Isabella died of general pyaemia, an often fatal form of septicemia, three days after a suppurating abscess was found on her thumb.

222 *That December* . . . Henry died at 84 Upper Leeson Street, Dublin, on 12 Dec 1887. See 'Calendars of Probate and Administration', Dublin.

223 *'fed up with England'*. . .*Time* magazine, 14 Apr 1930. Otway's will was unsuccessfully challenged by his brother Alfred – see NA, TS27/794.

CODA: DO YOU ALSO PAUSE TO PITY?

226 *'The address . . . wd be sufficient.'* Letter EWL to GC, 13 Apr 1858.

SELECT BIBLIOGRAPHY

UNPUBLISHED SOURCES:

Court for Divorce and Matrimonial Causes file J77/44/R4, containing papers on the Robinson divorce, NA

Court of Chancery file C15/550/R24, *Robinson v Robinson*, NA

George Combe's journals for 1856, 1857 and 1858 (MS 7431), NLS

Journal of Robert Chambers (Deps 341/30 and 341/33) and authors' ledger (Dep 341/289), NLS

Journals and letters of Henry Robinson's sister Helena Waters and her family, WG Papers

Letters from Mary Drysdale to Jane Williams, in the Clyde Company Papers at the State Library of Tasmania, Hobart, Tasmania, Australia

Letters of Charles and Bridget Walker and Henry Curwen in Curwen family archives (refs DCu/3/31, DCu/3/81 and 3/7), Cumbria Record Office and Library, Whitehaven, Cumbria

Letters of William Copland and Mary Drysdale to John Murray, John Murray archive, NLS

Letters to and copybook of George Combe between 1850 and 1858: letters by GC from 1850 to April 1854 are in MS 7392; from April 1854 to June 1858 in MS 7393. Letters to GC cited in this book are in MS 7350, MS 7365 and MSS 7369–7374, Combe Collection, NLS

Letters to and from Catherine Crowe in the Catherine Crowe Collection, Templeman Library, Kent University, Canterbury, Kent

Parish records for Ashford Carbonel, Hereford Record Office, Hereford, Herefordshire

Parish records for Ludlow, Salop Record Office, Shrewsbury, Shropshire

Parish records for St Pancras, London Metropolitan Archives, London

Records of the House of Lords, HO/PO/JO/9/9/382–448 (17 June 1859 to 13 June 1861); papers relating to the appeal against the Divorce Court verdict, HLA

PUBLISHED SOURCES:

Newspaper reports relating to the Robinson trial and other divorce cases, June 1858–March 1859: *Caledonian Mercury*, *Daily News*, *Daily Telegraph*, *The Era*, *Examiner*, *Liverpool Mercury*, *Manchester Times*, *Morning Chronicle*, *Morning Post*, *Nottinghamshire Guardian*, *Observer*, *Reynolds's Newspaper*, *The Times*

Acton, William, *The Functions and Disorders of the Reproductive Organs, in Childhood, Youth, Adult Age, and Advanced Life, Considered in the Physiological, Social, and Moral Relations* (London, 1857)

Allan, Janice M., 'Mrs Robinson's "Day-Book of Iniquity": Reading Bodies of/and Evidence in the Context of the 1858 Medical Reform Act', *The Female Body in Medicine and Literature*, ed. Andrew Mangan and Greta Depledge (Liverpool, 2011)

The Annual Register 1858 (London, 1859)

Anon., *A Handy Book on the New Law of Divorce and Matrimonial Causes* (London and Dublin, 1860)

———'Moor Park, As It Was and Is', *New Monthly Magazine*, Vol. 104 (May 1855)

———'Moor Park Hydropathic Establishment [a Prospectus]' (1856)

———[Charles Dickens], 'Our French Watering-place', in *Household Words*, Vol. 10, No 12 (4 November 1854)

———[Marianne Young], *Sketches of the Camp at Aldershot: also Farnham, Waverley Abbey, Moor Park* (Aldershot, 1858)

———'The Working of the New Divorce Bill', *The English Woman's Journal* 1 (1858); 'Act to Amend the Divorce and Matrimonial Causes Act of Last Session'; and 'Matrimonial Divorce Act', *The English Woman's Journal* 2 (1859)

———'The Divorce Court at Work', *Saturday Review* (31 December 1858); and 'A Month in the Divorce Court', *Saturday Review* (8 January 1859)

———'Divorce a Vinculo; or, the Terrors of Sir Cresswell

Cresswell', *Once a Week* (six-part series beginning 25 February 1860)

Anonyma, *The Serpent on the Hearth: a Mystery of the New Divorce Court* (London, 1861)

Arnold, A. J., *Iron Shipbuilding on the Thames, 1832–1915: an Economic and Business History* (Aldershot, 2000)

Auerbach, Nina, 'The Rise of the Fallen Woman', *Nineteenth-Century Fiction*, Vol. 35, No 1 (June 1980)

Baxter, R. D., *National Income* (London, 1868)

Beizer, Janet, *Ventriloquized Bodies: Narratives of Hysteria in Nineteenth-Century France* (Ithaca, 1994)

Bell, Acton [Anne Brontë], *The Tenant of Wildfell Hall* (London, 1848)

Bell, Currer [Charlotte Brontë], *Jane Eyre: an Autobiography* (London, 1848)

Benn, J. Miriam, *Predicaments of Love* (London, 1992)

Bennet, J. H., *A Practical Treatise on Inflammation of the Uterus, Its Cervix, and Appendages, and on Its Connection with Uterine Disease* (third edition, London, 1853)

Berrios, G. E., and Kennedy, N., 'Erotomania: a Conceptual History', *History of Psychiatry*, Vol. 13, No 52 (December 2002)

Black, Adam, and Black, Charles, *Black's Guide Through Edinburgh* (Edinburgh, 1851)

Blodgett, Harriet, *Centuries of Private Days: Englishwomen's Private Diaries* (New Brunswick, 1989)

——— *'Capacious Hold-All': an Anthology of Englishwomen's Diary Writings* (Charlottesville, 1991)

Bostridge, Mark, *Florence Nightingale: the Woman and Her Legend* (London, 2008)

Boyle, Thomas, *Black Swine in the Sewers of Hampstead: Beneath the Surface of Victorian Sensationalism* (New York, 1989)

Braddon, Mary Elizabeth, *The Doctor's Wife* (London, 1864)

Bradley, James, Dupree, Margaret, and Durie, Alastair, 'Taking the Water-Cure: the Hydropathic Movement in Scotland, 1840–1940', *Business and Economic History*, Vol. 26, No 2 (1997)

Bulwer-Lytton, Edward, *Confessions of a Water Patient* (London, 1845)

Bunkers, Suzanne L., and Huff, Cynthia A. (eds), *Inscribing the Daily: Critical Essays on Women's Diaries* (Amherst, 1996)

Carter, Kathryn, 'The Cultural Work of Diaries in Mid-Century

Victorian Britain', *Victorian Review*, Vol. 23, No 2 (1997)

Carter, Robert Brudenell, *On the Pathology and Treatment of Hysteria* (London, 1853)

Chase, Karen, and Levenson, Michael, *The Spectacle of Intimacy: a Public Life for the Victorian Family* (Princeton, 2000)

Collins, Wilkie, 'The Diary of Anne Rodway', *Household Words*, Vol. 14, Nos 330–31 (19–26 July 1856)

——————*The Woman in White* (London, 1860)

——————*Armadale* (London, 1866)

Colp Jr, Ralph, *Darwin's Illness* (Florida, 2008)

——————'Charles Darwin, Dr Edward Lane, and the "Singular Trial" of Robinson v Robinson & Lane', *Journal of the History of Medicine*, Vol. 36, No 2 (April 1981)

Combe, Andrew, *Observations on Mental Derangement: Being an Application of the Principles of Phrenology to the Elucidation of the Causes, Symptoms, Nature and Treatment of Insanity* (Edinburgh and London, 1831)

Combe, George, *The Constitution of Man Considered in Relation to External Objects* (Edinburgh and London, 1828)

——————Translation from the French of Josef Franz Gall's *On the Functions of the Cerebellum* (Edinburgh and London, 1838)

——————*A System of Phrenology* (fifth edition, Edinburgh and London, 1843)

——————*Life and Correspondence of Andrew Combe, MD* (Edinburgh, 1850)

——————*The Relation between Science and Religion* (Edinburgh and London, 1857)

Craik, Georgiana, *My First Journal* (Cambridge and London, 1860)

Creaton, Heather, ed., *Victorian Diaries: the Daily Lives of Victorian Men and Women* (London, 2001)

Crowe, Catherine, *The Night Side of Nature; or, Ghosts and Ghost Seers* (London, 1848)

Curwen, John F., *A History of the Ancient House of Curwen of Workington in Cumberland* (Kendal, 1928)

Dallas, Eneas Sweetland, *The Gay Science* (London, 1866)

Darwin, Charles, *On the Origin of Species by Means of Natural Selection; or The Preservation of Favoured Races in the Struggle for Life* (London, 1859)

Dawson, Gowan, *Darwin, Literature, and Victorian Respectability* (Cambridge, 2007)

Delafield, Catherine, *Women's Diaries as Narrative in the Nineteenth-Century Novel* (Farnham, 2009)

Dickens, Charles, and Lemon, Mark, *Mr Nightingale's Diary: a Farce in One Act* (Boston, 1877)

Dillon, Brian, *Tormented Hope: Nine Hypochondriac Lives* (Dublin, 2009)

Durie, Alastair J., '"The Drugs, the Blister and the Lancet are all Laid Aside" – Hydropathy and Medical Orthodoxy in Scotland, 1840–1900', *Repositioning Victorian Sciences: Shifting Centres in Nineteenth-Century Thinking*, eds David Clifford, Elizabeth Wadge, Alexandra Warwick and David Willis (Cambridge, 2006)

Emmerson, George, *John Scott Russell* (London, 1977)

Esquirol, J. E. D., *Mental Maladies: a Treatise on Insanity*, trans. E. K. Hunt (New York and London, 1845)

Fenn, Henry Edwin, *Thirty-five Years in the Divorce Court* (London, 1911)

Flaubert, Gustave, *Madame Bovary: Moeurs de province* (Paris, 1857); trans. Eleanor Marx Aveling as *Madame Bovary: Provincial Manners* (London, 1886)

Flint, Kate, *The Woman Reader, 1837–1914* (Oxford, 1993)

Foss, Edward, *Biographia Juridica: a Biographical Dictionary of the Judges of England from the Conquest to the Present Time* (London, 1870)

Fothergill, Robert, *Private Chronicles: a Study of English Diaries* (Oxford, 1974)

Gay, Peter, *Education of the Senses: the Bourgeois Experience, Victoria to Freud*, Vol. I (Oxford, 1984)

General Medical Council, *The Medical Register* (London, 1859–95)

Gibbon, Charles, *The Life of George Combe, the Author of 'The Constitution of Man'* (London, 1878)

Groneman, Carol, 'Nymphomania: the Historical Construction of Female Sexuality', *Signs: Journal of Women in Culture and Society*, Vol. 19, No 2 (Winter 1994)

Hager, Kelly, *Dickens and the Rise of Divorce: the Failed-Marriage Plot and the Novel Tradition* (Farnham and Burlington, 2010)

Healy, David, *Mania: a Short History of Bipolar Disorder* (Baltimore, 2008)

Holmes, Ann Sumner, 'The Double Standard in the English Divorce Laws, 1857–1923', *Law and Social Inquiry*, Vol. 20, No 2 (spring 1995)

Hoppen, K. Theodore, *The Mid-Victorian Generation, 1846–1886* (Oxford, 1998)

Horstman, Allen, *Victorian Divorce* (London, 1985)

House, Madeline, Storey, Graham and Tillotson, Kathleen, eds, *The Pilgrim Edition of the Letters of Charles Dickens, Vols 6–9, 1850–61* (Oxford, 1988)

Hughes, Edward, *North Country Life in the Eighteenth Century, Vol. II: Cumberland and Westmorland, 1700–1830* (Oxford, 1965)

Huff, Cynthia, *British Women's Diaries: a Descriptive Bibliography of Selected Nineteenth-Century Manuscripts* (New York, 1985)

Humpherys, Anne, 'Coming Apart: the British Newspaper Press and the Divorce Court', *Defining Centres: Nineteenth-Century Media and the Construction of Identities*, eds Laurel Brake, William Bell and David Finkelstein (London, 2000)

Jameson, Anna Brownell, *The Diary of an Ennuyée* (London, 1834), originally published as Anon, *A Lady's Diary* (London, 1826)

Lane, Edward Wickstead, *Hydropathy; or, the Natural System of Medical Treatment: an Explanatory Essay* (London, 1857)

————'Thesis: Notes on Medical Subjects, Comprising Remarks on the Constitution and Management of British Hospitals, etc.' (Edinburgh, 1853)

————*Medicine Old and New* (London, 1873)

————'Letter read by Dr B. W. Richardson FRS at his lecture on Charles Darwin FRS in St George's Hall, Langham Place, 22 October 1882' (privately published)

————*Hygienic Medicine: the Teachings of Physiology and Common Sense* (London, 1885)

Laqueur, Thomas, *Solitary Sex: a Cultural History of Masturbation* (New York, 2003)

Leckie, Barbara, *Culture and Adultery: the Novel, the Newspaper and the Law, 1857–1914* (Philadelphia, 1999)

Maclaren, Angus, *Birth Control in Nineteenth-Century England* (London, 1978)

Macqueen, John Fraser, *A Practical Treatise on Divorce and Matrimonial Jurisdiction Under the Act of 1857 and New Orders* (London, 1858)

Marcus, Stephen, *The Other Victorians: a Study of Sexuality and Pornography in Mid-Nineteenth-Century England* (New York, 1966)

Martens, Lorna, *The Diary Novel* (Cambridge, 2009)

Martin, Philip W., *Mad Women in Romantic Writing* (Brighton, 1987)

Mason, Michael, *The Making of Victorian Sexuality* (Oxford, 1994)

Mulock, Dinah, 'The Water Cure', *Dublin University Magazine* (April 1855)

——————*A Woman's Thoughts about Women* (London, 1858)

——————*A Life for a Life* (London, 1859)

Munro, J. Forbes, *Maritime Enterprise and Empire* (Woodbridge, 2003)

Nead, Lynda, *Myths of Sexuality: Representations of Women in Victorian Britain* (Oxford, 1988)

Norton, Caroline, *A Letter to the Queen on Lord Chancellor Cranworth's Marriage and Divorce Bill* (London, 1855)

Overton, Bill, *The Novel of Female Adultery, 1830–1900* (Basingstoke and London, 1996)

The Oxford Dictionary of National Biography (Oxford, 2004)

Phillimore, John George, *The Divorce Court: its Evils and the Remedy* (London, 1859)

Poovey, Mary, *Uneven Developments: the Ideological Work of Gender in Mid-Victorian England* (Chicago, 1988)

Ray, Phyllis M., *Ashford Carbonel: a Peculiar Parish; A Brief History* (Ludlow, 1998)

Richards, Graham, *Mental Machinery: The Origins and Consequences of Psychological Ideas, Part 1: 1600–1850* (London, 1992)

Robertson, Thomas William, *My Wife's Diary* (London, circa 1854), an adaptation of a French play by Adolphe d'Ennery, first performed in England under the title *The Wife's Journal*

Rose, Phyllis, *Parallel Lives: Five Victorian Marriages* (New York, 1983)

Rosenman, Ellen Bayuk, *Unauthorized Pleasures: Accounts of Victorian Erotic Experience* (Ithaca, 2003)

Russett, Cynthia Eagle, *Sexual Science: the Victorian Construction of Womanhood* (Harvard, 1989)

Sato, Tomoko, 'E. W. Lane's Hydropathic Establishment at Moor Park', *Hitotsubashi Journal of Social Studies*, Vol. 10, No 1 (April 1978)

——————'George and Charles Drysdale in Edinburgh', *Journal of Tsuda College Tokyo*, Vol. 12 (1980)

——————'Charles Robert Drysdale in 1848–69', *Journal of Tsuda College*, Vol. 13 (March 1981)

——————'George Drysdale's Supposed Death and *The Elements of Social Science*' (in Japanese), *Hitotsubashi Ronsu,* Vol. 78, No 2 (August 1977)

Savage, Gail, 'The Operation of the 1857 Divorce Act, 1860–1910', *Journal of Social History* (1988)

——————'Erotic Stories and Public Decency', *The Historical Journal,* Vol. 41 (2 June 1998)

Secord, James A., *Victorian Sensation: the Extraordinary Publication, Reception, and Secret Authorship of Vestiges of the Natural History of Creation* (Chicago, 2000)

Shanley, Mary Lyndon, 'One Must Ride Behind: Married Women's Rights and the Divorce Act of 1857', *Victorian Studies*, Vol. 25 (spring 1982)

Shortland, Michael, 'Courting the Cerebellum: Early Organological and Phrenological Views of Sexuality', *British Journal for the History of Science*, Vol. 20 (1987)

Shuttleworth, Sally, *Charlotte Brontë and Victorian Psychology* (Cambridge, 1996)

Smethurst, Thomas, *Hydrotherapia; or, The Water Cure* (London, 1843)

Smith, Roger, *Trial by Medicine: Insanity and Responsibility in Victorian Trials* (Edinburgh, 1981)

Smith, W. Tyler, *Manual of Obstetrics* (London, 1858)

Spencer, Herbert, *Social Statics; or, The Conditions Essential to Happiness Specified, and the First of Them Developed* (London, 1851)

Stack, David, *Queen Victoria's Skull: George Combe and the Mid-Victorian Mind* (London, 2007)

'A Student of Medicine' [George Drysdale], *Physical, Sexual, and Natural Religion* (London, 1854), reprinted as *The Elements of Social Science* (the thirty-fifth edition, published in 1905, includes a memoir of George by Charles Drysdale)

Stone, Lawrence, *Road to Divorce: England 1530–1987* (Oxford, 1990)

——————*Broken Lives: Separation and Divorce in England, 1660–1857* (Oxford, 1993)

Swabey DCL, M. C. Merttins, and Tristram DCL, Thomas Hutchinson, eds, *Reports of Cases Decided in the Court of Probate and in the Court for Divorce and Matrimonial Causes: Vol. I* (London, 1860)

Tallent-Bateman, Charles T., *A Home Historical: Moor Park, Surrey* (privately published, 1885)

Tanner, Tony, *Adultery in the Novel: Contract and Transgression* (Baltimore and London, 1979)

Taylor, Jenny Bourne, 'Obscure Recesses: Locating the Victorian Unconscious', *Writing and Victorianism*, ed. J. B. Bullen (London, 1997)

————and Sally Shuttleworth, eds, *Embodied Selves: an Anthology of Psychological Texts, 1830–1890* (London, 1988)

Tennyson, Alfred, *The Idylls of the King* (London, 1859)

Thomas, Keith, 'The Double Standard', *Journal of the History of Ideas*, Vol. 20, No 2 (April 1959)

Tidswell, Richard Thomas, and Littler, Ralph Daniel Makinson, *The Practice and Evidence in Cases of Divorce and other Matrimonial Causes* (London, 1860)

Tilt, E. J., *On Diseases of Menstruation and Ovarian Inflammation* (London, 1850)

————*The Change of Life in Health and Disease* (London, 1857)

Turner, E. S., *Taking the Cure* (London, 1967)

Vicinus, Martha, ed., *Suffer and be Still: Women in the Victorian Age* (Bloomington, 1972)

Wood, Ellen, *East Lynne* (London, 1861)

Wood, Jane, *Passion and Pathology in Victorian Fiction* (Oxford, 2001)

van Wyhe, John, *Phrenology and the Origins of Victorian Scientific Naturalism* (Aldershot and Burlington, 2004)

Young, Marianne, *Aldershot and All About It, with Gossip, Literary, Military and Pictorial* (London, 1857)

Charles Darwin's correspondence at www.darwinproject.ac.uk

ACKNOWLEDGEMENTS

My thanks to the staff of the British Library, the London Library, the National Archives and the Wellcome Library in London; to the staff of the local record offices in Hereford, Reading, Shrewsbury and Whitehaven; to Pauline Dunne at the National Archives in Dublin and to Alison Metcalfe at the National Library of Scotland in Edinburgh. For permission to quote from their archives, thanks to the Trustees of the National Library of Scotland, to the Cumbria Archive & Local Studies Centre (Whitehaven) and to the Tairawhiti Museum in Gisborne, New Zealand. Many thanks to Meg Vivers for sharing her excellent research into the Robinson family; to Mark Robinson for his information about his great-great-grandfather; and to Phyllis Ray and Ruth Walker for passing on their knowledge of the Walkers. For arranging for me to look round some of the houses in which Isabella Robinson and her friends lived, I am grateful to Clynt Wellington in Surrey; to Ann and Freddy Johnston in Ludlow; and to Florence Shanks and Lucinda Miller in Edinburgh.

Thanks to all the friends and family who have helped me with this book, among them Lorna Bradbury, Alex Clark, Toby Clements, Will Cohu, Tamsin Currey, Robert Douglas-Fairhurst, Claudia FitzHerbert, Miranda Fricker, Stephen Grosz, Victoria Lane, Ruth Metzstein, Sinclair McKay, Daniel Nogués, Marina Nogués, Tasio Nogués, Stephen O'Connell, Kathy O'Shaughnessy, Robert Randall, John Ridding, Wycliffe Stutchbury, Ben Summerscale, Juliet Summerscale, the late Peter Summerscale, Lydia Syson, Frances Wilson, Keith

Wilson, the mothers who meet at the Coffee Cup in Hampstead and the writers who meet at the Novel History Salon in Bloomsbury. Thank you especially to my son, Sam.

A big thank you to my agent, David Miller, as ever; to his colleagues at Rogers, Coleridge & White, including Stephen Edwards, Alex Goodwin and Laurence Laluyaux; and to Julia Kreitman of The Agency in London and Melanie Jackson in New York. My thanks to Richard Rose for his excellent suggestions and advice. Thank you to everyone at Bloomsbury in London for making the publication process such a pleasure, among them Geraldine Beare, Richard Charkin, Jude Drake, Sarah-Jane Forder, Alexa von Hirschberg, Nick Humphrey, Kate Johnson, David Mann, Paul Nash, Anya Rosenberg, Alice Shortland, Anna Simpson and – particularly – my editor, Alexandra Pringle, whose guidance has been invaluable. Many thanks also to the other publishers who have supported this project: George Gibson and the rest of Bloomsbury in New York, Ann-Catherine Geuder in Berlin, Dominique Bourgois in Paris, Ludmila Kuznetsova in Moscow, Andrea Canobbio in Turin, Sofia Ribeiro in Lisbon and Henk ter Borg in Amsterdam.

INDEX

A NOTE ON THE AUTHOR

Kate Summerscale is the author of the number one bestselling *The Suspicions of Mr Whicher*, winner of the Samuel Johnson Prize for Non-Fiction 2008, winner of the Galaxy British Book of the Year Award, a Richard & Judy Book Club pick and adapted into a major ITV drama. Her first book, the bestselling *The Queen of Whale Cay*, won a Somerset Maugham award and was shortlisted for the Whitbread biography award. Kate Summerscale has also judged various literary competitions including the Booker Prize. She lives in London.